MW01002451

RACE PREJUDICE

RACE PREJUDICE

BY

JEAN FINOT

TRANSLATED BY

FLORENCE WADE-EVANS

NEGRO UNIVERSITIES PRESS
NEW YORK

Originally published in 1906
by Archibald Constable and Co. Ltd., London

Reprinted from a copy in the collections
of the Brooklyn Public Library

Reprinted 1970 by
Negro Universities Press
A DIVISION OF GREENWOOD PRESS, INC.
NEW YORK

SBN 8371-2909-5

PRINTED IN UNITED STATES OF AMERICA

FOREWORD TO THE ENGLISH TRANSLATION

THE theory maintained in this work may seem perhaps somewhat bold. But when I think of the two principal classes of readers who are called upon to judge it, my fears are calmed.

On the one hand, those who only speak in virtue of facts, and who take their stand on the value of arguments, will be with me entirely. They will very soon perceive that the author has treated one of the most burning topics in the future of international relations without any preconceived idea. On the other hand, those who allow themselves to be influenced by the good and generous sentiments which lie at the bottom of every well-balanced soul, will be grateful for a conclusion, wherein the cause of human dignity and fraternity is made to triumph. The judgments passed on this work (which appeared quite recently in France) by the critics of the French Press and other eminent Continental minds reassure me further as to the welcome which the great English public will give it. Civilisation, or, if it be preferred, Anglo-French humanity, does it not show at present in Europe most reassuring tendencies in regard to the harmonious evolution of justice between races and peoples?

England, which first dared to enter into alliance and friendship with a yellow people, and afterwards to render to it the tribute of admiration which it deserved, and, with England, France, which now for a long time has conceded the rights of citizens to black peoples, are destined to direct and some day bring to a successful issue the emancipation and the lifting up of the so-called inferior races.

May I be allowed to urge yet another plea for the indulgence of my readers? The author of this book had the honour of being among the first who preached in France the Anglo-French *rapprochement* and friendship. When my first works appeared in 1901 on that subject, mocking voices were raised to show the impossibility of an *entente* between *two races* which were so inherently different and, presumably, antagonistic!

Among other things, special stress was laid on the innate (?) enmity which existed between the Bretons and the English. But it was precisely Breton journals and my Breton friends who were the most zealous in defending this work of fraternity between two peoples so closely connected by common thoughts and common preoccupations. The *Times*, in a remarkable article on my efforts in this direction (November 1st, 1902), was right in maintaining that it is often sufficient to breathe on the subjects of our discord to see them vanish. The union of a few men of goodwill has succeeded in overcoming the stupidity of the theory of races and of age-long prejudices! For it is often enough not to believe certain conventional lies in order to render them nil and harmless.

Anxious only for truth on the subject of races, we meet on our way with the triumph of justice, equality and fraternity. These three principles are seen to be more inseparable in this domain than anywhere else. All those who bow before their beauty and practical value will easily forgive me the somewhat tedious routes which lead towards what I consider to be the only really scientific solution of the struggle between peoples who differ in origin, colour and blood.

JEAN FINOT

Paris, 1906.

CONTENTS

BY WAY OF INTRODUCTION

The method of the work and its genesis.—The importance of the subject.—The man God and the man Beast.—Towards truth.

I

THE conception of races, once so innocent, has cast as it were a veil of tragedy over the surface of our earth. From without it shows us humanity divided into unequal fractions. There are aristocratic and superior peoples, peoples chosen to govern and to be admired. There are others, inferior, slaves of the first, enduring the suspicion and contempt which come to them from all sides.

From within this same falsely conceived science of races likewise encourages hatred and discord among the children of the same common country.

On one side, organic inequality (*anthropology*), based on the data of a science badly defined and subject to all kinds of error; on the other, anthropo-psycho-sociological inequality (*anthropo-sociology* or *psychology*), which, in addition to the unsteady foundations of the former, introduces a phraseology borrowed from fantastic and ephemeral doctrines. Finding it impossible to identify races with our modern nationalities, which are mixtures *par excellence* of the most diverse ethnical elements, the doctrine of races endeavours to divide peoples according to their component parts. No longer able to set races in opposition to one another from outside, it incites them to quarrel from within. In examining the shape of skulls and noses within the frontiers of the same country, it tries to frighten us by revealing hostile elements wrongly amalgamated. These populations, we are told, group themselves according to their craniological and nasal peculiarities, and only marry in virtue of principles favoured by the anthropologists !

The new doctrines, being derived from passion and from passions, can only maintain themselves by the audacity of their originators and want of reflection on the part of their adepts. True science, violated and deterred from its object, is transformed into a fair for depreciated and adulterated merchandise.

The sanguinary instincts which slumber at the back of our conscience, being thus encouraged and emboldened by the supposed necessity and benefits of hatred, are allowed free play. It is in the name of science that we speak to-day of the extermination of certain peoples and races as well as of certain social classes, on the ground of their intellectual or morphological inferiority.

Where the divergences of skull or colour are silent, anthropopsychology begins to speak in favour of inequality on the ground of contrary and hostile temperaments, aspirations, and mentalities. Men are in this way thrown into groups not only by reason of their features, which are infinitely various, but also because of acts done in the past and of acts which they omitted to do, and even of those which one may deem them capable of doing in the future !

Pretexts for mutual strifes have become innumerable. The Americans tell us that no way is possible of making "white" virtue enter into the "black" body of a Negro. The Germans maintain the necessity of exterminating, if not the Slavs, at least the Poles, whom they regard as culpable for not wishing to lose themselves in the German stock.

Russians frighten us with the dangers which the "Yellow Race" presents for the future of the Whites. Turks massacre Armenians from the same motives as the Russians persecute the Jews and the Finns.

Every land has its furious "nationalists," who add to their contempt for the foreigner a similar contempt and hatred for some section of their compatriots. In the meantime pan-Slavism, pan-Germanism, pan-Anglo-Saxonism, pan-Magyarism, pan-Americanism, and many other ethnical concentrations, often seek and always find reasons for sacrificing those who stand in the way of their unmeasured appetites, which appetites are dissimulated under the falsehood of unity of blood and common civilisation.

People against people, race against race, mind against mind, citizen against citizen; cries of battle, persecution, and extermination on every side !

What truth is there in these doctrines, which are declared to be scientific ? Fed by vulgar passions, they influence politics from people to people, from citizen to citizen, and indirectly affect all our social and moral existence. Probe the motives of international life as well as those of the inner development of every civilised land, and you will perceive what weight these fictitious conceptions of race possess !

Currents of thought sway humanity like those of the atmosphere do a balloon poised in mid-air.

On the reality or unreality of this principle, which dominates at the present hour the secret or avowed aspirations of the peoples, depends the whole of their future. Peace among peoples and the crown of such a peace—that is, the vast solidarity of mankind, the dream of the future—can in any case only triumph when founded on the conviction of the organic and mental equality of peoples and races.

If only from this point of view, our work deserves to attract and to retain the attention of the reader.

Above these considerations, however, soar the claims of scientific truth. Are there really irreducible differences between races and peoples ? Are there really superior and inferior peoples in an anthropological or psychological sense ?

II

The extent of our thesis seems almost illimitable. The science of races, properly speaking, includes the science of man. In virtue of this, all its numerous ramifications deserve to find their place. There are, to begin with, a dozen natural sciences. In speaking of human morphology, how can we forget anatomy, biology, and physiology ? To understand the relative value of races, can we leave out hygiene and pathology? We have, moreover, anthropometry, with its principal section, cephalometry. After that come anthropology itself and ethnography, inasmuch as this last is in immediate contact with the first.

We cannot understand the man of to-day without examining the man of yesterday. Since he is only a simple link in the evolution of things, his near and remote parentage must be included under survey. Geology and palethnology on one side, and on the other the sciences of the animal and the vegetable worlds, should likewise not be forgotten.

Moreover, since we are dealing with a psychic and intellectual being, we must also examine him in the manifestations of his intellect and conscience. We are thus bound to find room for psychology, sociology, and with them statistics, criminology, the history of sciences and inventions, etc. What shall we say, lastly, of history, which ought to furnish us with the key to the evolution of races; and of political geography, the function of which should be to throw light on the problem of their diffusion over the earth?

The science of races in these circumstances assumes the aspect of an immense empire summing up the intellectual and biological evolution of man across the ages. This conception, although imposing, is far too complex and too obscure. Would it not be better to sacrifice much of its ephemeral grandeur for the sake of clearness and precision? If we thus limit the grand horizon, and reject everything which does not enter directly into our domain, might we not present our problem in a simpler and more convincing manner?

In considering the method of our work, we have thought fit to adopt one which would throw the most light on its genesis and its slow elaboration before arriving at its definite expression. The reader in this way has the advantage of assisting at the development of an idea as though it were the formation of a living being.

We begin with the act of birth. In the presence of doctrines more and more exclusive and dogmatic on the inequality and the inevitable struggle between races, the author sets himself to find the arguments for and against this theory.

We have only chosen as guides impartial doubt and direct observation, using, moreover, the no less impartial study of facts observed by others. Attracted by the vast movement created around the prophets of inequality, we enter into their temples.

We do our best to understand their arguments and their grievances (Chap. I), in order to distinguish what truth or error may reside in their pessimism. But how is this to be attained ?

Let us apply ourselves to the animal and vegetable world, and let us find out what races and variations come into being in this *milieu*; how they are born, what is their length of years, and above all in what way they are distinguished from human races (Chaps. II and III).

Armed with these data, we endeavour to examine human divisions (Chap. V). Bewildered by the chaos of general classifications, we have recourse to those more precise ones which are based on the divergences of human forms. Without any preconceived idea, we study the numerous compartments in which anthropologists of every kind have enclosed the different branches of humanity (Chap. VI), and at last, seeing how fictitious and purely imaginary these limits are, we try to sum up our doubts to the best of our abilities (Chap. VII).

As our first essay proves unfruitful, we turn to other fields in order to find some glimmers of truth. As we question in their turn the *milieu*, cross-breeding, the law of organic co-ordination, and the intellectual life of humanity, they answer us with reassuring affirmations on human equality (Part II). Resisting the conviction which is thus forced on our mind, we submit it to a kind of inspection by questioning that astounding science which under the name of anthropo-psychology or sociology has done most to destroy the ideas of human equality.

We proceed to consider in the first place the psychology of peoples, this mother more serious of aspect and more balanced than her fickle child, anthropo-sociology. We see her, however, a prey to flagrant contradictions and disfigured by numerous falsehoods (Part III). We then return to the source from which she derives these poisonous elements. To analyse the value of modern peoples, it is first necessary that anthropo-sociology or psychology should know the value of their principal constituents.

Inasmuch as they base their oracular deliverances on the voice of blood, which speaks across the field of history, they should at least be able to distinguish its essential characteristics. Do they know anything about it ?· And what do they know ?

We now arrive in the midst of Aryans, Gauls, and the so-called Latins, which are worlds of which they never cease to speak as the best explored and the most perfectly known (Part IV).

From every side we get sarcastic replies, railleries, and contradictions ! Surely, we say to ourselves, this quasi-science proceeds in a very strange fashion. Instead of going from the known to the unknown, she follows the opposite route and builds on mysterious and unfathomable chasms. After admitting that the past mocks her, does not the present by chance decide in her favour ? Is it a fact that peoples condemned to a mixture of blood perish irremediably from an intellectual and biological point of view ?

The example of France comes under our notice as a striking protest against all such exaggerations (Part IV, Chap. IV). But if superior peoples do not degenerate after cross-breeding, may not inferior ones be raised to the height of the so-called privileged races ? If that were the case, would it not be a convincing answer in favour of the inanity of all the doctrines of irreducible racial gradations ?

Besieged by this doubt, we pass on to the Negroes (Part V), who are relegated to the most humiliating place on that ladder where human beings are artificially arranged. Here a new wonder awaits us, for these semi-monkeys, by the intellectual progress which they have realised in these last years, give a finishing stroke to all those declamations on the subject of the acquired or innate intellectual inferiority of particular peoples and races.

III

Truth at last seems to smile on us. In summing up our impressions by the way, we perceive that they assume the form of a precise and comforting affirmation. Surely human beings, who in the past sinned through too much pride, are anxious to expiate their faults by an excess of modesty. The " gods on the earth " of long ago are wrong in identifying themselves on all points with the most backward animals. Some time ago they despised the links which unite them to the two kingdoms; nowadays they exaggerate the resemblances and forget the distinctions. After having believed for a long time that the earth is the centre of the universe, and that man, its king, incarnates in himself the finality of nature, we are now victims of a defect equally extreme in an opposite sense. We have forgotten to take into account intellectuality, which gives man a peculiar position in the evolutionary chain of existence. Under the sublime forms of soul, conscience, and thought, it places a peculiar stamp on our life, and furnishes us with innumerable motives and a field of action without limits. Although differentiating our souls, it still preserves their unity owing to the analogous essence of their biological basis, and in this way prevents any such division of the human race as would render a return to unity impossible. On the other hand, what we call civilisation, this synthesis of progress realised by our intellectuality throughout the ages, has it not always militated against races and human inequality ? Is it not civilisation which dissolved primitive societies founded on unity of blood, and which established as a principle the commingling of all with all, the general " pan-mixture," the universal "half-breed " ?

The attraction of mutual interests has replaced prejudices, and frontiers have disappeared like the sacrosanct privileges of castes and social classes. Where, then, is the refuge of pure and superior races in the anthropo-sociological sense, if these ever existed ? How can they be portioned out, and especially how can we appreciate the value of an element which is henceforth beyond all investigation ? For even the appeal to the past proves unfruitful.   It only answers us in contradictory fragments.

When one meditates with the gravity which becomes man on all these problems on which his destiny depends, the heart-rending cry of Goethe's Faust comes back to one's memory— "Alas! alas! thou hast shattered with thy terrible blow the wonderful world of external divinities! It falls, it dissolves in ruins! O thou, powerful among the children of the earth, rebuild it more beautiful than ever."

Part I

THE INEQUALITY OF HUMAN BEINGS

RACE PREJUDICE

CHAPTER I

THE GOSPEL OF INEQUALITY AND ITS PROPHETS

I

INEXORABLE doctrines on the inequality of human beings, adorned with a scientific veneer, are multiplied to infinity. Based on craniological differences, the largeness or smallness of the limbs, the colour of the skin or the hair, &c., they endeavour to appeal to a sort of pseudo-science, with its problematic laws, unexamined facts and unjustifiable generalisations, as a guarantee of their audacious theories. The number of these theories is incalculable. To use the expression of Charles the Bold, they are like a "universal spider," traces of which are visible in every sphere of our life of action and thought. Despotic, cruel, and full of confidence in their laws, the creators and partisans of all these doctrines do their best to impose them as dogmas of salvation and infallible guides for humanity.

Among these doctrines, which are so diverse and yet so alike on their fantastic sides, those which are founded on the craniological variations of men have exercised the widest and most lasting influence. They also have the greatest number of adherents and the most zealous.

It was Count Gobineau who laid the foundations (*Essai sur l'inégalité des races humaines*, 1854; 4 vols). His work, which constitutes an enthusiastic pæan in favour of so-called superior races and a merciless condemnation of those styled inferior, is a veritable arsenal of arguments from which all the champions of the persecution, oppression and extermination of weak peoples and races have drawn.

Of an inquiring mind, learned, however, in mere odds and ends, a mediocre stylist and a savant far too paradoxical, Gobineau was never taken seriously in his native country of France. Men saw personified in him a combination of Amadis and Don Quixote, those heroes of dreams and adventures so dear to his imagination. Treated as a diplomatist among savants and as a savant among diplomatists, he himself was the cause of the discredit into which his works fell, by the publication of doleful and whimsical poems of 20,000 verses !

His *Amadis* has perhaps done more to depreciate his name than the flagrant contradictions with which his *Essai sur les races* and his *Histoire des Perses* abound. To these one must add his tales and novels of studied extravagance, such as *Akrivia Phrangopoulo* and *Le Mouchoir Rouge*. A brilliant talker, a delightful man in his worldly relations, Gobineau easily made people forgive his faults as a writer. In Paris people forgot his "graphomania" to remember only his social gifts. The writer as well as his literary works would have sunk altogether into oblivion, had not fate willed that he should meet Richard Wagner towards the end of his stay in Rome.

The great musician was profoundly moved by the divine grace of "Gobinism" which, after proclaiming the division of men into superior and inferior, placed the sceptre of royalty in the hands of the Germans. What must have struck the Master most forcibly was that France was suddenly relegated to the subsoil of humanity and her population destined to irrevocable decadence. The first among Germans was singularly flattered in being at the same time, as a consequence of the Gobinistic religion, the first among human beings. Thus Gobineau, whilst still living, had the good luck of being borne by Wagner's genius into his divine Walhalla. The genial musician, who was at the same time a somewhat naïve philosopher, was astonished at this new key which opened for him the enigma of the decadence of peoples. Instead of his old dogmatic explanation, the abuse of meat, here is offered him a plausible solution, namely, the mixture of races. As long as the Aryans came from Asia to make good from time to time the waste of superior blood so Gobineau taught him, humanity maintained a certain level. But their immigrations having ceased, humanity becomes a prey to an invading corruption. The brachycephalic multiply like vermin and repulse the dolichocephalic on every side. Ruin threatens them in all directions. Who will escape it? The purest perhaps—that is to say, the Germans and the English.

Gobineau taught that the inequality of races (whose meeting forms a nation) sufficed to explain all the connecting links of the destinies of peoples. The philosophy of humanity is reduced to this absolute truth that everything which is great, noble and fruitful on the earth, that is, science, art and civilisa-tion, springs exclusively from one sole thought and belongs to one *sole family*, the various branches of which have ruled in every civilised country in Europe. And this chosen people, this divine family, is none other than the Aryans, of whose legendary existence and fictitious influence we shall speak later on. According to Gobineau, of the seven chief civilisa-tions of the world,[1] six belonged to the Aryan race and the seventh, that of Assyria, owed the Iranian renaissance to the same race. What is modern civilisation if not that which was created by the Germanic races which in the fifth century succeeded in transforming the genius of the West? But these Germanic races were simply Aryan races. They were endowed with all the energy of the Aryan variety. Gobineau sententiously affirms that this was necessary in order that they might fulfil the part to which they were called. After these Germanic races, he tells us elsewhere, "the white species had no more power and activity to give. The Teutons completed the discovery of the globe and they took possession of it by making it their home before spreading it with their *half-caste descendants*."

The multiplication of humanity by way of mixture of races

---

[1] These seven civilisations are represented, according to Gobineau, by (1) the Indian, a branch of the white Aryans; (2) the Egyptian, which was created by an Aryan colony from India which settled on the Upper Nile; (3) the Assyrian, with which were associated the Jews, Phœnicians, Lydians, Carthaginians, and Himyarites; the Zoroastrians and Iranians who ruled in nearer Asia under the names of Medes, Persians, and Bactrians, constituted a branch of the Aryan family; (4) the Greek, likewise founded by Aryans; (5) the Chinese, an Aryan colony from India, introduced civil life there; (6) the ancient Italic, whence sprang Roman culture, and which was a mixture of Celts, Iberians, Aryans and Semites; and (7) the Germanic, essentially Aryan.

soon resulted, however, in a howling promiscuity, and our prophet cannot find words violent enough to denounce such defilement. This poor Aryan clay in this manner became lost as far as one could see! "After the age of the gods, when it was absolutely pure, the age of heroes, where the mixtures were slight in form and number, and the age of nobles, it advanced more or less promptly according to localities towards the definite confusion of all its elements owing to its heterogeneous unions." There remains, alas! nothing but hybrids. The portion of Aryan blood " which alone upholds the structure of our society " is thus being absorbed. And when the last pure drops of this privileged blood shall have disappeared, we shall enter into the "*era of unity*, the era of general and universal mediocrity, that is to say, into the all but nothingness." This will be the fearful dissolution of the Apocalypse, the reign of mournful and desolate darkness! "Human herds, no longer nations, weighed down by a mournful somnolence, will henceforth be benumbed in their nullity like buffaloes ruminating in the stagnant meres of the Pontine marshes"!

The creator of "Parsifal" greatly relished this philosophical synthesis of humanity. His optimistic temperament, however, revolted against this inevitable fatality. What! Are all men on the road to decadence and savagery! Can there be no salvation for the Ideal! And here Wagner appeals to the Divine Redemption which baffles Gobineau's pagan mind. The Aryan hero, the Saint, shall win back the world by the contemplation of the Saviour on the Cross!

But the theory of Gobineau still holds its own, strong and unassailable for his faithful adherents. The pessimism and bitterness which are the sap of this theory continue to afford strong nutriment to all the branches which issue from its trunk.

His admirers thus never cease being haunted by this tragic vision which poisoned the life of their master. For all of them, the impure races, recruited from among the brachycephalic, rush, like the Huns devastating ancient civilisation, to the assault of the pure races, the Aryans, who are regarded as angels from heaven. On all sides they only hear the groanings of the great and noble, the noise of towns falling in ruins and the anguish of the highest who are passing away. Like the medieval chroniclers who in terror of Attila depict him, now with the snout of a pig and now as the scourge of God, they show us the earth attacked and consumed by human insects representing everything which is most ignoble and most repugnant.

II

A condemnation of principle, however, weighs on all these ethnological dramas which end invariably like the fifth act of a third-rate tragedy. All the heroes slaughter one another and only monsters remain to crush underfoot the Good, the Noble, the Soul, and Humanity.

Let us say, however, that Gobineau never attempted to dissimulate the motives which led him to write his *Essai*. For him indeed it was only a matter of bringing his contributions to the great struggle against equality and the emancipation of the proletariat. Imbued with aristocratic ideas (did he not even impose on his contemporaries his own genealogical tree, the ramifications of which extended to the first Vikings who invaded France?), he thought it useful to oppose to the democratic aspirations of his time a number of considerations on the existence of natural castes in humanity and their beneficial necessity.

We can easily understand that this exaggerated, dark and ill-balanced picture which claimed to destroy everything which we admire and love as progress and civilisation, buoyed up by an empty phraseology and generalisations clashing with acknowledged facts, only indifferently convinced those pre-disposed in their favour. Even the anthropologists of that time showed themselves very refractory to the objurgations of this new " Scourge of God."

It has been found that Gobinism displayed too much pessimism in the face of too little knowledge, and that even its ideas of barbarous and inferior peoples lacked clearness. Since the brachycephalic, more vigorous and healthy, succeed in exterminating the fairhaired dolichocephalic, the future must belong to them and civilisation has only to range itself under their banner. After all, can one so easily destroy the work of so many centuries of progress? Does not history show that evolution is only the eternal linking of the past to the present and that life is born of death? Why then grieve over the triumph of those who must necessarily triumph? We are tempted to repeat to Gobineau those memorable words of Marcus Aurelius to Verus. "If the Gods have willed the Empire to Cassius, Cassius will escape us, for thou knowest the saying of thy great grandfather, 'No prince has slain his successor.'"

This is also perhaps the reason why France was insensible to the apprehensions expressed by Count Gobineau. Germany was all the more stirred by them. Having entered the Wagnerian Olympus, Gobineau became one of its divinities. His cult soon assumed the form most likely to glorify the writer and his theories. An association, the *Gobineau Vereinigung,* composed of many Germans and of some French, undertook to popularise his name and ideas. All the fruits of his many-sided muse were carefully translated into German and in addition to these, some unpublished works as well, which Gobineau's sense of decency had compelled him to relegate to the bottom of his desk. Thus the Gobinistic cult arose. The members of his church set before themselves the duty of proclaiming the glory of their prophet and the profundity of his views. They were filled with zeal. According to Professor Schemann, the present President of the Gobinist Society, the author of the *Essai sur l'inégalité des races* is as great a philosopher as he is a great poet, a great moralist and a great orientalist. His admirers will even honour him so much as to declare that he is a "German"!

Gobineau never ceased making ravages into the brains of his adopted fellow-countrymen. The notion of superior and inferior peoples spread like wildfire in Germany. German literature, philosophy, and politics were profoundly influenced by it. In the name of the salvation of the superior race, that is, "the Germans," it has been attempted at Berlin to justify the proceedings of the conquest of the new provinces and their Germanisation to the utmost extent.

The disciples of Gobineau like Ammon[1] and Chamberlain[2]

---

[1] *Die Gesellschaftsordnung und ihre natürlichen Grundlagen* and *Die natürliche Auslese beim Menschen.*

[2] *Grundlagen des XIX Jahrhunderts.*

have only enlarged on their master and prophet. According to Ammon, the dolichocephalic, incited by some irresistible attraction, go into the towns. There the élite of Humanity are to be found. Unfortunately, the harmful atmosphere of large human agglomerations succeeds in killing off men with narrow skulls, so that their number is constantly diminishing. Democrats with round skulls (the brachycephalic) take their place and so the level of humanity falls.

Chamberlain, although of English origin, is likewise received in Germany with open arms, whereas England makes light of his sanguinary theories. He also like Gobineau glorifies Germany and is glorified in return. There is something strange in this spontaneous and enthusiastic naturalisation which Germany tenders to a pure Gascon like Gobineau and to a no less pure Englishman like Chamberlain.

Is it a case of that innate relationship of ideas of which Goethe speaks? Chamberlain, however, attaches less importance to the anthropological basis and lays special stress on the sociological and psychological data. We shall, however, have occasion to consider this theory later on.

French by origin and German by adoption, Gobineau had the incomparable honour and glory of inspiring many writers and savants and thus of influencing in a very vivid way the life of a whole people. He created a nucleus of ideas which is far from being extinct.

Humanity, always more sensitive to evil than to good, always more attentive to voices which preach hatred than those which proclaim love, has tamely followed the teachers of inequality and still follows them.

The theory, however, maintained by Gobineau, decidedly lacked a scientific veneer. The works of Darwin had not yet appeared. Thanks to Darwin, the scholastic method of Gobineau will soon be galvanised.

III

Selection with its corollaries enters the scene with Galton,[1] who proclaims the exclusive influence of the factor of race in human evolution. His studies lead him even to a sort of fatalistic

[1] *Inquiries into Human Faculty.*

belief. He regards inferior races as a human misfortune which it is necessary to combat at all costs. To him we owe "the aristocracy of eugenics," those men of privileged skulls, scions of superior families, who are called by destiny to all the good things in life. The State ought to watch tenderly over their multiplication, encourage their marriage, facilitate their existence and even provide for the future of their progeny !

Numerous English and American savants side with Galton and Darwin in preaching their gospel of the survival of the fittest and the benefits of selection. We do not intend to analyse the works of all these authors of more or less repute and popularity, for their number never ceases to grow, while the direction of their thought takes more and more fantastical turns. But in order to characterise the value of their tendencies we shall speak of the most influential among them as they come. Thus, for example, according to Professor Haycraft,[1] the differences among men correspond with those among animals. By selection it would be possible to produce men as dissimilar as the bulldog and the old Sussex dog or the tumbler and the wild pigeon. In every .case humanity must only be reproduced by choosing the best among its specimens. The author in consequence praises contagious diseases, alcoholism and other afflictions from which humanity suffers because they possess for him the merit of killing off the most feeble; and thus making room for the aristocratic products of humanity.

But if English and American writers have specially deduced from it practical conclusions as to the amelioration of public health, the gospel of human inequality has assumed in France and Germany still stranger aspects.

In France it is Vacher de Lapouge who justly passes as the most authoritative representative of the new doctrine. Faithful to his principles and convinced of their justice, he defends them in all his works[2] with seriousness and ability worthy of esteem. As jurist, zoologist, psychologist, physiologist and anthropologist, the author appeals to all the sciences for argu-

---

[1] *Darwinism and Race Progress.*

[2] See among others his *Selections sociales* (a course delivered at the University of Montpellier in 1888), his Memoirs on *l'Hérédité dans la Science politique*, the origins of the *Ombro-latins*, the neolithic Pygmies of Soubes, etc., etc.

ments in favour of his doctrine.   Coming later than Gobineau, he depends on the theory of selection which is conspicuous by its absence in the *Essai sur l'inégalité.*   In M. Vacher de Lapouge, the new doctrine finds a most eloquent defender, and it is enough to examine his books in order to know all the weapons which his co-religionists, both adepts and learners, will afterwards use.

According to Lapouge and his disciples, the morphological and characteristic differences of races or principal species are equal and even greater than those which exist among the *most distinct species* of the canine, feline and coleopterous orders.   The two fundamental elements in the present populations of the West, the European and Alpine man, have in this sense clearly marked differences.

In the case of the first, the cephalic index is from 72 to 76, and that of the bare skull from 70 to 74, with tendency to increase by the widening of the front part of the skull; general conformation, longilinear.   In fact we have before us a dolicho-cephalic in all his beauty.

He has great needs and works without ceasing in order to satisfy them.   " He earns money more easily than he can save it.   He accumulates wealth and loses it with ease.   Adventurous by temperament, he dares everything, and his audacity assures his incomparable success.   He fights to fight, but never without an afterthought of the profit to be gained thereby.   He is logical and never wastes his words.   Progress is his greatest desire. *In religion he is Protestant*, and asks only that the State respect his activity.   He is to be found in the British Islands, and still constitutes the dominant element in Belgium (maritime), Holland, Germany (near the North Sea and the Baltic), and in Scandinavia.   In France, and especially in Germany, he enters as a secondary element, but still an important one, into the population of the plains.   At an altitude above 100 metres, he is rarely found." [1]

To speak in a more concrete way, his race is known as Indo-Germanic, European, Indo-European, *Aryan*, Kymric and Galatic.   There are about 30 millions in Europe and 20

---

[1] Note that the description of Lapouge is based on that of Linnæus (*Systema naturale*).   Thus for the European we have albus, sanguineus, torosus, pilis, flavescentibus prolitis, levis, argutus, inventor, &c., &c.

millions in America. The number of half-castes approaching
the type is equal or somewhat more.

Leaving on one side the too technical apparatus borrowed
from zoology, we keep to the most general terms, the most pronounced characteristics and the most obligatory in order to
give a clearer idea of the value of this division.

Let us take the Alpine man. His medium masculine height
is from 1ᵐ60 to 1ᵐ65 ; the medium cephalic index of the
living, 85 to 86, of the bare skull, 84 to 85. Thick-set, brevi-
linear, brachycephalic, brown or medium colouring of the skin,
hair, iris and beard. Frugal, industrious, economical, remarkably prudent, he leaves nothing to chance. Rarely a mere
cipher, he still more rarely attains talent. He is very suspicious,
but is *"easily caught with words."* He is the man of tradition
and of what he calls good sense. He adores uniformity. In
religion he is willingly Catholic. In politics, he has only one
hope, the protection of the State, and one tendency, to level
all who surpass him without ever feeling the need of lifting
himself. The frontiers of his country are often too broad for
his sight. He finally succumbs to all the vices of which we
accuse our middle class. He corresponds with the Celto-Slavs
and the Turanians. The race of pure Alpines does not exceed
from 50 to 60 millions. For the most part they appear to us
under a hybrid form resulting from the cross-breeding between
the Homo Alpinus and the Homo Europæus.

Do not let us despair, however. His strong characteristic is
the widening of the back part of the skull with a more or
less marked flattening of the same part, which shows itself
in the third month of his fœtal life. A crossing effected with
an Alpine ·gives a significant and manifest result, viz., the
shortening of the length of brain and skull and the exaggeration
of the width.

To confine oneself to depicting humanity as divided into
these two capital sections, the Alpine and the European man,
would be unworthy of any self-respecting anthropologist. M.
Lapouge, as a savant who understands his duties, insists in
addition on the *contractus* man, a small race whose face and
skull are discordant and whose index of bare skull is only from
77 to 78. He dates from neolithic times. He preceded the

Homo Alpinus, to whom indeed he gave birth by mixing with the *Acrogonus.* The *Contractus* men still exist in Central Italy. As for the *Acrogonus,* he is one of M. Lapouge's exclusive creations. He is even strongly convinced that men of this type existed in the Quaternary epoch. What are the proofs? How can we doubt their decisive value when M. Lapouge affirms that he possesses certain samples with "very marked characteristics"! Their peculiarities are the widening of the back part of the skull, the raising of the parietal bumps and the almost vertical falling of the sub-obeliac profile. In its modified form of *Acrogonus cebennicus,* this type is frequently met with in the Ardèche, le Gard, Lozère and Aveyron. There are no less than a million of them!

Whatever may be the number of the divisions and the subdivisions of the human race, Lapouge says that whoever forms part of any one of them is under the influence of the merciless law of heredity. "Its extent is as universal and its force as irresistible as that of gravity." This heredity operates without limit, as is shown by the frequent cases of atavism. In the embryogenic evolution of a man, there is only the repetition of ancestral evolution as far back as possible. Before assuming the human form or that of a mammifer or of a worm, every organised being has been a simple bubble with two leaflets or rather a simple cell with an imperfect nucleus.

In arriving at the conclusion of the unity of the world and of the intimate relationship between all organic matter, we are taught that all the phenomena of heredity which are seen in the animal and vegetable worlds are also present in the evolution of humanity.

But how can we measure the respective value of the races before us?

IV

This depends, before everything else, on what we desire to bring to perfection in man, that is to say, his beauty and physical vigour, and also his cranial capacity, which to the anthropologists is equivalent to his intellectual capacity. In using the more or less certain conquests of palæontology, geology

and historic anthropology, we see that races whose cephalic
index is below 70 are always to be found leading humanity,
and are followed by races whose cephalic index is as much
as 90 or 95. Now the ideal cephalic index is nearly always
accompanied with fair hair, great height and other marks of
superiority.

Peoples gifted with these ideal qualities have left beneficent
traces in the history of humanity. They were in the past the
ancient Greeks and Romans. To-day their mantle has fallen
on the Anglo-Saxon peoples.

In general, the upper strata of every nation carry distinctive
traits of their noble origin, whilst in the lower strata these
traits are conspicuous by their absence. Between these two
extremes float the "uncertain" classes who have inherited
many virtues of the one and retained many vices of the other.

The philosophy of history, as well as the problem of human
politics which is so complex, are thus very much simplified.
All trouble and effort for the perfecting of humanity is reduced
to this, namely, the increase of the number of superior types
at the expense of the inferior types.

But what is really happening ? Let us listen to the complaints
of this school of anthropologists.

By a cruel fatality, impure or inferior elements nearly always
eliminate the pure or superior elements. It is thus that the
brachycephalic drive away the dolichocephalic, who emigrate
more and more from Europe and go to the New World.
The Aryans are giving way to Turanians. In the Old World
only England remains with the noble type of primitive
Europeans.

This disappearance of the superior elements owing to emigration and exhaustion is the prelude to the great evils which
are threatening humanity.[1] The decay of Europe is before us,
an inevitable decay. The future of a people, like that of all

---

[1] The anthropologists of this school, revelling in pure fantasy, easily subordinate their scientific conceptions to the interests and passions of the moment.
The German branch of the school, especially after the victories of 1870, found
the "noble" type in the Germany of the conquerors. In like manner French
nationalists, whose scientific partisans are under the influence of Gobineau
and his followers, regard the future of France with despair ! Its superior
elements, they tell us, are drowned in the immigration of other non-Aryan
elements, who are on that account vile and inferior.

peoples, does it not depend on the quality of those who comprise it ? Nothing is more natural. From the moment the moral or intellectual level of a people sinks, from the moment when its fate depends on "inferior" ethnical elements, its star pales and threatens to go out, For the factor of race, so say the prophets of human inequality, exceeds all the other factors of evolution. It is true that race also involves a host of other elements, such as climate, the historical past, and the degree of civilisation. But their influence fades in that of the dominant factor of race, just as the wills of courtiers vanish in that of their master. Why, for example, does not modern Greece resemble ancient Greece ? It is, they tell us, because the cephalic index of modern Greeks has gone from 76 to 81, and so they can no longer produce great men ! M. Lapouge, with that assurance which is characteristic of this sort of science, adds that if the ancient Greeks (with a 76 index !) could suddenly revive, in less than a century the Acropolis would once more become the centre of civilisation. As the Greeks of Homer, by their disappearance, brought about the fall of Greece, so the "Aryan" Romans of Livy, with their ideal cephalic index, by giving way to the brachycephalic, brought about the ruin of the Roman Empire.

Universal history is thus reduced to the history of the variations of cerebral structures. These variations are epoch-making. Wherever the dolichocephalic came, there prosperity and a great civilisation arose together with the mastery of surrounding peoples and even that of the world. When the "inferior," the brachycephalic, made an irruption into the State, they straightway brought in decadence in all its forms.

Why did Gaul fall under Roman domination ? It was because the Gaulish aristocracy was destroyed by the Romans. In its place Gaul was flooded with the brachycephalic. And so it will be throughout the centuries. Their incessant invasion will degrade the French genius and diminish its superiority. As French society becomes physiologically and intellectually weaker, power falls into the hands of individuals drawn from the people, from quarters which are more and more brachycephalic. French intelligence declines and the irremediable

decadence of its nobility brings this unfortunate land to
servitude and death.

What will you do with a race whose skull indicates a
scandalous width !

M. de Lapouge paints the future for us in still gloomier
colours.

" I am convinced," he cries,[1] " that in the next century (that
is to say, the twentieth century !) millions will cut each other's
throats because of one or two degrees more or less of cephalic
index. This is the sign which is replacing the Biblical *shibboleth*
and linguistic affinities, and by which people will recognise one
another as belonging to the same nationalities and by which
the most sentimental will assist at the wholesale slaughter of
peoples."

This manifest sign which is to distinguish the slayers from
the slain makes us ponder ! We know that when we examine
with the naked eye individuals who submit with all good grace
to our investigations we are often mistaken by several degrees,
and when done with the help of the most exact instruments, the
same thing happens unless we are guided by a sure method
which has stood the test of time. Again, it is also necessary to
know whether the dolichocephalic are brown- or fair haired, with
long or short faces ! But these considerations do not stand in
the way of the author of *L'Aryen.* It is there especially that
M. de Lapouge gives free play to his apprehensions as to the
future of the Teutons. Frightened before the invasion of the
brachycephalic, who have supplanted the noble race of narrow
skulls " as a bad penny drives away a good," he foretells a Cossack
Europe and the approaching end of brachycephalic peoples like
France, Poland, Turkey, or Italy. We console ourselves, however, with the thought that North America is likewise destined
to a prompt and doleful end. But this catastrophe, according to
M. de Lapouge, will be due to the fact that "feminism " rages
there with fury. In short, we are upon the eve of a universal
slaughter.

[1] *L'Anthropologie et la Science politique* (Revue d'Anthropologie, 1887).

V

With a touching courage and with a simplicity of sentiment which disarms us, the French anthropologists of this school lay particular stress on the misfortunes which threaten France, whose destiny is apparently to become enslaved to other peoples.

There are only two nations which find grace before the unpitying severity of these judges. Sometimes it is the English and sometimes the Germans. The persuasive warmth with which they comment on their origins and their historic evolution, and with which they predict a more and more brilliant future for them, reminds us very much of the foresight of fortune-tellers who are acquainted with their clients' circumstances. All these theories, which arose in the nineteenth century at the time of the greatest expansion of Great Britain and Germany, only corroborate the fact of the prosperity of these two peoples who had already arrived at the summit of their fortune. Thus all the data of English and German prosperity are made to enter into the anthropological domain like stones brought to the construction of a building. Every historical fact and every victory of the English and German peoples serve as material for the vast edifice of human inequality. We learn, for example, from the studies of Bernard Davis and Rolleston, which are founded on skulls discovered in England, that the insular neolithic folk were dolichocephalic in the best sense of the word. Their cephalic index varied between 70·3 and 72·8. They were also fairhaired. The tribes which came to unite themselves with this élite of peoples (between 155 and 900 before Christ) were likewise of the same noble origin. They were dolicho-blond tribes from Gaul. Do you not marvel at this injustice of fate that successive invasions have only augmented the proportion of this privileged blood! As waters run to the rivers and the rivers to the sea, the children of the dolicho-blond march towards this land of promise. They first come with the Romans, then with the invasions of the Angles, Danes, Norwegians and Saxons. It is true that the Norman Conquest later on introduced a respectable number of brachycephalic and brownhaired dolichocephalic, much inferior to the fairhaired variety, but these have been gradually eliminated by the superior element, and as the fairhaired dolichocephalic get the upper hand, England becomes a conqueror and colonises whole worlds. In the interior of the land, especially where the brownhaired dolichocephalic dominate, we perceive poverty and intellectual arrest among the inhabitants. A danger, however, threatens this terrestrial paradise, namely, emigration, which takes away the fairhaired dolichocephalic in particular. As their number diminishes, the proportion becomes very favourable to the accursed brachycephalic and the brownhaired dolichocephalic. If these last ever get the upper hand, abrupt will be the ruin of Great Britain!

This impartial summary of the cerebral inequality of human beings reduces itself to this, that there is a chosen people or rather a chosen race, namely, the Aryans. They comprise all the good human qualities both moral and physical. The greatness of a people is directly dependent on the number of these exceptional mortals who are found within its frontiers.

The problem of national politics which is to be solved consists quite simply in the augmentation of the beneficent type and in the elimination of the "regressive" and noxious type. A well-organised State ought even to place a premium on the fairhaired dolichocephalic, and give special encouragement to their reproduction. In applying the well-understood principle of zootechny, it would not even hesitate to make use of certain ingenious methods intended to facilitate social selection.

M. Lapouge[1] thus advises Aryans, or, as he calls them, "Eugenics," to arrange themselves for the defence of their race. Elsewhere[2] he gives them lessons on rigorous selection for the purpose of obtaining in a limited time individuals answering to the anthropological ideal. He even goes to the extent of zootechnic and scientific reproduction. A small number of male reproducers of the élite type is to be chosen, and their spermatozoids used for artificial generation in superior women deserving of this honour.

With his rigorous and scientific precision, the author estimates

[1] *Hérédité dans la Science politique* (Revue d'Anthrop., 1888).
[2] *Sélections sociales.*

that by his system a male reproducer *will assure 200,000 births.*[1]

With a thousand of these privileged males, there would be enough to reform a whole country after two generations !

It goes without saying that to preserve this precious blood and together with it the so dearly acquired cephalic index of the fairhaired, we must not shrink from the establishment of "specialised" and "separated" classes. By following the example of the Jews, who only marry among themselves, the ideal of the procreation of "eugenics" could be easily realised. Even the assistance of legislation could be avoided. In any case this last must not interfere with the regeneration under-taken by the fine "eugenic" flower of the people !

In their ardent desire to find a new method of salvation, the anthropo-sociologists of the school of Gobineau have completely forgotten that it already exists and has exhibited results for centuries. Has not India realised from time immemorial the boldest conceptions of the reformers of modern races? It is there that a large field of experimentation has been established, the results of which dispense European peoples from an imita-tion, which at least would be superfluous.

The Indian castes have in their cruel exclusiveness nothing analogous on the earth. The Sudras, who are at the bottom of the human scale, have been treated from time immemorial as the brachycephalic could never be treated in Europe. Marriage with Sudras was strictly prohibited, and even simple contact with these unfortunates was considered a mortal sin. They were strictly forbidden to read the sacred books, and those who were unfortunate enough to go near them were strictly to avoid even their noxious breath. Ratzel[2] even tells us that certain of these castes were objects of greater contempt than animals. The Pulayas of Travancore were not allowed to look at the Brahmans from a distance less than 96 feet. When employed at public works, they were obliged to wear visible signs of their caste in order to be recognised at a distance, and so to prevent men of noble extraction from coming too dangerously near. In

---

[1] According to Lapouge the sperm may be diluted with impunity in certain alkaline liquids. The solution of a thousandth part in a proper vehicle is efficacious in a dose of two cubic centimetres injected into the uterus.
[2] *Völkerkunde*, II.

crossing the highroads, the Pulayas were compelled to hide themselves at the approach of travellers of another caste. This sentiment of inequality has so profoundly influenced the Indian conscience that it has been frequently observed that men have died of hunger rather than touch food which had been contaminated by the touch of Pulayas. As time went on, the sentiment of exclusion grew, and the original castes multiplied themselves into numerous sub-castes, whose intercommunication presented insurmountable difficulties. The *Kshatriya* (the old warrior caste) has been divided into 590 sections, which are in a state of mutual strife owing to questions of precedence and superiority. The sub-castes of Brahmans amount to a fabulous number, and between these, proud and haughty, in Benares, and the outcasts of Orissa who walk about almost naked, there is a great gulf fixed.

What then has been the result of this "ideal" separation of the population, of this unrestricted worship of the blood of ancestors and of the excessive purity of race and of races?

The vast country of India has been from all time the prey of those who would take possession of it. From the days of Alexander, who humiliated and conquered it, its masters have only changed names. The Scythians (1st cent.), the Arabs (7th cent.), the Afghans (12th cent.), the Mongols (14th cent.), then the Portuguese, followed by the Dutch, who gave way to the French, who themselves were supplanted by the English, here we have the series of conquests inflicted on hundreds of millions of people by invaders whose number was often only one in a thousand to that of the inhabitants.

Impotent with regard to enemies from outside, India was conspicuous for a kind of intellectual stagnation. It was indeed a land of misfortune and death. The hope of India is precisely in the introduction of modern ideas, which contribute towards breaking up its aristocratic organisation of castes and making the principles of fraternity and human equality prevail.

History is rich in examples which prove that all these divisions among inhabitants are always accompanied by a weakening of the sense of solidarity and the absence of all patriotism.

It would undoubtedly be the same in Europe if the ideas on the fatalities involved in anthropological origin and origins were ever to triumph.

VI

Nevertheless, in spite of the readiness with which all propaganda of hatred is received, this organic inequality between peoples inheriting the same civilisation must sooner or later be broken against an insurmountable obstacle.

Inasmuch as the fairhaired people with narrow skulls, that is, the dolichocephalic, only number about 50 millions out of the 400 millions who at present occupy Europe, how will they succeed in becoming masters?

What is to be done with those particular brachycephalic and brownhaired dolichocephalic who are determined not to disappear?

What is to be done with their progeny? In their burning desire to save the future of humanity, the priests of this new cult go so far as absolutely to forbid the majority of men and women from getting children. The most lenient among them are content to allow abortion and infanticide, if not to impose it. Here their courage fails them. Where, however, the French anthropologists fear to tread, those of Germany step forward with frenzied zeal. Savants like Ammon advise that the same methods which European civilisers use in the case of negroes and savage tribes should be used in the case of those whom they consider "degraded" in the matter of race. Let them be soaked with spirits supplied gratis, let them be attracted to places where debauchery is rampant, let them even be led to contract all kinds of diseases; and so exhausted, depraved and enfeebled they will finally disappear from the earth.

Certain anthropologists, however, allow themselves to fall into despair. M. R. Collignon,[1] for example, although quite convinced that the law of Ammon is equally applicable to France, threatens us, however, with the certainty of brachycephalic success. It is quite true, he says, that the struggle of classes in modern society is only the struggle between races of

[1] *Mem. de la Soc. d'Anthrop.*, Vol. I., 1893.

narrow and round skulls, that is, between the dolichocephalic and the brachycephalic. On the one side we have the people with narrow skulls who are comparatively only new-comers on French soil, a race of innovating mind, adven irous, and in another way as active in these times as were their far-back ancestors in the period of the barbaric migrations. On the other side we have their predecessors, viz., the brachycephalic, more peaceful and *attached to the soil by fate*, being only agriculturists. They represent in our collectivity the economic, reflecting and *conservative* mind! How then are we to reconcile these extremes? A fatal struggle must arise between them, incited by their contrary origins and aspirations. The final triumph in the course of centuries or of millions of years will certainly in France belong to the brachycephalic. Nevertheless these must not rest too much on their laurels!

This pessimistic fatalism contains some consolation. Inasmuch as we know beforehand the inevitable final result, it becomes useless to excite ourselves against these poor brachycephals. But all the doctrinaires of this school do not find resignation so easy! Nott and Gliddon,[1] struck by the hateful rôle which the brownhaired and the roundskulled play in social evolution, express this retrospective regret, that if Napoleon had beheaded all the demagogues who were not fairhaired, the French government would have achieved the same solidity as that of Germany and England! "Death to the brownhaired!" is the cry of these two American sociologists, for life is only possible for them under military governments. When the yoke of this form of servitude is removed from their shoulders, they become discontented and start revolutions.

These "lovers of the incredible," to use an expression of Tacitus, are thus not deficient in matter for their priesthood They remind us somewhat of that Roman emperor who, having received the gift of an unusual kind of doll, fell madly in love with it, proclaimed it a supreme divinity and honoured it with numerous sacrifices.

Human inequality, having in this fashion become the object of a veritable cult, is glorified in all its forms. Every pretex

[1] *Types of Mankind.*

is acceptable to these priests of misfortune, anxious to chant the glory of their sombre deity. Narrow skull or round skull, brown hair or fair hair, prognathism, long hands or short, the form of the nose or the eye, are all so many opportunities for proclaiming the providential divisions among human beings and the necessity, if not the benefit, of their inevitable hatreds.

Having come back to the level of beasts, man seems to have had a giddy fall. He is treated as a simple animal or plant, as though his brain and conscience and centuries of intellectual evolution had never existed for him. The history of to-day as that of to-morrow assumes the aspect of those tragic thermal baths where the best among mortals die or will die. If these philosophers of inevitable inequality are to be taken at their word, the world is on the highroad to ruin, unless perchance it is saved by chaos. Whilst to some of them, the angels (*i.e.* narrow skulls) are disappearing and the monstrosities (*i.e.* round skulls) are pouring in, to others uncertainty lowers over us in the form of unceasing strife. The inferior races, hurling themselves against the superior, will succeed perhaps in exterminating them or perhaps, again, they themselves will be overwhelmed. But in any case a dark cloud of peril awaits us. Yellows, Blacks, Jews, Anglo-Saxons, Pan-Germanics, Pan-Slavs, &c., surge from all sides, all redolent of quarrels, hatreds and wars. Moreover the height of misfortune is this, that when two races are in competition, it is the inferior which triumphs (Lapouge).

Notice that everything is banded against the success of the superiors. The advent of democracy with its ideals of liberty and equality is only one of the many great calamities in store for the peoples. What are these democrats if not brachycephalic and brownhaired, in fact barbarians, who do not grasp the beauty of an " eugenic " régime, that is to say, the rule of the fairhaired élite ? Democracy tends towards the exclusion of the latter, and in every case to reduce them to its own level. The anthroposociologists tell us that the barbarians are no longer relegated to other quarters of the globe. They live near us, or rather above and below us, in the basement and in the garret. The poor world is thus menaced from above and below.

What an agreeable prospect for the humanity of to-morrow !

In the face of all this, what becomes of the dignity of man, the needs of the spiritual life and the victories of science ? We leave for the moment these abstract considerations, and turn towards the science which is responsible for having bred all these doctrines which darken the modern conscience.

CHAPTER II

ANIMAL RACES AND HUMAN RACES (ANALOGIES AND DIFFERENCES)

I

WHEN we examine the conditions which accompany the birth of new races in the vegetable and animal world, we easily see how great is the gulf which separates them from human races. Neither the origins of the differentiation of humanity nor the striking peculiarities of its subdivisions, nor their successive evolution, nor the transplantation of different races and their return to the place from which they started, nor the factors which cause external changes in men, are identical in the three kingdoms.

There is an element which above everything else rules in humanity, viz., the moral element. Considered as mentality, conscience or soul, it exercises a decisive influence on the formation of human divisions and gives them special marks by which they may be distinguished. As the moral reacts on the physical, in a manner as powerful as it is incontestable, humanity evolves under the decisive influence of a factor which belongs to it alone, and which for this reason does not allow the same laws to be applied strictly to it which hold good in the two other kingdoms.

This moral element supplies man with a formidable weapon in the struggle for life. Far from being a passive product of external circumstances, man often creates them, especially for his own profit. This privilege which all men hold in common, however dispersed over the world, not only provides them with a characteristic of abstract identity but also prevents the differences produced by the influence of the varying *milieux* from creating fissures which would destroy the unity of the human race.

What is still more significant is that in the long evolution of humanity we nowhere meet with those strange phenomena which have given rise to the theories concerning the mutation of species, or, still better, the "explosive transformation" of Standfuss or the "spasmodic progress" of de Vries.

To understand the essential differences which separate animal races, it would be well to study the origin and evolution of species according to the new theories which have modified that of Darwin. It is all the more necessary to examine this side of the question, because all modern partisans of human inequality draw their arguments from the doctrines of Lamarck and Darwin. Hypnotised by the gigantic and constructive work of the Darwinian school, they have failed to consider its incomplete or problematic sides. In translating into the vital domain of humanity its teachings and conclusions they have applied without mercy all the deductions made by Darwin in what concerns animals and plants. But, as we shall see, the principal theory having received some mortal blows, the anthropological generalisations which are mainly due to the help of the shattered doctrine, are thus threatened with ruin.

Let us state, however, that the principle of evolution or of transformation has escaped almost unscathed from all the battles which have surged round Darwinian science. Discovered in the first place by Lamarck and Geoffroy Saint-Hilaire it is to-day universally accepted.

It is Lamarck who first maintained in a scientific [1] manner the descent of species.[2] A great number of savants sided with Lamarck, but it is Darwin's glory to have demonstrated the truth of transformation and to have imposed it on the learned world.

Without regarding it as a fixed mathematical law, modern

[1] *Philosophie zoologique*, 1801.
[2] Darwin points out in his historic notice which prefaces the *Origin of Species*, that Dr. Erasmus Darwin, his grandfather, had in his *Zoonomy* (1794) anticipated Lamarck in this matter. Goethe and Geoffroy Saint-Hilaire maintained the same ideas about the same time. But all these precursors had rather the presentiment of this truth without being able to demonstrate it scientifically. They played the same part with regard to the theory of Evolution as Raspail with regard to the science of Pasteur.

science accepts it in the main as an inevitable hypothesis to explain the essence of the evolution of species.

But while admitting this fundamental position until the contrary were proved, naturalists were unable to agree on the why and wherefore of transformation. The great originality of the Darwinian theory was to have found the key to it in *natural selection*.

Selection and heredity fix the characteristics acquired by a living being in the course of its existence. These are the two levers of this theory, which has revolutionised the natural sciences as well as sociology during the last half century.

But owing to the methodical observations made since the appearance of Darwin's *Origin of Species,* his theory was first contested and then entirely rejected.

To explain the changes wrought in this sphere, let us take the classical example of the giraffe and let us see how the Darwinian school and its successors explain the appearance of its long neck and the length of its front legs.

II

We know Lamarck's theory. The chief cause of modifications is the use or non-use of organs.

The heredity of results occurring under these conditions, that is to say, the heredity of characteristics thus acquired or lost, completes the work of transformation. The giraffe, living in places which were not fertile, only found its pasture on trees. It was therefore obliged to stretch its neck in order to browse the leaves. Its neck, owing to this habit, became considerably longer, and its forelegs became longer than the hind ones.

Darwin introduced as a corollary the selection of favourable variations. Giraffes, which thus succeeded in lengthening their necks, were the only ones which survived in time of famine. In mixing they gave birth to this new species which is quite distinct from the other types of hoofed animals. Therefore, according to this school, to obtain a new species, we must first admit (*a*) the appearance of a new quality; (*b*) the heredity of this quality; and then we must be convinced that nature, like a good breeder, anxious that this quality should not disappear,

presides at the pairings which are directed to perpetuate the
new variation !   What perplexes us most is the infinite number
of these pairings which is necessary to fix the new variation.
Since it is a matter of variations which are trifling and almost
impossible to grasp, and which can only produce results
naturally going from good to better in the course of centuries,
we must admit a conscious force which is constantly preoccupied
with the realisation of its ideal, and which is jealously watching
its forward march.

How many thousands of centuries does it not take to explain
the presence of a variation in any animal or plant whatsoever !
We are reminded of Lord Kelvin's exclamation of complaint that
the Darwinian theory multiplies to excess the age of the globe
which is already so old !   Yet geology by no means grudges time
to the existence of the globe.   This author declares that the con-
solidation of the crust of the earth took from ninety-eight to two
hundred million years.   According to M. Croll, sixty millions of
years have passed since the deposit of Cambrian formations.
This generosity of geologists, however, is insufficient to honour the
cheques whose payment is demanded by the Darwinian theory!

But the representatives of the neo-Darwinian school (Wallace,
Weismann, Galton, Pflüger, Strasburger, Kœlliker, etc.), in
examining this phenomenon closer, have found that the explanation, however attractive it may appear, does not correspond
with facts.   They question with reason not only the length of
the giraffe's neck obtained as the result of efforts made to reach
the leaves of high trees, but also the heredity of the long neck
acquired under these conditions.   This hypothesis having been
upset, men have tried to construct on its ruins another explanation no less improbable, but still more complicated.   A few
years have been enough to give a finishing-stroke to
Weismannism and to its transformist metaphysics.   Owing
to the works of Hugo de Vries, the celebrated Dutch botanist,
a new theory has triumphed, which at the present time has
almost all the suffrages of the naturalists.

III

We have seen above that since the Darwinian theory finds it impossible to give us convincing proofs of the two principal bases of its hypothesis, serious doubts have been entertained as to its truth. It not only fails to prove that in stretching its neck the giraffe has added to its length (acquired characteristic), but it cannot prove that the giraffe, after acquiring this neck, transmits it to its descendants (heredity of acquired characteristic).

But how can we explain the appearance of so strange a species of hoofed animals ? Sudden variations is the explanation called in, or, as M. de Vries has it, *spasmodic progress*. (See on this subject the works of Huxley, Mivart, Bateson, Clos, and, lastly, the *Theory of Mutation* by M. de Vries). All these savants admit with Agassiz the spontaneous appearance of species at a given time under the influence of certain special conditions. It is thus, for example, that a mixed animal world appears suddenly in the time of the first fossiliferous strata. These sudden variations, which have played so considerable a rôle in the formation of the fauna and flora of all epochs, have not disappeared in our days. Numerous examples of the explosive birth of variations will be found in Cuénot, Bateson and de Vries. Among the Echinoderms, the species of Ophiures, with six, seven, or eight arms, and the tetramerous and trimerous Crinoideans and the Asterias with numerous arms, reproduce exactly the sudden variations which appear from time to time in the normal pentamerous species (L. Cuénot). In the secondary epoch the sudden appearances are seen both of gigantic Dinosaurian lizards like the Brontosaur, which are as large as four or five elephants united, and also of quite little ones resembling small birds.

The first placental mammifers appear at the commencement of the tertiary period in a spontaneous fashion, and after giving rise to a variety of forms nearly as rich as those of the mammifers of to-day, they disappear altogether.

To explain the appearance and disappearance of all these species by way of Darwinian selection it would be necessary to extend the duration of our planet by several millions of centuries.

Darwin himself saw this lacuna in his theory. He asks himself why it is that each geological formation, in each of the strata which compose it, does not overflow with intermediary forms. He is reassured with the thought of the extreme insufficiency of geological documents.[1]

He admits before everything else, with Sir Charles Lyell, an interminable duration of time which must characterise the existence of our globe. In order to admit it, he takes his stand on the immense volume of rocks which have been raised over vast extents. He is also consoled by thinking of the thickness of sedimentary formations. These attain, for instance, in certain parts of Great Britain, according to the calculations of Professor Ramsay, as much as 72,584 feet.[2] When we consider that between the successive formations extremely long periods have elapsed, during which no deposit has been formed, fantastical estimates of the time which our planet must have lasted are arrived at. It touches close upon eternity, so Darwin tells us.

But geology and palæontology have little information to give us on the subject. There is nothing astonishing in this. Organisms which are entirely soft do not remain in a good state of preservation; shells and bones lying at the bottom of the water are swept away in time. Science can therefore only show us forms and species which are incongruous. The science of geology presents gaps which may perhaps be filled as time goes on. But at present it leaves us more ignorant than it instructs. Moreover the facts which it offers are often vague and uncertain. According to Lyell's comparison, the geological archives furnish us with a history of the globe incompletely preserved, written in an ever-changing dialect, and of which we possess only the last volume, treating of two or three countries alone. Some fragments or chapters of this volume, and certain scattered lines on each page, are all which have come down to us.

Whereas some seek the first traces of organic life in the oldest Silurian beds, others seek to throw back their appearance by many millions of years. New strata are constantly being discovered, the number of formations augmented and at the

---

[1] *Origine des Espèces*, Chap. X.
[2] Paleozoic strata, 37,145; secondary strata, 13,190; tertiary strata 2,340, etc.

same time the first appearance of organic life is being thrown back. Darwin therefore finds a basis for his theory in the fact that if given positive, palæontological proofs, negative proofs have no value whatever. But if we cannot conjecture the future from the past, yet the past still authorises us to come to conclusions with regard to the present. It is possible, therefore, that palæontology will some day justify Darwin by supplying his theory with numerous intermediary varieties, this essential basis of his edifice; but for the time being these are altogether lacking, and therefore it is difficult to espouse his cause.

An *aggravating circumstance* is that the most authoritative representatives of geology and palæontology, these two sciences to which Darwin makes constant appeals, declare themselves openly against this theory. The same applies to his forerunners and also to his contemporaries, Cuvier, Agassiz, Murchison, Falconer and Sedgwick.

IV

M. de Vries advances a more plausible theory—that of the sudden and clearly defined transformation of species. With him it takes the form of "mutation of species," instead of "individual variations" as with Darwin. The species appears, and exists a certain time. Subject to specific change, it gives rise to a new species which shows itself suddenly under the action of determined causes of which the reason escapes us. The primitive species from which it comes lives for some time near that to which it gave birth and then disappears. But the variety so created is so different from the mother-species, that their crossing remains sterile if not impossible. The celebrated botanist goes on to give a number of remarkable experiments which enabled him to justify his theory. He was particularly successful in proving it by means of the evening primrose (*onagre biennal*). This plant, brought to Europe about the beginning of the seventeenth century, is very widely spread in Holland. It was reported in 1875 that near the little town of Hilversum this plant displayed an exceptional vigour and a readiness to multiply itself beyond measure. De Vries

concluded that the species must be passing through the period of
its spasmodic mutation.   After having isolated this plant in the
Botanic Gardens at Amsterdam, he placed it under very strict
observation during fourteen years, from 1886 to 1900, and towards
the end of this year he found that out of 50,000 plants, 800 new
ones had appeared belonging to *seven* new and unknown *species*.
These species were perfectly distinct from the mother-species.

But more than this.   There is no doubt that if new species
are left near the mother-species, they will be brought back, bit
by bit, to a medium type, if not to the old one.

In order that a new species may take a definite form and
survive, it is necessary to isolate it.   It is only then that its
forms become fixed, and when fixed give rise to a new morphological species.   L. Cuénot, who insists on this necessity, points
out several kinds of causes which would thus save the new
species.   There is first the geographical isolation which erects
impassable barriers between the mother-species and the new
species, and thus prevents all crossing.   But this isolation may also
be produced by physiological causes, of an anatomical order (as
in the case of the dog, the jackal, and the wolf), where differences
such as that of height make it impossible to couple two
animals like the Newfoundland and the pug-dog; and again,
sexual incompatibility which produces very feeble fecundity, if
not absolute sterility in cross-breeding.   For many species
which only present the most minute physiological differences
become sterile once they have crossed, as in certain species of
coleoptera, and of wasps, &c., &c.

This same phenomenon is frequently observed among plants.

De Vries' theory has, however, every chance of being victorious
in modern science.   Simultaneous or later observations made
in other countries only confirm it.

M. Armand Gautier's discoveries are to be noticed in particular.[1]

In speaking of the analysis of the pigment of red wines and of
their numerous varieties, he comes to striking conclusions on
the origin of species and of races.   He also brings forward this

---

[1] *Mécanisme de la variation des êtres vivants*, in 1886, as also his remarkable
memoir on the *Mécanismes moléculaires de la variation des races et des espèces*,
published towards the end of 1901.

curious phenomenon, that great variations giving rise to the appearance of species and races do not proceed from continuous and insensible changes, but from vast modifications which appear immediately and without transition. Thus the ordinary *Aralia* with seven-lobed leaves suddenly produces branches with simple leaves which may be multiplied without slips. On a bi-coloured lilac with violet-blue flowers there suddenly appeared (in 1901) a single branch of flowers of lilac sagelike red or purple (observation made by L. Henry).

In the world of insects M. Gerard observed the same phenomena. Numerous variations of wings have suddenly appeared. Communicated by way of heredity they have caused the birth of new races. Examples of this kind abound in the animal world.

V

The school of Darwin explains this phenomenon as a kind of atavism, that is, a return to the primitive type, due to a tardy aptitude to revert. We know how this word, often void of meaning, always very mysterious and whose virtue consists in explaining the unknown by the unknown, has been abused. What is this inexplicable force which, dormant for centuries, like the Sleeping Beauty in the wood, suddenly wakes up, to drop again into an indefinite sleep? For, on the one hand, there is no regression, since these freaks in evolution give birth to new species and races. Whilst, on the other hand, the researches made by A. F. Ledouble, S. Pozzi, E. Rabaud, &c., on anomalies and freaks have demonstrated before everything else that in the number of anomalies there is a large quantity which lies completely outside the atavic theory. Those which remain are reduced to the new adaptation by the aid of a new characteristic, the resemblance of which to the atavic trait is only superficial. In other cases there is only a relationship, a continuation of characteristic traits which have never ceased to belong to the given species.[1]

[1] See, for example, the curious experiments of Tarnier, who produced polydactyly (supernumerary fingers) by simply exciting the tissues. Also of M. Boinet, who explains, with the aid of radiography, that no connection exists between any bone whatsoever of the wrist and the supernumerary finger; of Rabaud, in microcephaly, such as the arrest of the brain's growth, &c., &c.

So-called anomalies of reversion are, in short, only new organs created on the ruin of old ones. To say that their cause is atavism is to invoke nothing. The appearance of ancestral characteristics in domestic animals which have returned to wild life, a fact which plays a part in Darwinian atavism, is easily explained by the influence of changed circumstances. In tearing the animal from the influence of its proper *milieu*, we have reduced it to the influence of other conditions. When once these conditions cease to act the animal takes back its own characteristics. It is useless to invoke a mysterious force as long as we can rest on such an evident and plausible cause. The same applies to the domestic plants. As long as we specially manure the ground which nourishes their roots, as long as we take these roots out and protect them from the extremes of heat and cold, as long as we clear away the other vegetation which dispute the ground with them, and even remove noxious insects, they develop in a certain way. When this protection is withdrawn and the plant is abandoned to itself, there is no wonder that it should return, for this very reason, to its old ways.

Let us add, however, that the theory of evolution has nothing to lose by the disappearance of this cumbersome factor, atavism.

In the march of progress, atavism, acting as a stumbling-block, constituted, if not a menace of death, at least a kind of general paralysis. This sudden reversion bore traits of weakness, for by it progress involved a retrograde action contrary to its essence, which is to march forwards. Freed of this impediment, the law of progress becomes a true law of nature, astonishing in its simplicity and clearness.

CHAPTER III

SPECIES, VARIETIES AND RACES IN THE ANIMAL AND VEGETABLE WORLD

I

BEFORE drawing any conclusions from the present hypothesis of the origin of species, let us see how they as well as varieties and races originate. What is the manner of their creation, and what are the essential differences which separate them? In the first place, what is species? A mass of specific characteristics which are transmitted from generation to generation by heredity. When among individuals of the same species certain differences are established, they give rise to varieties or races. These differences are concerned in the first place with characteristics of a second order, and are distinguished subsequently by their lack of fixity. These fleeting characteristics can thus disappear and the individuals who are deprived of them return to the primitive type of the species.

The causes of variability are many. The first place must be given to the direct action of the climate, which involves that of nourishment and mode of life. According to Darwin, the principle of selection plays a prominent part, as we have seen. It is nature which is operating on a large scale, continuously, and for long lapses of time. Man also tries to do the same thing on a small scale in imitating the work of nature. Darwin, applying the theory of Malthus, affirms that means of subsistence increase in arithmetical progression, whereas living beings multiply themselves in geometrical progression. This multiplication would be so rapid that no country, not even the surface of sea and land combined, could contain all the beings born from a single pair after a certain number of generations. There is thus a perpetual struggle for room, a struggle for life. The fittest prove victorious, and certain of their advantageous qualities becoming hereditary give rise by *natural selection* to the origin of varieties and species.

This hypothesis of selection and of the heredity of acquired characteristics is, as we have seen, much battered by the science of our day. Its place has just been taken by that of sudden or spontaneous variations. These appear under the influence of causes whose essence escapes us.

New races in the domestic state are obtainable either by coupling two distinct varieties (*métissage*) or two species more or less related (*hybridation*). The results of coupling depend greatly on the conformation of the sexual organs of the respective individuals. Moreover, it is this which constitutes the fundamental difference between the species and the variety or race.

Most naturalists go so far as to consider a distinction between varieties as a distinction of species from the moment when the coupling remains systematically sterile. We are ignorant of the cause of this sterility. We only know that certain changes happening in the life of animals or plants affect in a certain way the reproductive system and produce sterility.

According to Darwin, fecundity not constituting a special distinction between species and varieties, it is necessary to admit a general identity between the progeny of the two species crossed and that of the two varieties.[1] He tells us that mongrels and hybrids resemble each other in a striking way, not only because of their variability and their property of absorbing each other mutually by repeated crossings, but also by their aptitude to inherit the two parent forms. Starting from there, Darwin states the importance of this somewhat fictitious division, for the species of to-day are only the varieties of yesterday.

But let us put aside this academic discussion on the subject of the origin of species or races, and let us rather see what internal changes have accompanied the appearance of a new race or species. In this domain, as in many others of the theory of transformation, we have succeeded in digging the soil,

[1] *Origine des Espèces, Hybrides et Métis.*

and getting nearer to truth. Whereas Darwin was occupied in particular with the changes of external forms and confined himself to simple morphology, we now know, thanks to the experiments made by many French and foreign savants, the profound and internal revolution of the organism which ordinarily accompanies external variations. It will be sufficient to grasp the significance of these phenomena and to compare them afterwards with those which are seen in the racial modifications among men for us to gain a singularly powerful argument in favour of the equality of human beings.

Holding faithfully to our method, we confine ourselves for the time being to setting forth the present state of the question, reserving the right of applying these acquired truths afterwards.

II

It was while making his ingenious researches on the colouring matter of wines, on the alkaloids of tobaccos, and on the diverse animal albumens, etc., that M. Armand Gautier, the learned author of *Mécanisme de la variation des êtres vivants*,[1] arrived at his luminous conclusions. According to him, every time there is variation and production of a new race, not only do the external, anatomical and histological characteristics of the new being vary, *but even the structure and composition itself of its plasmas,* or at least the immediate products of their *fonctionnement.*

This change takes place both in the reproductive cells and in the vegetative cells (somatic). In short, a new race means a profound variation of plasmas.

We know, moreover, the striking analogy between vegetable races and those of the animal world. The origin of species and variations appears in the two worlds under analogous conditions. The analysis made with regard to modifications undergone by plants gives consequently the right of drawing conclusions as to those which animal variations and species must undergo. Studies made concerning plants, which are easier

---

[1] See especially his *Mémoire*, read Nov. 16, 1901, at the *Congrès international de l'hybridation de la vigne*, held at Lyons.

from the point of view of experiments, are striking with regard
to their final exactness.

But in comparing the different varieties of cultivated vines
M. Armand Gautier has established[1] that each variation of
vine stock possesses specific colouring matter, proper to itself,
which can be distinguished at the same time by its chemical
characteristics and by its centesimal composition. Their
differences do not stop there, for the internal changes which
accompany the appearance of new races of vines are most
numerous. If the colouring matter of different vine stocks is
examined, certain of them will be found soluble in pure water
(le Petit Bouschet), whereas others remain insoluble. Some
become, after their preparation, insoluble in alcohol (Carignan),
whilst others precipitate acetate of lead into blue indigo
(Teinturier or Carignan), others into dark green (Aramon).

Similar phenomena are found in examining other plants.
Let us take, for instance, different kinds of pines and we shall
see here also the essential internal modifications which divide
them. Thus the Maritime pine of the Landes gives a resin
which throws to the left the line of polarised light, whilst that
of the Australian pine throws it to the right. The different
kinds of acacias produce special gums, as other trees of other
varieties give different tannins. According to the observations
made by M. Charabot and M. Ebray, the variety of peppermint
known as basilic produces a dextrogyrate essence of which the
smell is quite different from that of the levogyrate essence of
ordinary mint. Thus the examples furnished by the comparison
of colouring matter and gums might be multiplied to infinitude.
These principles characterise species and varieties. What do
these essential differences which separate them signify? It is
that the cellular plasmas from which all these principles have
issued have equally undergone profound variations. The
modification of cellular plasmas occasions in its turn the
modification of the cells which are derived from them.

[1] Here, for example, are the colouring matters of different vine stocks :—

Aramon	$C^{46}H^{36}O^{20}$
Carignan	$C^{42}H^{40}O^{20}$
Grenache	$C^{46}H^{44}O^{20}$
Teinturier	$C^{46}H^{40}O^{20}$
Petit Bouschet	$C^{45}H^{38}O^{20}$
Gamay	$C^{40}H^{40}O^{20}$, &c.

III

Let us make an incursion into the animal world, and we shall see an analogous change in the composition of their plasma varying according to species and race.   The comparative analysis of their albuminoid matters brings out this startling truth, that species or race signifies here also change of plasma in the same way as vines change their colouring matter.   It is thus that the albumens of the horse and of the mule vary in the same way as do those of monkey and man.

The recent studies on antitoxins and *anticorps* have also confirmed and extended this theory.   The hæmoglobin of the blood in passing from one animal to another differs every time, as is demonstrated by its crystalline forms, its secondary properties and the hematines which are derived from it (P. Cazeneuve quoted by A. Gautier).

What does this signify, if not that the variations which characterise the appearance of species or of race are very profound ?   In acting on the albuminous plasma, the serum of the blood in animals or tannins, the colouring matters or catechines of plants, they succeed in making an impression on the whole being.   All the constituent molecules of the individual are attacked by them.   In one word, it is not a matter of an external change, but of a profound revolution undergone by the whole being.

If we pass to the supposed races of men, we shall see that this essential condition of the formation of varieties is completely lacking.   The anthropologists have not succeeded in finding the essential variations in the composition of the blood between men of yellow, black and white colour, of broad and narrow skull, of the smallest cranial capacity and those of the most astonishing greatness !

What is no less conclusive is that the part which the composition of blood plays in demonstrating the difference between race and species is known.   It is only the blood of beings belonging to the same variety and to the same race which may be injected into them with impunity.   Thus the blood of a hare may be injected into the organism of a rabbit, or that of a mouse into that of a rat, but the blood of man may not be injected into the organism of a dog, a horse, or any other animal whatsoever.   Neither can the blood of an animal be injected into the veins of a man.   In all these cases the foreign blood, not being able to unite, will be destroyed, or will destroy the organism which has received the injection.   On the other hand, the blood of a white man or a negro may be injected into the organism of a yellow man, or that of a negro into the blood of white or yellow.   It goes without saying that the form of the skull, as well as the other grounds on which the anthropological divisions of human beings rest, plays as negative a part as the colour of their skin.

CHAPTER IV

THE DISTINCTIONS BETWEEN HUMAN VARIATIONS AND THOSE OF THE OTHER TWO KINGDOMS (*continued*)

IN the desire to apply to man the ideas derived from the modifications undergone by plants and animals, inevitable errors are readily made. Analogy does not constitute identity. The anthropologists have pursued a wrong course in identifying human variations, which are all superficial, with those radical and intrinsic ones which appear as the result of evolution or spasmodic progress. For reasons which it will be necessary to consider again, man shows in comparison with other living beings a quasi-physiological permanence which is moreover in perfect harmony with the hypothesis of transformation. Man, it is true, is above everything else the product of millions of years of evolution, undergone by the first plasma. He is subsequently the late product of a geological epoch, which has followed so many preceding transformations realised on our globe. But once having appeared in his present form, he has scarcely varied morphologically, since the far-back period when we first trace his marks on the earth. Without wishing to divine the reasons of his organic persistence, it is enough to state that man is far from presenting as many traits entirely dissimilar from his primitive stock, as we recognise in examining the representatives of the other worlds. Nowhere is this phenomenon seen in man, which is so general elsewhere. If everywhere the number of varieties tends to augment and to differentiate more and more, the human species alone is an exception to this rule.

What then are varieties if they are not species in way of formation? It is enough to transport an animal or vegetable group into a new country, to see with what rapidity its morphological structure changes in adapting itself to the changed conditions of its existence. Can the same be said of man?

It is generally admitted that each being tends to progress, that is to say, to perfect itself. In what does progress consist? Beings in evolving place themselves in a more and more intimate harmony with their surroundings. Looked at from this point of view, man is no exception to the rule admitted with regard to all other organic creations. What varies is the form of progress. In nearly all organised beings it is restricted, according to the definition of von Baer, to the specialisation of the different parts of the body, conformably with their functions as with the extent of these differentiated parts. In a word, everything is reduced to the augmentation of the differentiated members which must be specialised in the functions assigned to them in the economy of the organism. Only allowing that for vertebrates progress is specially limited to the perfecting of their intellect, it would be *a fortiori* the same in the case of man. Is he not the intelligent being *par excellence*? Moreover his royal position in nature, which he has acquired in the course of his existence, having become his owing to this unique factor, it is very natural that progress in his case should manifest itself solely in this particular.

On the other hand, having acquired a morphological organisation fitted to render him the greatest services in the struggle for life, man only needs to guard its normal working. Here again his intellect serves him as a guide and a sure regulator. This explains why we notice so little change in him since the earliest traces of prehistoric man. The skulls which, like the organs of mastication, have served in particular to distinguish men, present no perceptible differences.

Men of past epochs did not give birth to species analogous to those of the animal or vegetable world. As we shall see later on, the bases of distinction between human beings are sometimes fictitious, sometimes superficial and always deceptive. The reason for this phenomenon is evident. Man has evolved under the influence of intellectual and psychical factors. The progress which has been particularly marked in this domain has left the morphological domain almost intact. When modifications appear they are of a transient nature and in every case realisable by other men when placed in like conditions.

The animal life of man, in whatever latitude, has always had to reckon with his brain or his soul, whose influence neutralised the action directed against his physiological unity. Man from all times has been driven to dominate external obstacles and to subjugate them to the profit of his own individuality. These efforts of his common mentality have given him analogous or rather identical traits. This is one of the principal reasons which make humanity one and indivisible. Its distinctions will always be concerned with superficial details. These, coming as the result of momentary circumstances, disappear with them, which is an additional proof that they do not touch the essence of his being.

It is thus that so many phenomena which in other worlds characterise the appearance of races and varieties perish before human resistance. For instance, the preponderating influence which parasites exercise on the birth of new races is known ; under the influence of certain insects acting on plants these are transformed into new varieties. According to the observations of M. Marin Maillard,[1] the flowers of the *Matricaria inodora*, when attacked by the *Perosnospora Radii*, assume the form of the double flowers of the Radiæ.

We could quote other innumerable examples.

All these variations in plants are complemented by the anatomical changes of the vegetative or floral organs. The mass of these modifications go so far as to constitute new species or races.

We know the imposing number of the diseases of a parasitic nature which ravage humanity. Nevertheless, neither under the influence of the bacteria of yellow fever, nor those of syphilis or diphtheria, does man as a species degenerate, nor does he rise to the formation of a new variety. If the individual is hurt or destroyed, the human species remains intact. When the majority of its members are assailed by the action of certain destroying parasites, a people naturally begins to show signs of

[1] *Recherches sur les cécidies florales.*

physical decadence. But it is sufficient that the cause of the evil should disappear in order that this apparent decadence might disappear also. We have seen it among people who are victims of malaria, after the marshes have dried and the parasites of this malady have been annihilated. Whatever may be the virulence of the evil, it never causes the appearance of a new species of men nor the disintegration of humanity.

CHAPTER V

THERE are as many anthropological schools as there are divisions among men. Their arbitrariness is obvious. It is sufficient to examine their foundations to see their fantastical character. Whereas some only try to divide humanity into four strictly distinct branches, others, more generous, go so far as to present hundreds of divisions and subdivisions. The multiplicity of all these systems and the impossibility of defending these outrageous and extravagant hypotheses are so many warnings to unprejudiced people to guard themselves against these quasi-scientific discoveries. What increases the difficulty of locating oneself in this labyrinth is that every classification, whatever its value, is decidedly vague and idealistic, for with rare exceptions human beings as anthropological types or divisions are everywhere commingled.

The incessant migrations in the past, as well as the mutual interpenetration of peoples in modern times, make a pure race answering to the ideas of the theorists almost impossible of discovery.

Let us add that specialists themselves, who undertake the difficult task of splitting humanity into ethnical races and groups, are rarely united on the nature and the essential characteristics of these groupings. For it is as easy to find the pure type of any zoological species as it is hard to find one in the world of man.

When, after having adopted a precise definition on the subject of any race, it is believed that a representative in flesh and bones has been found, many characteristics are seen which mark him off clearly from the type which he *ought* to incarnate

Real life, without otherwise considering the superior interests of anthropologists, has endowed him with one or many traits which sometimes distinguish him slightly from others and sometimes fix him decidedly in an ethnical group from which he ought to be fundamentally separated. The more the many cases are studied of individuals matured in some human agglomeration, the more is it seen that in all real instances they are attached by visible or invisible links to all those from whom it is desired to detach them.

After all, has not the historical evolution of peoples placed an invincible obstacle in the way of all these divisions ? With the exception of primitive or entirely savage peoples, the number of which is insignificant, the countries which have played or are playing, or are destined some time to play, a part in the march of humanity, have become the scene of an infinite mixture of peoples, groups and races. Wherever we turn our eyes we nowhere see anthropological groups, but ethnical agglomerations created by community of language or that of economical, social, political and religious interests.

Sheltered on the same soil, bound together by common interests, connected by unions of blood and family, evolving under the influence of analogous conditions of psychic and moral surroundings, exposed and condemned to undergo the impress of so many conditions of heredity and of the formation of their physiological, intellectual and moral type, the component parts of a people, which last is a purely abstract expression, become finally similar to one another in spite of the diversity of their origins. Owing to the influence of inter-breeding, practised almost unconsciously, they lose their essential differences, if ever they had them. Owing to the influence of the conditions of an identical life they acquire a common type, resulting from so many factors, which have fashioned the human species.

The more one reflects on the matter, the more it is perceived that if the division into races ever had its cause in a distant past, it has lost them in the course of history. As humanity advances, the theory of races recedes. The two only form a game of see-saw, the one end going up as the other goes down. It is thus that theoretically the science of races seems to be condemned beforehand, when regarded without the partisanship of a school or of blind human pride. The type of race conceived in irrealisable conditions must necessarily be somewhat fictitious if it is to be considered outside of its historical past. Strictly speaking, we can understand the speculations of a palæontologist who, taking his stand on fossil remains, tries to reconstruct by their aid certain contrary types of men, but with greatest difficulty can we conceive the attitude of a modern anthropologist who, in the face of some of the inhabitants of different European countries, finds it necessary to lodge them in opposite camps. Whereas his attempt at division, based on an uncertain science, fastens on all sorts of transient and deceptive traits, the unity of civilised man which lies behind this mirage laughs at all these subterfuges and presents itself in smiling harmony to impartial observation.

In the first place, what is a human *race*, this type of differentiation to which it is desired to bring back humanity? When this term, race, is used in speaking of domestic animals, its meaning and bearing are easily grasped. But the life of human beings, evolving under the influence of so many distinctive elements, does not allow the use of the same term. It is to man that the theory maintained with so much talent by Lamarck is particularly applicable, viz., " The classifications are artificial, for nature has created neither classes nor orders nor families nor kinds nor permanent species, but *only individuals.*" Moreover it is enough to examine the individuals composing an ethnical group in order to see that there are more differences between them than between races conceived as opposing unities.

Herbert Spencer [1] also tells us that classifications are only subjective conceptions to which no demarcation corresponds in nature. Their only purpose is to limit and arrange the matters submitted to our researches, in order to facilitate the work of the mind. Unfortunately, this logical process, the purpose of which should be to simplify our studies by assisting the memory, acquires in the eyes of the profane a real and independent existence. A simple symbol under these conditions receives a soul and becomes a living entity. In classification, which is the logical means of grouping these facts, one gradually becomes accustomed to see an expression of real life. The four or forty

[1] *Principles of Biology.*

races or sub-races are thus deemed to represent to our eyes real and essential divisions. With the assistance of the defects of our mentality, those very persons who knowingly used the logical method of division become afterwards its first victims. By using this two-edged sword, anthropologists succumb to their own reasoning. They often begin by speaking of races as artificial categories and end by treating them as fixed barriers between human beings. Entirely subservient to their mental divisions which have been created by reasoning, they forget that each being has its own individuality, and that the individual is the only objective reality. They forget, in addition, that race is only a conception of our mind, the consequence of subjective thought, depending as much on our faculties as on the weakness of our reasoning. Moreover, they also express our sentiments of like and dislike.

We thus perceive a whole series of obstacles rising before the man who classifies.

When he happens by chance to unite in himself an impartial spirit, vast knowledge, the patience of an observer, and a superhuman perseverance in collecting facts, he must not forget that his edifice is only a simple mirage of logical processes. Its construction is limited by his conscience and by his weak and fallible reasonings. For (and we cannot insist sufficiently on this point) race is only an abstract image, the existence of which does not lie outside our brain.

II

The word " race " is of modern origin. Its fanatics, it is true, find it in Hippocrates himself, but in that far-back time the term " race " cannot have had the signification which we attribute to it in our day. Topinard only notes it about the year 1600. François Taut, notably in his *Trésor de la langue française*, seems to be the first who used it in the modern sense. " Race comes from radix, a root (so he tells us), and refers to the extraction of man, dog or horse. We say they are of good or bad race."

With Buffon the idea of race enters into the world of science. Let us note this singular fact that the illustrious author of the

Histoire naturelle générale et particulière [1] is much nearer the truth in his definition of race than many savants of our time. Race, to him, is only a variety caused and fixed by climatic influences, food and habits. But this fixity is subordinate to the *milieu*, according to Buffon. It "persists as long as the *milieu* remains and disappears when the *milieu* changes." From Buffon's time likewise, the scientific researches on the varieties which are met with in the human species might be dated. In following the movement inaugurated by him, Daubenton published his curious memoir on *le Trou occipital dans l'homme et les animaux*, and Camper, the famous Dutch physician, his *Dissertation sur les différences réelles que présentent les traits du visage chez les hommes de différents pays et de différents âges* (1791). Having conceived his work more from an artistic point of view (for the author's purpose was to provide artists with the means of comparing the heads of men of different races), Camper afterwards enlarged his field and included the animal world as well. It is to him we owe the famous "facial angle," which was to engender subsequently hundreds of anthropometrical measures. Almost at the same time as Camper, Blumenbach brought out his *Decades VIII. craniorum diversarum gentium* (1790-1808). The start was given. From almost everywhere there came from that time studies on races with their various definitions and classifications.

The beginning of the nineteenth century was the epoch of great travels and fruitful explorations. It was likewise the epoch of the blossoming of the natural sciences. The struggle revolving round the unity and the plurality of the human species set going several generations of savants. Does humanity descend from a single primitive type (monogenesis) or has it several distinct ancestors (polygenesis)? Here is a quarrel which has brought us a most imposing literature.

Let us state, however, that polygenesis is being more and more proved to be erroneous, the theory of the evolution of species having given it a mortal blow. But all the vicissitudes of this desperate struggle reacted on the science of races. If the multiplicity of human origins had triumphed, what arguments there would have been in favour of the superiority of certain human stocks over others ! There was even a time when slave merchants and the barbarous governments which protected their commerce used polygenesis to justify the traffic in Negroes, who were regarded as having originated outside white humanity.[1] Fortunately, as the science of man advanced, polygenesis lost ground. To-day the question of the unity or plurality of our species appears to be postponed. Let us take this opportunity of stating that this dispute has only a purely theoretical value from the point of view of our thesis. As we shall see later on, inasmuch as all these differences between human beings are lost under the influence of the *milieu*, the doctrine of equality may be defended in spite of and even in opposition to the upholders of polygenesis.

With this imaginary enemy actually in its death-throes, and with the ground of discussion thus cleared, the philosophy of races anticipates nothing but profit. Consequently, as Darwin[2] remarks, it becomes a matter of indifference whether the diverse human varieties are designated under the name of races or whether the expressions species and sub-species be used. · Let us, therefore, put on one side the species of the upholders of polygenesis, and occupy ourselves with human races properly so called.

Everything which we have said above of their abstract and conventional value makes us assume the ease and spontaneity with which they are born and divided. In reality a dictionary of races, according to the anthropologists, would require a thick book with thousands of names and as many headings.

The wherefore of this diversity is often only to be found in the desire to be distinguished from one's forerunners or to bewilder the crowd. It would, without doubt, be wearisome to examine them from every point of view. Only the curiosity and the vogue which certain systems have enjoyed could justify such an examination. We shall quote some of them according to

---

[1] The theory of monogenesis is defended with a wealth of the most convincing arguments by Prichard in his classical *Researches into the Physical History of Man* (1837 ; 5 vols.), and in the luminous study of Quatrefages, *l'Espèce humaine.* The two authors seem to us to have completely exhausted the subject.

[2] *Descent of Man.*

the notoriety of their authors and the value of their definitions. The mass of them will show us their purely conventional significance.

III

According to I. Geoffroy Saint-Hilaire, the word race comprises "a succession of individuals born of one another, and distinguished by certain characteristics which have become permanent." Let us note, however, that *permanence* does not mean *fixity*, and therefore this definition has the merit of being distinctly liberal in the sense of the continual variability of human beings. Prichard goes still further in this direction, and adds that "the collected individuals forming a race present certain characteristics more or less common to all, and transmissible by heredity, whilst the origin of these characteristics is left on one side and held back." According to Quatrefages, "race is an aggregate of individuals resembling one another, belonging to the same species, having received and transmitting by way of generation the characteristics of a *primitive* variety." The word *primitive* clearly betrays the thought of the ardent defender of the unity of the human species, for his definition leads us to believe that from the beginning of humanity there were clearly established varieties! This is the idea which prevails in the writings of the upholders of polygenesis. According to Pouchet, for example, the word race means "the *different natural groups* of the human family."

All modern anthropologists, however, only see in human races varieties bound together by certain common characteristics. Broca is equally careful to add that this more or less direct relationship between individuals of the same variety "does not solve, either affirmatively or negatively, the question of affinity between individuals of different varieties."

Nevertheless, after descending from these heights, we see what a gulf often separates these definitions from their application. For even the broadest of them which concede most to the specific characteristics of the variations, appear to make amends for having used the word race which is so inappropriate to human beings.

Under the influence of the analogous use of the term which

is also applied to the animal world, there arises in our mind the conception of identity between human races and animal races. Interest and passion, which are absent when we are concerned with the other two kingdoms, enter here with such force that they finally create clouds which completely hide or in any case modify the real import of the term. For, because human varieties are defined in the same way as animal and vegetable varieties, it does not follow that they are identical. We have already seen that, on the contrary, the distinctive traits are as clearly marked and defined in the other kingdoms as they are transitory among human beings. Thus in the animal or vegetable world, when there is a salient characteristic which sharply separates from its surroundings a group or race, such a characteristic is constant and as stable as possible. It is met with in its fixed form throughout the whole of the variety, and its permanence and rigorous stability constitute the essence of the variety. Is it the same with human beings? Here not only do the individuals *not* resemble the type which ought to incarnate the race, but this type of race itself is, according to Lamarck's just statement, only a product of art.

Moreover it is sufficient to remember the fact of intelligence which cements the unity of the human species. Its influence even fashions their morphology. Only this circumstance makes the application of the term race to men and animals in a similar sense impossible. Yet our mental necessity which forces us to classify and arrange facts is the cause of this fatal division of humanity. But in order to avoid the inconvenience, we must do away with this identity of terms. The word race appears to us, for the reasons indicated, quite inappropriate. The identity of the word implies for simple minds an identity of phenomena, which makes us understand the ease with which the masses come to conceive of human and animal races in the same light. To avoid confusion in our ideas, the cause of the confusion must be destroyed. Instead therefore of the term " race," that of " *human variety* " should be used in preference. Moreover its definition should take into account the facts established by the science of man. Inasmuch as the distinctive traits of human varieties are the products of the *milieu*, which, after having created them, can afterwards destroy them, this circumstance of first importance should likewise not be omitted in the definition. From this point of view, a human variety may be defined as *a group of individuals bound together by certain permanent characteristics and distinguished by other passing traits from other human groups*. The permanent characteristics in this case are those characteristics which are common to the whole of humanity. The passing characteristics are those distinctions which are only the effect of the many circumstances amassed by the *milieu* and which are merely of a temporary nature. This definition has the advantage of laying special stress on the unity of humanity and of setting in relief the important distinction between human divisions and animal divisions.

IV

The necessarily vague sense in which the word race is used by all authors has facilitated the appearance of numerous classifications. The meaning of definition is "to state the attributes which distinguish a particular thing and which pertain to it to the exclusion of everything else." [1] Now, as we shall see later on, nature has certainly sown distinctive and exclusive traits with an exasperating profusion amongst all human varieties. A race has sometimes one and sometimes ten or twenty qualities analogous or dissimilar to that which it is desired to contrast with it. How then can it be distinguished from the mass of the others and given its proper definition? It becomes still more difficult to classify all the human varieties. How is it to be done?

This demarcation of human beings is somewhat like the task which would fall on a mathematician to find the number of the different combinations into which twenty persons placed round a table could be formed. We know, for example, that the placing of twelve persons can effect 479 million combinations, whilst an additional person would bring the number up to 6,500,000,000. If one adds still another person, the fourteen could effect 91,000,000,000 combinations. When we come to fifteen persons, the number of possible combinations

---

[1] Littré's *Dictionnaire de la Langue française*.

attains the fantastic figure of 1,350,000,000,000. Now, the number of the elements which enter into the classification of human beings is very considerable. The anthropologists of the ship *Novare* (see the works of Weisbach) adopted forty-two methods of measurement, whilst anthropological instructions generally demand from observers from twenty to forty necessary data. Broca takes note of thirty-four of the first order, Topinard eighteen necessary and fifteen optional ones, whereas Quetelet points out forty-two in his *Anthropométrie*. And when it is considered that though essential they are not identical in all authors, the possibility and the facility with which human races may be created at will can be easily imagined! Far from being astonished at the number already extant, we must bless Heaven for having preserved us from a thousand million races and consequent classifications!

Let us, however, endeavour to quote several of the most scientific, now that their purely relative value has been shown by all that we have said above.

Let us begin with that of Linnæus, who still appears in modern anthropology under diverse forms. According to him, man comprises three different sections, viz., *sapiens*, *ferus* and *monstruosus*. The first is subdivided into Europeans with fair hair, blue eyes and white complexions; the Asiatic with blackish hair, brown eyes and yellowish complexion; the African with black and woolly hair, flat nose and thick lips; the American with tawny complexion, black hair and beardless chin. The man *ferus* (savage) is mute, hairy and walks on all fours, whereas the man *monstruosus* is divided into plagiocephalic and microcephalic.

Professor Blumenbach popularised the word *Caucasian*, which applies to a whole human variety originating in the Caucasus. This term was maintained by Cuvier, who, as against Blumenbach, admitted only three instead of five races (Caucasian, Mongolian and Negro). He multiplies, however, the subdivisions. Thus with him the white or Caucasian race has three branches: Aramean (Semitic), the Indo-pelasgian and the Scythotartar. The Mongolian branch comprises the Chinese, Kalmucks, Manchurians, Japanese, Coreans and the inhabitants of the Caroline and Marian Islands.

Bory de Saint-Vincent, starting from the position that Adam

was only the father of the Jews, divided humanity into fifteen species, and these in their turn into a number of races and sub-races.   Let us add that it is the Arabian species which has the signal honour of sheltering the descendants of Adam, who are divided into Jews and Arabs, whereas all the other species, Hyperborean, Australian, Columbian, &c., are outside these privileged limits.

Subsequently the classifications in being, multiplied and rami-fied to suit the convenience of savants and of their more or less exact notions of human conformation and qualities, varied from the three races of Cuvier, the four of Leibnitz and Kant, and the nine centres of Agassiz, and at length reached a hundred. Even a hundred and twenty have been proclaimed in certain anthropo-logical congresses.

Isidore Geoffroy Saint-Hilaire divides human beings into *orthognathic* (oval face with vertical jaws), *eurignathic* (high cheek bones, Mongolian type), *prognathic* (projecting jaws, Ethiopian type), *eurignathic and prognathic* (cheek bones far apart, projecting jaws, Hottentot type).

Gratiolet distinguished *frontal, parietal* and *occipital* races, characterised by the prominence of the front, middle and back parts of the skull and brain.

According to Huxley, men are divided into two capital sec-tions, the *ulotrichi* with woolly hair and the *lesostrichi* with smooth hair.

Certain anthropologists would divide humanity according to the facial profile. Warushkin[1] in this way discovers the Mongolian, African, European and Juvenile profiles. The first is weak in two ways, horizontal and vertical.   The second is weakly developed horizontally, but strongly accen-tuated vertically. It is found among the Negroes and Austra-lians. The European type is distinguished by a profile strongly marked in both ways. The Juvenile profile, which is proper to Slavs and youths, is strongly accentuated horizontally, but slightly vertically.

As the science of man develops, the desire to classify and simplify the collected facts encourages more and more numerous demarcations of men.

[1] *Ueber die Profilirung des Gesichtsschaedels.*

As morphology is no longer sufficient for this task, they have recourse to the psychological and mental life in order to find in them new standpoints. Thus it is that the ideal tendencies and aspirations of human beings are taken into account and so contribute to render more difficult the pass in which the classifiers find themselves. Among the anthropo-psychologists with whom we shall be occupied later on, the number of divisions becomes incalculable, for fancy and caprice replace in a decided manner the measurements of the savants. We remember in this connection the attempts of M. Fétis to divide humanity according to the musical systems of its representatives, and that of César Daly advocating, with the same object in view, the differences according to architectonic works.

The few facts noticed are sufficient to reveal the vague interest of all these divisions. To give a more exact idea of them we shall proceed in an anatomical order. We shall examine man according to the essential parts of his body and we shall study the consecutive divisions founded on them. The systematic *study* of the salient parts of our organism allows us to grasp vividly the difficulties which the science of races has to combat. As the essential divisions of human beings have their starting-point especially in the head and the comparative conformation of its parts, their *analysis* will singularly facilitate our task. For let us not forget that the skull and the brain, prognathism and the facial angles have furnished for their part nine-tenths of all the divisions and of all the systems of inequality among human beings.

CHAPTER VI

THE DIVISIONS OF HUMANITY FROM A CRANIOLOGICAL POINT OF VIEW

I

THE skull has served as a starting-point for a whole series of divisions among human beings, adopted by the anthropologists of all countries and of the most diverse schools. In its more or less defined forms, natural frontiers of separation among men, united under so many other aspects, were thought discoverable. The various forms of the skull in this way caused humanity to be divided into more opposed categories than could have been done by their different modes of living or thinking.

Craniometry, this important branch of anthropology, henceforward assumed an altogether overwhelming position in the science of human races. With its fellow, cephalometry, it is responsible for the innumerable errors with which modern anthropology overflows.

Cephalometry gives the head measure of a living being or of a corpse, whereas *craniometry* only takes account of the bare skull. With reference to measurements, there now exist numerous instruments as well as complicated methods. Unfortunately measurements of the skull continue to be made by all sorts of amateurs who are ignorant of this important fact, that, from a simple amusement, craniometry has almost become a science, and one of very technical complexity. The lack of method and of elementary ideas which characterises the works of so many amateur anthropologists results in particular in a lack of unity and cohesion in their observations. This robs their easy and superficial generalisations of all credibility.

Even those who have recourse to special instruments do not know how to use them. Thus a large number of measurements made are often grotesque, and nearly always useless, because each investigator has used the instruments in his own way. When the instruments are the same, there is need to be careful not to change methods in the course of the research. These quasi-experimentalists, however, adopt measurements condemned by experience, and neglect others which are indispensable. They compare numbers which have only in common the names of the headings under which it is desired to place them. In this way considerable errors and shocking inexactitudes are made which disconcert the specialists and engender ridiculous ideas among the ignorant. Truth is only saved through errors which are " gross as a mountain, open, palpable." This seems paradoxical, but is nevertheless true, for these superfluities and extravagances of science enter even into the works of comparative anthropology and create hopeless confusion in the thought of credulous readers. The doctrinaires, then, rejoice in the essential differences which separate not only the brains of savage and civilised men but also the inhabitants of two neighbouring communities. Science, which generally rebels against monstrous mistakes, allows itself to be duped by errors apparently trivial, which, once admitted into its domain, cause incalculable complications. A specialist in cephalic anthropometry, who would show up the innumerable faults and inexactitudes with which the works of the best known anthropologists swarm, would have before him the labours of a new Hercules.

Of the immense mass of craniological estimates there would perhaps only be a vast chaos of errors which would make any positive conclusion impossible. It is enough to say that even two specialists, accustomed to technical methods of measurement, can make serious mistakes in working on the same subject if they have not taken the precaution of harmonising their methods at the beginning.

The anthropologists in general seem to be faithful to the popular dictum which identifies a strong head with a big one. But without espousing Aristotle's paradox that the smallest heads are also the most intelligent, and that man arrives at greater intelligence than other animals merely because the dimensions of his head are relatively smaller, we must nevertheless repudiate the forced relativity of the head's bigness to its intelligence. Professor Parchappe, in his luminous *Recherches sur l'encéphale, sa structure, ses fonctions et ses maladies* (1836), used later on by Broca, opposes with many confirmatory proofs the necessary connection between imbecility or idiocy and a decided smallness of head. He stated, for example, after a number of comparative measurements, that of the fifty heads of men of normal intelligence which he had studied, seven had inferior dimensions to those of the imbecile subjected to observation, whereas thirteen of them had dimensions very slightly superior. On the other hand, the head of an intelligent woman was found to be perceptibly inferior to the dimensions of the head of an idiot. Parchappe concludes from this that intelligence can manifest itself in its normal degree in a head whose volume is inferior, equal, or only slightly superior to the volume of the heads of idiots. Even among these last, and among classified imbeciles, the degree of intelligence is not in proportion to the bigness of the head. Thus, in his list of imbeciles, the feeblest, whose head was only in horizontal circumference 460 millimetres, proved to be the most intelligent of the group, for he alone spoke and knew the value of money.

II

The measurement of an essential element like the cubature of the skull, made according to the same method, can give results differing to the extent of 100 centimetres. The differences of the occipital length of the same head may present differences of about 20 millimetres. The result depends not only on the difference of instruments but also on the way of measuring the parts submitted to examination. An anthropologist as circumspect as M. L. Manouvrier formulates even this bold conclusion, "that it is imprudent to use the anthropometrical figures collected by observers whose method of work is not known *de visu* unless it is found that they served a practical apprenticeship in a laboratory or with a master whose method is known, or, still better, unless they have *minutely described their mode of operation.*" [1]

It is sufficient then to take note of the complicated processes of measurement as practised in the anthropometrical laboratories of our time, to perceive how much the value of these hasty generalisations on the human races is to be suspected.

Most of the treatises on our organic inequality appear forgetful of the fact that the size and form of the skull depend in the first place on the physical constitution. On the other hand, the cephalic index is not always at one with the form of the skull which ought to result from it. Sergi,[2] for instance, has demonstrated that a skull which, according to the measurement of the index, ought to be dolichocephalic might be brachycephalic and *vice versa*. Nor can reliance be placed on the division of the skull's height by its length, for "a skull which on examination appears developed in height may, on the contrary, be low if of notable length" (Giuffrida Ruggeri). The same anthropologist, perceiving the great variability of the skull, suggests a classification of skulls according to morphological, ethnical and sexual variations, physical constitution, variations on the ground of atavism and infancy, and, lastly, individual variations. Manouvrier dwells on the difficulty of connecting the numerous variations of the skull with the variations of intelligence or character. According to him "it is absolutely erroneous to make of the variations of the cephalic index a sort of phrenology of races, for no biological fact justifies it." "On the contrary (he tells us), the variations of the cephalic index are the most insignificant physiologically. In the brachycephalic, the skull gains in breadth what it loses in length."

On the other hand, it must not be forgotten that many peoples have had their skulls altered under the influence of purely mechanical causes.

The custom of deforming the head in order to give it a narrow shape, which seemed to be *à la mode* long before the

[1] See L. Manouvrier's *Céphalométrie anthropologique* in the *Année psychologique*, 1899.
[2] *Specie e varieta umane.*

time of Gobineau and Ammon, was in past time much in vogue. Hippocrates speaks of the macrocephalic folk who, as the result of artificial deformation, had long heads. The heads of children from their tenderest age were subjected to pressure by means of bandages and with the aid of mechanical pressure. In time, Hippocrates tells us, the change became natural.[1] Strabo, Diodorus Siculus, Pliny, &c., confirm this custom. Sidonius Apollinarius himself tells us with a mass of details which he brings to bear on the matter how the members of a people who came from the Scythian plains (the Huns) succeeded in giving to their heads the form of a cone.[2] According to Amédée Thierry,[3] certain peoples overcome by the Huns imitated their custom of deforming the skull in order to resemble them, whence sprang the numerous traces of this custom which is met with even in our days.

We also find in the old books of Adrian Spiegel of Brussels,[4] &c., J. Bodin,[5] &c., curious indications concerning the processes adopted by Belgians to possess skulls like the dolichocephalic heads of their Germanic conquerors. They bandaged the heads of adults, but they commonly began by tightening the heads of the new-born.

Lagneau believes that he can trace the Toulousian deformation of the skull to the Volci or Galates or Belgæ, of the northern Germanic race, whereas Broca ascribes it to the Kimmerians. According to Foville,[6] this cranial deformation is found among the inhabitants of the departments of Aude, Haute-Garonne, Tarn, &c.

In Limousin such a custom also exists. Among the descendants of the ancient Lemovices, according to M. Blanchard, the custom of using very tight bonnets in order to give the head a long shape still exists. This allowed more room

---

[1] Hippocrates, *On airs and waters*, Vol. II.
[2] *Panegyric of Anthemius.*   [3] *Histoire d'Attila et de ses successeurs*, Vol. II.
[4] *De humani corporis fabrica.* Venetis, 1727.
[5] *Methodus ad facilem historiarum cognitionem.* Amstelodami, 1850.
[6] *Déformation du crâne*, 1834, quoted by Lagneau in his *Anthropologie de France* : "The head being submitted from infancy to the circular constriction of a fronto-occipital bandage which depresses the coronal and the bregmatic fontanel, there results a diminution of the encephalic capacity and the reduction of the frontal lodge. The anterior cerebral lobe, depressed above and in front, lengthens from the front to the back at the expense of the parietal lobe." See also Broca's *Sur la déformation toulousaine du crâne*.

for memory, according to the precepts of the Jesuit Father, Josset, which are very popular in that district.

It must also not be forgotten that the form of the skull may change under the influence of diet. This is at least what Nathusius, Nyström[1] and so many other observers affirm. Darwin had already[2] taught us that the skulls of many of our improved and domesticated races had varied perceptibly, and he quotes in addition to pigs diverse races of rabbits and many races of fowls.

It must likewise be remembered that there is a perceptible difference between the skulls of men and those of women. This demarcation has an importance which deserves consideration. Many German savants who have made a special study of the craniological differences between the two sexes of the German people have certain typical traits to show us on this subject. A. Ecker dwells on the specific structure of the female skull, especially in what concerns the vertex (the most elevated point in the skull's arch). According to Welcker, the skull of German women is in general narrower and flatter than that of the men. Virchow even tells us that this difference exercises a decided influence on the cranial configuration, for in progeniture, where maternal influence predominates, the skull, including that of male infants, is affected by the cranial structure of the mother. If the fact observed by Virchow was authentic, humanity would have before it fresh prospects for the evolution of skulls and their—infinite differentiation.

III

Since the time that Gobineau and his followers allowed themselves to be hypnotised by the conformation of the human brain, science has made singular reports. It has found in the first place that dolichocephaly, so much envied and sought after, is especially to be found among savage and primitive peoples. To attribute to these the first rank among human beings would no doubt be extravagant.

[1] *Formenveraenderungen des menschlichen Schaedels* (Arch. f. Anthrop., 1902).
[2] *Variation des animaux et des plantes*, Vol. II.

The dolichocephalic index under 76 is to be found in particular among Hottentots, the Krous Negroes, the Muchikongo and Bakongo (73) and the Ashanti, in Africa; the Papuans of New Guinea (74), diverse Australians, the islanders of the New Hebrides and the Tasmanians, in Oceania; also among Hindu tribes (Kota, Badagas, Todas of Nilghiri), the Ainos of Saghalien, the Pathans of the Punjaub, &c., in Asia; the Eskimos, Hurons and Botocudos, &c., in America; whereas in Europe it is especially the Corsicans and Portuguese who appear to embody the ideal of M. Gobineau and M. Lapouge (74 and 76).

The sub-dolichocephalic are represented among the Bushmen, Hausas, the M'Zabites, and other African tribes; among the islanders of Sumba, the Kurds, Japanese, Ostiaks, Turkomanns, Northern Chinese, Tartar Highlanders, &c., in Asia; the inhabitants of the Solomon Isles, the Marquesas Isles, divers Polynesians, &c., in Oceania; divers Indians, half-caste Algonquins, the Eskimos of Alaska, Iroquois, Sioux, Fuegians, in America. All these tribes find their equals in Europe in cephalic index among the Flemish Belgians, the French of Roussillon, Sardinians, Sicilians, Spanish Basques, &c.

Let us now pass to the mesocephalic (between 79 and 81·8). The Dutch and the Normans in Europe correspond with the Chinese of the South and the Bororo of the Amazon basin, whereas the inhabitants of Provence (81·7) correspond with the Áracanians or the Teleoutes in Asia (81·8) and the Omaha in America.

The French of the department du Nord (80·4) are on the same level with the Crow Indians (America), the Nicobarians and the Tipperds of Tchittagong (in Asia). Our Limousians and Périgordians, to whom anthropology ascribes an index of 80·7, correspond with the Nahuqua of Brazil and the Battas of Lake Toba, &c.

The sub-brachycephalic (between 82 and 84·8) are represented with the same abundance among the people of Java, Coreans, Annamites, Patagonians, Polynesians of Tahiti or Pomotou, as among the Italians in general, Magyars, Ruthenians, Tcherkesses, the Great Russians, Belgian Walloons, Russian and Galician Jews, Laplanders, the Badois, Votiaks, Bretons, the half-savage tribe of Mordwa (Russia), the Tartars of the

Caucasus and the French in general. If it is a question of the hyper-brachycephalic (over 87), the craniologists tell us that they are to be found among the Roumanches of Switzerland and the Khirgiz-Kasaks, as well as among the French of La Lozère, Cantal and Haute-Loire, the Jews of the Daghestan and the Lapps who inhabit the extreme north of Scandinavian lands.

What conclusion can be drawn from this except that all these craniological measurements teach us almost nothing concerning the mental capacity and the moral value of peoples?

Admitting that these anthropometrical calculations are absolutely and strictly exact, one is forced to draw odd deductions with reference to the respective value of races.

We are driven to place on the same level the Bushmen and the French of Roussillon, the Teleoutes and the French of the department du Nord, the Nahuquas of Brazil and the French of Limousin and the Périgord; the Mordwa, the Tartars and the Votiaks, on the same level as the French in general, the most representative type of European thought and civilisation!

On the other hand, the champions of the organic inequality of races, in desiring to hurl back these conclusions, see themselves spoiled of that which they have proclaimed as the most solid part and basis of their theory. For what is there left to them when once the cephalic index is gone?

IV

The world wherein our intellect is formed is always very mysterious. In spite of so many efforts made by the immense departments of the science of man, we are always reduced to suppositions more or less well founded whenever it is a matter of defining the sources, development or the deviations of thought. The wherefore of the mind of a genius escapes us. We can scarcely state the reasons for the mental arrest of an idiot or a cretin. The science of the localisation of our intellectual capacities follows a difficult path and its conquests are far from being definite.

In the meantime everything is subject to doubt and contradictory interpretation. Is our intellectual development in direct dependence on the volume of our heads? Is man the most intelligent among living beings because his brain presents the most advantageous proportion? The general belief is ranged on this side and rests with pride on this advantage of human beings, who thereby proclaim their superiority in the animal scale. Yet the relation of the brain's weight to that of the body is not so advantageous in the case of man as is generally supposed. It is true that, the proportions being equal, the anthropoid ape shows a relationship three times less and a dog ten times. But take the case of a cat and a lion. Whereas in the cat the relation of the brain's weight to that of the body is 1 to 106, the same relation in the lion is 1 to 546.[1] Must we conclude from this that the cat is five times more intelligent than the lion? On the other hand, it is known that the smaller the animal the greater is the relationship of the brain's weight to that of the body. This once admitted, can it be deduced that small animals are relatively more intelligent than animals of great height?

In order to escape from this strange conclusion, we have seen physiologists like M. Charles Richet admit the existence of a permanent intellectual element in relation to the varying cerebral mass. Dogs, whether big or little, have an equal intelligence notwithstanding their different cerebral mass. This ingenious explanation cannot be considered satisfactory. Where is the place of this constant mass which is designed to complete and to manifest this intellectual element, and what are the conditions of its activities?

It is thus that even in the case of animals we find ourselves limited to a number of hypotheses. Yet the facility with which physiologists can operate on living beings should decidedly simplify the problem and diminish its mysterious sides. Now there is only one truth which is imposed indisputably on us with regard to the animal world, and that is, that the weight of the brain corresponds in no way with the degree of intelligence.

It is the same with men, and Broca was right in deeming it

---

[1] E. Dubois, *Sur le Rapport du poids de l'encéphale avec la grandeur du corps chez les Mammifères*, Bulletin de la Société d'Anthropologie, 1897.

absurd to make the degree of intelligence depend on the dimensions of the head and consequently on its forms.

But if the extent of the cerebral volume does not solve the question, it must not be forgotten that the weight and the conformation of the skull vary and progress with instruction. The same rule applies to the brain as to the other organs of the body, which grow and develop with exercise. Now this fact is of great importance, although most anthropologists have forgotten it, for, if this question of exercise, manifested by increase of volume, is once formulated, it will be easy to draw from it certain important conclusions.

Professor Parchappe was, perhaps, the first to have the idea of the connection between the volume of the head and the work which it undergoes. After having taken a number of measures on the heads of men entirely devoted to the study of letters and science, professors and masters, placed much above the mediocre by their talents of writing and speaking, he contrasts with them measures taken on the heads of men who from childhood had been exclusively engaged in manual toil, and whose intelligence had received no culture whatsoever. The circumstances of age and height being about the same, Parchappe found that in the case of the first the head was perceptibly larger, and concluded in favour of the influence of intellectual exercise.

Following Parchappe, Professor Broca also dealt with the direct influence which the exercise of the mental faculties exerts on the volume of the head. In a memoir, published in 1873, he states that the systematic exercise of the mental faculties is favourable to their development, and that, consequently, it is possible to increase their power by special training. After having taken the attendants in the Hospital of Bicêtre as basis for comparison, and placed them in a line with the house-surgeons (doctors and chemists), he arrived at results similar to those obtained by Parchappe. All the measures of the whole head are markedly in favour of the house-surgeons, men of education, as compared with those of the attendants whose intellectual culture had been neglected.

The conclusion of Broca is formal, viz., " The house-surgeons have more voluminous heads. The education which they have received has exercised their brain and has been favourable to its development." This development is particularly noticeable in the front lobes of the brain, and to this greater development of the frontal region the greater part of the largening of their heads is due.

Elsewhere Broca, astonished by these results, informs us that education not only makes man better but it makes him superior to himself. "*It enlarges his brain and perfects its forms.*" To spread instruction, therefore, is to ameliorate the race.

M. Lacassagne and M. Cliquet, who undertook later the task of verifying these observations of Broca,[1] arrived at conclusions clearly identical. After having operated with a simple *conformateur* (which hatters use to take the shape of the head) on 190 doctors or medical men, on 133 soldiers who had received the elements of instruction, on 72 soldiers who could not read, and 91 prisoners, they stated that :—

1. The head is more developed among educated people who have exercised their brains than among the illiterate whose intellects have remained inactive.

2. Among educated people the frontal region is relatively more developed than the occipital region.

With reference to the same subject, the activities of Professor Enrico Ferri, as shown in his *Homicide,* must be mentioned. In this book he compares the head-measures of students and soldiers, and finds that the cranial capacity is much greater among the former. The researches of Vitalis, Galton and Vann, &c., only confirm the theory maintained by Parchappe and developed by Broca.

V

As Virchow has shown, the head must broaden with time in order to make room for our increasing knowledge. As the brachycephalic or rounded form possesses the advantage that it can relatively contain more cerebral mass in smaller space, the future belongs to the broad skulls, that is, to the brachycephalic! Nyström supports this theory with a curious measurement made on 500 Swedes, who are the dolichocephalic

[1] *Annales d'Hygiène publique,* 1878.

people *par excellence.* Individuals intellectually but little developed are particularly dolichocephalic. Of 100 brachycephalic persons, 58·4 belonged to the educated classes and 41·6 to the uneducated. Of 100 dolichocephalic, 76·5 were of the less cultured and 23·5 of the more cultured class.

The example of Sweden is not exceptional, for the same phenomenon is everywhere observable. When we examine entire populations according to their particular countries or provinces, we perceive that they are ranged according to three chief craniological types. According to Kollmann, of 100 modern Slavs submitted to craniological examination, 3 were dolichocephalic, 72 brachycephalic, and 25 mesocephalic; of 607 Germans, 16 per cent. were in the first category, 43 in the second, and 41 in the third. According to Virchow, of 100 North Germans, 18 were dolichocephalic, 31 brachy, and 51 mesocephalic. According to Clon Stephenos, of 100 modern Greeks, 15 were dolicho, 54 brachy, and 31 mesocephalic. Of 100 Venetians (Topinard) 17 were dolicho, 45 brachy, and 38 mesocephalic.

Deserving of notice is the fact that the same variety of types is found among primitive or semi-civilised peoples. Although negroes are deemed dolichocephalic, yet Topinard states that of 100 negro skulls, 38 were meso, and 6 brachycephalic. In the German collections of Chinese skulls, Ranke states that representatives of the three categories are found in the proportion of 12, 34, 54, &c.

What is the influence of thought on the increase of the number of the brachycephalic? It would no doubt be hazardous to say. But what is certain is that the skull is modified and varies according to circumstances.

This fact once demonstrated, we can scarcely state its full bearing. It follows in the first place not only that the encephalon can be enlarged by the effort of man, but also that the conformation of the skull is not fixed. With the enlargement of the frontal lobes and of the volume of the encephalon, the external form of the skull also enlarges. The stigma of race (if it be a stigma) must therefore often give way to the efforts or the idleness of our intellectual life. A systematic exercise of the brain can thus raise the cranial level of a representative of inferior brains, and often give him advantages over the representative of privileged or hereditary virtues. Nothing is more natural! Does not physiology teach us that every mental act involves a physiological cerebral act as an inevitable condition? In other words, to exercise the mind is to exercise the brain.

If then the yellow or black races for example are inferior to us in the matter of encephalon, which has not yet been proved, *nothing permits us* to say that they will remain so everlastingly. To deny this would be as absurd as to maintain that the brain preserves its form intact notwithstanding its educational activity or inactivity.

The modification of the craniological structure does not depend exclusively on intellectual activities. Professor Langer, the celebrated Austrian anatomist, has on this subject an hypothesis which deserves attention. According to him, the form of our skull depends in particular on our organs of mastication. Having made an enlarged drawing of the head of a new-born child, and having given it the dimensions of an adult head, which he places in comparison with the former, he shows how certain parts of the infantile head are perceptibly developed in detail under the influence of our masticating organs. Their mode of acting reacts on the skull, and Langer draws from this in an ingenious way its narrow or round form. Without wishing to subscribe to the whole of this hypothesis, which appears hazardous at first sight, we may nevertheless, without being charged with exaggeration, admit a partial influence which our masticating organs exercise on our craniological structure.

Milieu also exercises a decided influence on the skull. Virchow, E. von Baer, Ranke, and many other anthropologists explain the brachycephalic character of the Bavarians and other mountaineers by the conditions of mountain life. And when we study the rich variety of causes which influence cranial conformation, we see that skulls have intrinsically nothing fatal, nothing superior, nothing particularly noble. We can even formulate this axiom that man by his own will with the aid of factors placed at his own disposal can effect certain possible modifications in the human skull.

But let us suppose for a moment that the cephalic index

preserves all the essentials of a fixed character, and that it is transmitted by heredity across the centuries, and that we all have it just as it was with our ancestors of the neolithic age! Even in such a case it would be difficult to draw from it other conclusions than those which are drawn from a simple descriptive form. The cephalic index would have no more importance than a hand or a foot which exceeded a certain size!

In reality, when we study the influence which the form of the skull exercises on our mentality, we perceive its absolute nullity. The numerous authors who have not hesitated to base their philosophy of history as well as their systems of internal or international politics on the morphological differences of the skull, have never been able to point out to us why the brachycephalic form is incompatible with a very high mentality or very high morality.

In default of positive arguments which the adherents of this theory are very careful not to give us, we possess numerous negative proofs to the contrary. Brachycephalism never prevented Kant, Laplace or Voltaire from taking their place among the intellectual leaders of humanity. On the other hand, it ·has never been possible to show any correlation whatsoever between the value, extent or profundity of our thoughts and the craniological formation of the individual. In vain are we told of the dimensions of the skull, less (!) in the case of the brachycephalic. It is true that the skull is in this case less long, but is not this dimension royally compensated by the increase of breadth? The dolichocephalic thus gain in length what they lose in breadth! We have consequently before us a law of compensation which restores equilibrium if this last is really in danger.

In order to see of what little importance is the accentuation of the skull's length or breadth, it is sufficient to consider certain injuries to the brain and to examine their counter-effect on our mental faculties. Now it is incontestable even at a glance that it would be difficult to ascribe to the simple descriptive characteristics of the skull the importance which pertains to its alterations. Let us recall certain significant cases. Robert Hugues notes that of a man where a fragment of iron weighing one ounce had lodged for more than a year in the middle of an abscess in the front right lobe of the brain. Dr. Simon quotes the case of a woman of seventy-nine years where an autopsy revealed a needle in the left lobe which had penetrated entirely, and which penetration dated from early infancy, the woman having never shown any cerebral accident sufficient to attract attention. Myxoma and gliomata have been observed to attain the size of the fist before producing any appreciable symptoms. Hasse relates the fact of a fracture of the skull resulting in a bone splinter remaining in the brain throughout twenty-six years with impunity. Broca speaks of a cyst which, after attaining the size of a pigeon's egg, was found to have been for years in the back part of the left hemisphere without occasioning the least trouble of sensibility, of intelligence or of movement. Malinverni dwells on the case of an individual where the hard substance did not exist, the hemispheres being separated one from the other and the crested circumvolution altogether lacking. This man, however, appeared throughout his life to enjoy the use of his intellectual faculties to the full.

But let us pass on to craniological formation.

The brain, so specialists tell us, can undergo in its general form even abnormal variations without its functions appearing to be in any way affected thereby. Cerebral development can even experience with impunity a certain check as long as it succeeds in overcoming it, as we see in the case of the artificial deformation of the skull by partial pressure or in the case of pathological deformations caused by the premature synosteosis of a suture.

As for dolicho and brachycephalism, both are due to a cause which has nothing to do with cerebral development. In taking our stand on the present state of science, we can affirm with Manouvrier " that there are not in the whole of the human body morphological variations which are more insignificant physiologically."

It is enough to remember what has been said above in order to perceive the regrettable error of which the apologists or the traducers of long or wide skulls are the victims. This error once rectified, what remains to the upholders of the organic inequality of human races ?

VI

The skull has also been dealt with in order to arrive at distinctions of another nature. For this purpose savants have undertaken to measure its *capacity*. But what room for error there is here ! To obtain positive indications of cranial capacity they have thought it necessary to proceed to *gauging* and then to *cubature*.

These two different operations, it goes without saying, give results which are often very contradictory. By *gauging* we obtain the cranial contents, if one can thus express oneself, and by *cubature* its volume. In the first case the cranial cavity is filled with some substance afterwards weighed, and this weight gives the measure sought for. But what substance must one use ? Some use liquids and others solids. Water, sand, mercury, grains of glass, gun-shot, pearl barley, grains of white mustard, different kinds of vegetables such as haricot beans, peas, &c., have all been used and have produced numerous results of comparisons and errors. One might here repeat this tragical exclamation of Pascal : "Nothing shows us truth, everything deceives us ! The senses deceive the reason with false appearances and this same deception which they bring is returned to them again by the reason ; she ever takes her revenge." The diverse substances in the first place adhere to the sides of the skull in diverse ways. They arrange themselves in a different manner. Some leave too much space between themselves and others too little !

But now that the skull is filled we must proceed to the measuring. Here again the variety of methods produces the most contradictory results. Among the well-known anthropologists each drinks in his own little glass and uses his own method. Thus all reach different solutions, each being persuaded of the excellence of his own system and the defects of that of his neighbours. It is enough, however, to compare the results obtained by certain contrary methods in order to make clear the error of their starting point and the nullity of their conclusions with regard to the theory with which we are concerned. Broca, moreover, foresaw the danger which threatened the anthropologists in this matter and gave them good advice not to trust themselves too much to their fine conquests in the domain of cranial capacity.[1]

Let us take the works of Broca and many other anthropologists and try to compare their several estimates. If the Auvergnats, with their cranial capacity of 1598cc, are at the head of humanity, the poor Parisians, who are contemporaries of Broca, only follow the Lower Bretons. The Corsicans, whom we shall see to be so privileged in the matter of prognathism, approximate to the Chinese and Esquimaux.

According to the cubatures of Morton, the Negroes of Africa and Oceania are much superior to the Americans. The Maoris, who, when civilised, show themselves to be very intelligent and provoke the admiration of the Anglo-Saxons of Australasia, are equal (according to Barnard Davis) to the Negroes of Dahomey, the Kanakas, and the natives of the Marquesas Islands.

VII

The *weight of the brain* has provoked no end of enthusiasm among believers in the inequality of human beings. In the presence of the fact that there are brains exceeding 1,800 grams, as compared with others which do not attain 900, they have not been able to repress a cry of triumph. Nevertheless this basis of comparison is still more fragile than the many others enumerated above.

Let us not forget that the weight of the brain depends directly on the size of the organism. Without being proportional, this augmentation is a palpable and indisputable fact. Men of great height generally have a weightier encephalon. On the other hand, the weight depends on the age of the subject and on its sex. In the man (according to Boyde's calculations) the weight of the encephalon represents at the age of three months a fifth of the weight of the whole body ; a tenth at the age of five years and a half; a fifteenth at seven years ; a twenty-second at seventeen years ; and a thirty-third in the full-grown man.

[1] Broca, *Mémoires de la Société d'Anthropologie*, Vol. II., 2nd series : *Capacité du crâne*.

As we get older the weight of the encephalon diminishes perceptibly. From the forty-fifth year the brain begins to grow smaller, and at ninety has lost as much as 120 grams in man and less than 90 in woman (calculations of Broca, Topinard, &c.). The weight of the encephalon also increases with use and diminishes in default of all intellectual work.

The manner of weighing brains has also its importance. It is necessary to proceed with this operation directly after the decease of the individual, for it is known that even when kept in alcohol the encephalon loses part of its weight. On the other hand, there is no means of fixing differences of weight of the encephalon according to races, since this same weight varies in great proportions among the adults not only of a race but of a country, a town, and even of the same village. Among 519 European men, from twenty-five to fifty-five years old, and belonging to the least-favoured classes, the normal variations were in round numbers from 1,025 to 1,675 grams.[1]

In comparing the weights of the encephalons it is necessary in order to make the experiment conclusive to use infinite precaution. None of the theories based on this factor can resist the least criticism from this point of view.

The works of Wagner, Bischof, Broca, Manouvrier, and many others, have demonstrated in a way which allows of no doubt that intelligence influences the augmentation of the weight of the brain. According to the researches made by a learned Czeck, M. Matiegka (quoted by M. I. Deniker [2]), the weights of the brain vary according to the occupations. It shows on an average 1,500 grams in students, officials, doctors, &c., and descends to 1,410 among labourers.

The weight also depends on the height. According to F. Marchand, the weight augments with the height in both sexes and all ages. According to his calculations there is a proportion of 7·7 to 8·8 grams of brain in a man and 7·6 to 8 grams in a woman for each centimetre of height.

Even in admitting considerable differences in the weight of the encephalon among different races, we would only state the

---

[1] *L'Homme dans la Nature.*
[2] *Année physiologique*, by A. Binet, 1904.

well-known fact that these differ according to culture and height. But does this mean that they would be unable to exceed the scale attributed to them ?

Immediately we admit the possibility of the evolution of the brain under the influence of occupation, craniological differentiation loses its force. The truth is that the skull and the brain furnish no arguments in favour of organic inequality.

CHAPTER VII

OTHER DISTINCTIVE CHARACTERISTICS BASED ON THE HEAD

I. *Prognathism*

It is the same with what concerns the other craniological elements. As science progresses, its basis of operation becomes wider. It is no longer concerned with cephalic indices and other traits of similar significance.

Persuaded that there is a correlation between the different parts of our skull, science desires to consider them one and all. Before the imposing wealth of the combinations of so many organic varieties, it is seen how difficult, nay, rather unjust, it becomes to classify human beings according to one or more traits taken haphazard. The supreme economy of nature makes these hasty methods all the more disputable inasmuch as she holds in reserve a thousand means to put observation off its guard. With the exception of those organically diseased, normal humanity is with difficulty divided into clearly marked categories. If it is desired, without taking one's stand on the simple form of the skull, to perceive in it some intellectual capacity or predestination, a series of corollaries must be immediately introduced which break down this brutal division and disclose its inanity.

Let us stop before another characteristic trait, viz., *prognathism*, which has also been adopted by many anthropologists as a means of classifying human beings. It is known that this division of heads, with or without *prognathism*, ought, in the eyes of its authors, to correspond with a nobleness or baseness of origin, with a superior intellectuality, or one which is limited for evermore. For prognathism, like brachycephalism, is an hereditary stain and serves as a distinction between the privileged races and pariahs.

Prognathism, as we know, is the protuberance of the face in front of the brain, in the horizontal position of the skull. This slight inclination of the facial profile can only be measured at first with much difficulty. On the other hand, it has scarcely any relation with the development of the brain. Prognathism presents a whole series of variations, beginning with that which is limited to the nasal region such as is met with so often in Jews, and to the modifications which include the super and sub-nasal regions. Therefore, those who consider prognathism as signifying lack of intelligence, or simply inferiority of mind, allow too much to the Jews, who are " prognathic."

Moreover, all the classical types which are placed before us as models of plastic beauty and moral character are abundantly endowed with it. We elsewhere meet with the so much dreaded prognathism among royal families like the Bourbons, who ought exactly to combine nobility of birth and superiority of origin.

The wider observation of prognathism discovers it under all latitudes and among all peoples. Certain of its most accentuated forms are merely to be found in immediate correspondence with stature.

But if all anthropologists insist much on prognathism, they are rarely in agreement as to its significance. According to current opinion, it is only a matter of the elongation and projection of the jaws (Prichard). But the prior question is to be found elsewhere. This particular formation of the jaws naturally varies according to the angle in which we place ourselves to observe it. This variety in the results of our observation raises another question, namely, that of a fixed and uniform measurement which can give authority to comparisons, and to the conclusions to be drawn from them.

Consequently we find ourselves before a veritable forest of definitions of prognathism and before a thousand and one methods of measurement. What must we include in the definition of a jaw ? What part of the face must enter into its category and contribute thereby to the results of comparison ? According to some, one must stop at the nostrils and cut off everything below them. Others only speak of the prognathism of the face, that is, above the nostrils. Whereas for certain anthropologists it is only a matter of the upper face, their opponents only include the lower jaw To some the dental system is of chief importance, whereas others attach no importance to it. Methods of measurement are also most contradictory. According to Virchow, it is enough to measure the two lines from the *basion,* one going to the nasal point and the other to the subnasal. We have again a series of diverse angles which have been popularised by Camper, Geoffroy Saint-Hilaire, Cuvier, Vogt, Welcker, &c., each of whom ought to present us with the answer to the riddle. We have lastly the method advocated by Broca, Topinard, &c.

It is enough to indicate this divergence of views and methods in order to understand the difficulty of piloting oneself through this labyrinth of definitions and of contradictory conclusions. Therefore, while doing justice to the efforts made by anthropologists of all schools to use prognathism as an element for the appreciation and comparison of races, it is difficult to attribute to their successes any importance whatever. Even admitting the absolute exactness of a method chosen anyhow and subscribing beforehand both to the method of measurement and to the results obtained, what useful conclusion can be drawn from it ?

Let us take for example the method adopted by Virchow, and let us pause a moment before his conclusions. We must in the first place conclude that inasmuch as the French, Chinese, Tartars, Lapps, Malays of the Moluccas, Gipsies, Kalmucks and Jews have all the same coefficient, 91, they must all be in the same boat. We must then rank the ancient Romans (fortunately it is only a matter of five skulls which were at Virchow's disposal) with their coefficient 98 behind the Kaffirs (97), and even lower than the Cossacks or the Malays of Sumatra (96). Here among others is a small conclusion which is separated from his bundle of measurements, viz., 30 Germans, 20 Japanese and twelve Russians are found in this respect to be all on the same level, *i.e.* 94.

According to Topinard, true prognathism is only prognathism

" *alveolo sous-nasal.*"   It is this sub-nasal region which alone must be taken into account when it is desired to discover the origin of a skull.   It alone furnishes the differential characteristics among human races.   Nevertheless this vaunted criterion is shown to be absolutely inefficient when we desire on its data to arrive at a graduated classification of races.   Its adepts proclaim, it is true, that all human beings are prognathic, and that the difference is only one of degree.   Thus the European races are such in a slight degree, the Yellow and Polynesian races much more so, and the negro races still more so.

But leaving on one side the measurements obtained on other skulls, let us turn towards Europe and compare the results obtained.   According to Topinard, the most favoured in this respect are the Corsicans (81·28).   The next to them are the Gauls (?), then 14 skulls from the Cavern of the Dead Man, only then the Parisians (78·13), followed by the Toulousians, Auvergnians, Merovingians, Finns, Tasmanians, &c.   The Chinese are discovered to be on the same level as the Eskimos, &c., &c.

At the head of humanity are the Guanches, superior even to the Corsicans !   Another statement which appears no less extravagant is that the least prognathic in Europe were the inventors of—the polished stone !

The progress and the intellectual efforts of so many generations would only tend in consequence to diminish our superiority acquired in the Stone Age, and to lead us back to a sort of fatal decadence.

It is enough to put forward this strange conclusion in order to see the scaffolding of figures prepared with so much care by the professors of prognathism fall in pieces.   It is true that they could reply that craniometry has nothing to do with the task of graduating human beings !   Bravo !   For in that case we could easily agree on the importance of this series of measurements which have only a purely descriptive value.   Inasmuch as its relative data do not allow us to classify human beings according to an illusory canon, this method loses in that way the extravagant character which they wish to assign to it.

II. *The Form of the Face and the Theory of Angles*

The head with the variations displayed by its different parts has given rise to the creation of numerous distinctions between human beings. They depend principally on the conformation of the skull and face.

Their structure may be similar and harmonious in the same way as they may individually display particular tendencies. The face, for example, may be elongated and the skull too, as in the case of Negroes, or both may be wide, as with the majority of the Yellow races.

We see in general a kind of harmony between the skull and the face, the latter being really only a part of the skull. This last is divided into two parts, the skull properly so called, which is the receptacle of the brain, and the face, which includes the chief organs of the senses and mastication. When we compare man with animals with reference to the whole skull, we perceive this chief difference which distinguishes them. The position of the human skull above the face, and also its volume, appears altogether to distinguish it from the animal skull, which is placed further back and possesses other peculiar traits.

Nothing, then, is more easy and attractive than the temptation to divide, under this heading, men and animals in general and men and monkeys in particular. Is it the same with the distinction between human beings?

We have under this heading numerous attempts to find in the form of the face a solid foundation for ethnical divisions. Above all, let us note the facial angle of Camper. In his *Dissertation sur les différences réelles que présentent les traits du visage chez l'homme de différents pays et de différents âges* (Paris, 1791), Pierre Camper teaches us that the facial angle (facial line or characteristic line of the face) varies from 70° to 80° in the human species. "Every thing which is above this comes under the rules of art, whilst everything which is below this resembles monkeys. If I raise the facial line forward, I have a classical head; if I make it lean backwards, I have the head of a negro." A no small consolation for the Negroes is that this line must be more inclined to have the head of a monkey, and still more so to have that of a dog. It is necessary afterwards to make a great effort of inclination to have that of a woodcock.[1] According to Camper, his angle allows us to distinguish in a very precise way the masterpieces of Greek art from those of the Romans. For while the facial angle, measured according to his method, gives 100° to the former, it gives only 95° to the latter.

Applied to the different races his measure in no way allows us to divide human beings into superior and inferior. The reason for it is very simple, viz., that individual differences leave far behind those between whites (85°), yellows (80°), or blacks (75°), as Camper formulates them. This fact comes out particularly in the subsequent refinements brought to the measurement of Camper's facial angle by Cloquet, Jacquart, Cuvier, or G. Saint-Hilaire. The difference of 5 which should separate human races, according to Camper, is increased to 10 by Jacquart among white representatives in the city of Paris alone.

In addition to the facial angle, anthropometry offers us a quantity of others due to the ingenuity of savants of all lands.

Let us note some as they come to our mind : the sphenoidal angle of Welcker; the cranio-facial angle of Huxley and of Ecker; the parietal angle of Quatrefages, the angle of Barclay, the metafacial angle of Serres, the angle of the condyles, the naso-basal angle of Virchow and Welcker, &c., &c. However curious the results obtained by this numerous series of measurements may be, they all resemble one another from that special point of view which for our present purpose is foremost. They do not allow us "to seriate" humanity into superior and inferior races. And if they fail to establish irreducible differences between races, they only end in securing the triumph of the theory of individual differences which divide human beings.

The attempt has also been made to determine the breadth, length, and thickness of the face, with the aid of divers methods which consequently vary frequently according to those who

[1] The angle of Camper is formed by two lines, one horizontal from the auditive canal to the root of the nose, the other tangent, called facial, from the forehead to the nasal bone. In other words, one of the lines is from the auditive aperture to the lower edge of the nostrils, and the other is to the most salient points of the face, the top of the forehead and the anterior face of the two lower incisives.

apply them. Without wishing to study their technical side, which would demand a special volume, we shall confine ourselves to dealing with certain results obtained within the limits of a particular method. It is thus that, according to Broca, the Parisians, with their facial index of 65·9, hold the mean between the New Caledonian Islanders, 66·2, and the Australians, 65·6. The Negroes, with their index of 68·6, are next to the Bretons (68·5), and the Auvergnats (67·9), &c. If we begin with the total length of the face and its bi-zygomatic breadth, as maintained by Pruner-Bey, the Scandinavians, with their 129 millimetres of length and 132 of breadth, are found between the Chinese (134 and 137) and the Germans of the South (127 in length and 131 in breadth). The New Caledonian Islanders and the Negroes approach the Germans, &c.

On the contrary, in having recourse to the naso-basilar line of H. Welcker, we shall find that this has the same length of 102 millimetres among the French and the Malays of Sumatra, as it has of 100 millimetres among the Chinese, Germans, Russians Cossacks, Mexicans, and Tartars; 99 among Hungarians Hottentots, and Gipsies; and that the Eskimos approximate to the Kaffirs, and the Papuans to the Jews! We have in fact before us one of those incongruous mixtures which prevents our arriving at any conclusion. If the naso-basal angle of Welcke and Virchow were taken as point of comparison, or the naso basilar line compared with the skull's antero-posterior circum ference of the two same savants, we should arrive at conclusion still more eccentric. From the point of view of the firs measure, the French occupy the mean (65·1) between the Turks (64·3) and the Kalmucks (65·8), and are then followed by the Chinese (65·9), who precede the Germans (66·2), who in their turn precede the Eskimos, the Hottentots and the Negroes.

With regard to the second measure, the French with their 398 millimetres occupy the mean between the Negroes (402 and the Australians (395), whereas the Germans (404) are between the Chinese (407) and the Kalmucks (403) ! ! !

The orbital index, popularised by Broca,[1] enjoyed and sti continues to enjoy a certain success. It is concerned with the

---

[1] *Sur l'Indice orbitaire*, Rev. d'Anthrop. 1879.

measure which is obtained in the following manner. After having measured the vertical diameter of the orbit, the result obtained is multiplied by 100 and is afterwards divided by the horizontal diameter. From this standpoint Broca divided humanity into three races according to the size of the index thus obtained, viz. the *Mégasèmes*, whose average index is 89 and over; the *Mésosèmes*, 83 to 89; and the *Microsèmes*, below 83. But when we pass from these general classes to their concrete application, we perceive here also as elsewhere that nature has not willed to establish privileged human races. The figures of the orbital index are displaced in a capricious way, and bring together peoples and races separated in our eyes by great gulfs. The Indians of North America elbow the people of Java and the Indo-Chinese; the Auvergnats the Negroes of Africa; the Parisians tread arm-in-arm with Negroes and Hottentots, &c.

Broca himself produces abundant proofs that the differences between individuals of the same race are greater than those which he had established between his three classes. We have seen that these are divided by a mean of 6 units, but Broca has found 108·33 in the case of a Chinese woman, 105 in an Indian Redskin, 100 in a Parisian woman and in a woman of Auvergne, &c. On the other hand, as we perceive, the same series includes whites, blacks or yellows, civilised and backward peoples, the brachycephalic and the dolichocephalic. Let us add, however, that the learned anthropologist, after comparing the orbital index in the case of men and monkeys, gave up the idea of finding in it any grounds for the graduation of human beings. In effect, if the quadrumana regarded from the standpoint of the orbital index can be also divided into méga-néso-, and microsèmes, the same index will reunite under the same measure the higher anthropomorphous beings with types which are as low in the scale as the lemurs.

Certain indications also have been attempted to be drawn from the comparison of the upper and lower jaws among different races; but, all things considered, it has only been possible to assign to them a purely descriptive value. The variations among individuals exceed in the same way in this particular those which it has been desired to establish among human varieties. On the other hand, the variety of forms

which the jaws assume, as well as the diversity of their relationship, make all generalisation difficult. We shall not leave the
human face without dwelling on the measurements of the nose
and ears, so important for descriptive anthropology.

III. *The Nose*

Its principal form as well as its numerous variations have
been much studied, and the results of these studies have served
for much disputed generalisations.

Broca, starting from the relation of the maximum width of
the nose to its total height, has gone so far as to attempt to
divide humanity into three different sections; the men with
long and narrow nose, the *leptorhinnians,* corresponding to the
white race; the *platyrrhinians,* with wide and low nose, a
characteristic peculiar to the black races; and lastly the
mesorrhinians, comprising the yellow races.

This indeed is the most important statement made under
the nasal heading. The measures of Broca have been taken
on 1,200 human heads belonging to diverse races. This is his
way of proceeding. After having multiplied by 100 the width
of the nose taken at the opening of the nasal chambers, he
compared it with the length between the spine and the naso-
frontal articulation. The result is what he calls the nasal index
The mean of the nasal index is 50·00, but it varies according to
races from 42·33 (Eskimos) to 58·38 (Houzouanas). Let us note
however, that the Eskimos enter into Broca's series of Whites
and the allophylian Whites, the Finns, the Esthonians and
also the Papuans, into the mesorrhinians. On the other hand
the individual differences here also are much greater than those
which separate human races. What is more essential is that
Broca does not state the age of his examples. The nasal index
however, varies with years, according to his own estimates
being 76·80 in the embryo; 62·18 in the developed fœtus; and
50·20 in a child of six.

The anthropologists who afterwards adopted different methods
of measuring, naturally discovered considerable discrepancies
among human races. Let us state that in general measure

nents are not made in a strictly exact way. With the lack of unity in the methods, an infinite variety of starting points accosts us. The results of all these investigations remain inconclusive. Everything which we know on this subject is reduced to visual impressions. We see that noses are often developed among white people in a prominent way, whereas they are flat and wide among the Blacks and Yellows. Topinard points out a number of considerations which it would be necessary to introduce into nasal measurements in order to arrive at serious results. Above all, the maximum height (transversal index), which is measured vertically from the root of the nose to its base, by means of a compass with a slide, ought to be insisted on ; also the width of the nose (antero-posterior index) from the points furthest removed from the wings of the nose ; the nasal prominence, which goes from its point to the sub-nasal point, &c., &c.

The base, nostrils and ridge of the nose are also very important. Thus for the ridge, the angle of its inclination, its rectilineal direction bent or bumped, convex (aquiline variety), concave (turned up), its form, roofed, rounded or flat ; for the nostrils, their form, elliptic, special or rounded, their plan, &c. ; the direction of their axis, antero-posterior, oblique or transversal, &c., &c.—all these are so many elements which cannot be neglected as principles of comparison. The multiplicity of all these data, of which each has its characteristic value, makes their application difficult, and the nose as a typical trait of comparative humanity still awaits a patient, exact and persevering savant who would be willing, perhaps at the expense of a lifetime, to consecrate to it a special work.

In the meantime we have monographs on details which tell us the differences in the nasal, transversal, antero-posterior index, &c. Let us not forget that all these operations still leave much to be desired, especially in what concerns the insufficient number of individuals who are representatives of races or of human varieties. Thus Topinard invented his nasal transversal index after having utilised for his measurements *one* Papuan, *one* Australian and a Cochin Chinese bust, &c. E. de Mérejkovsky, after having studied the ridge of the nose on a number of human skulls, arrived at the conclusion that it is much flatter among primitive peoples than among civilised. His index comprises the height of the nose from its root in a straight line to the angle of its inclination. The Polynesians in this case follow the Whites; then the Americans, the Melanesians, the Mongols, the Malays and the Negroes.

Topinard also distinguishes (a) the depth of the hollow of the root, which is considerable among the Melanesians, somewhat marked among the majority of Europeans, and faintly so among the Mongols, Arabs, and in the ancient Greek type (Venus de Milo); (b) the flat and crushed noses, peculiar to Chinese, Malays, Negroes, &c.; (c) the particular arch of the nose as broken and bent (among the Bourbons), more general among the Americans, and which takes an aquiline form peculiar to the Jews, the ancient Assyrians, and to the Arabs, with numerous subdivisions, &c.

In short, the nose furnishes a descriptive character which is rather interesting. But the insufficiency of its measurements and the defective methods do not allow us to found on their diversity a racial division among human beings. Similarly we must not forget that nasal morphology depends in particular on the configuration of the face and skull. In virtue of the law of the co-ordination of traits, it must be admitted that with the evolution of the skull the structure of the nose also changes.

IV. *The Ear*

It has also been attempted to deduce from the structure of the ear certain characteristic indications for the differentiation of races, but all these attempts have proved fruitless. Certain French anthropologists, it is true, teach us that the lobules of the ears are lacking in the ears of certain Kabyles in the province of Constantine, but they are forced to admit that the same phenomenon frequently appears amongst and near ourselves. The same applies to the oval or pretended " square " form of the Negroes. G. Fritsch, who made a particular study of the Bushmen, states that their ears have the same configuration as that of the Europeans, whereas Langer tells us the same thing of the Negroes.

The ears vary to infinitude in individuals but not in races. Their variations are even so characteristic that they may serve to identify individuals like finger-marks. It has been thought for a long time that the ears are placed higher up among certain tribes, which opinion is certainly well founded. The Copts and the ancient mummies of Egypt (Ebers, Dureau de la Malle) have been noticed in particular as distinguished for this odd position of the ears. But more exact measurements have deprived this legend of all credence. People wished to perceive in it a monkey characteristic (this phenomenon really exists among the gorillas), but this opinion had to be given up. Czermack, Langer, and Norton, to speak of these only, found that the famous ears of the mummies, as those of the Copts, are fixed on the head at the same height as among the Whites. What has justified this erroneous opinion is the conventional art of the Egyptians, who deemed this type of ear a sign of comeliness, for which reason they lavished them on nearly all their monuments.

People have also wished us to believe in a superior acuteness of hearing on the part of primitive or savage peoples, but according to numbers of works on this subject, we must decidedly renounce this distinction, which nothing justifies. Let us remember among others the experiments of Myers. He made use of a clock giving five strokes to the second, which could be as easily stopped as set going. His examples were thirty-five in number, of whom seven were little girls, twelve boys, and sixteen adults, all natives of Murray Island. This experiment, made with the aid of the members of the expedition organised by the University of Cambridge to the Torres Straits, has confirmed this fact, that in general the hearing acuteness of the natives submitted to observation was somewhat inferior to that of Europeans. According to Myers, the savages, when accustomed to distinguish the fixed series of sounds, were on the watch for them, and in this way found it easy to distinguish them more readily.

V

A conclusion forces itself on us when we compare the result
obtained by the measurement of all the parts of the head. I
is that the skull, which is subject to variations, leaves a1
impression during its evolution on the face which is only it:
complement, Consequently, inasmuch as we no longer se
about us any races which are clearly defined from a cranio
logical point of view, it is impossible that there can be an)
such races from the point of view of the other measurement
taken from the component parts of the head. The difference:
among individuals belonging to the same human variety ar
thus always greater than those perceived among races regardec
as distinct units in themselves.

The mixed type constitutes the salient characteristic o
modern humanity, especially that of Europe. We shall se
later on that this, being the result of a cross-breeding of nearl)
all the other races, must have with these many traits i1
common. This is particularly noticeable in the case of cranio
logical variations.

The European population presents a mixture of dolicho-
brachy-, and mesocephalic peoples. What is still mor
important is that all these types are dispersed throughou
the same countries, the same districts, and the same families
They are not seen, however, in their pure state. Men witl
narrow skulls have wide faces ; those with round skulls hav
narrow faces ; whilst between these two mixed types float th
" impure" to a degree still more surprising, for they reunit
numbers of traits which are really the prerogative of the dolicho
or brachycephalic divisions. Ranke has tried to group i1
clearly defined categories this mutual interpenetration of type:
and traits. The following are some of his divisions : (*a*) shor
heads with long faces (*dolichoprosope Brachykephalen*) ; (*b*
long heads with short faces (*brachyprosope dolichokephalen*) ; (*c*
long heads with long faces (*dolichoprosope dolichokephalen*); (*d*
medium heads with long faces (*dolichoprosope mesokephalen*)
(*e*) short heads with short faces (*brachyprosope brachykephalen*)
and (*f*) medium heads with short faces (*brachyprosope meso*

cephalen). Very naturally each of these sections is divided into sub-sections. Besides, the number of these categories could be multiplied to infinity. The essential thing is that these, reunited, should give us a gentle and imperceptible gradation which would result in a general craniological type. F. Kollmann tells us with reason that all the skulls of the inhabitants of Europe approximate so much to one another that one might speak of an *European skull*. If we say *European*, it is only a way of speaking. It is the civilised skull with which we are concerned, which is distinct from the skull of non-civilised and primitive peoples living outside civilisation and deprived of that cerebral exercise which civilisation imposes. Do not let us forget, however, that this distinction is not irreducible, for the savages of yesterday can easily become the civilised of to-morrow. They will profit in this quality of craniological evolution which accompanies the systematic and regular life of the intellect.

CHAPTER VIII

CONTINUATION OF DISTINCTIVE CHARACTERISTICS

I. *The Height*

HEIGHT is considered a sign of race in the case of animals, but can the same standard be applied in the case of man ?

We are aware that men vary in stature not only in different countries, but also in the bosom of the same family.

On the other hand, with rare exceptions (*e.g.* the Pygmies) human varieties show a kind of mean height which may be estimated at 1m. 630. Above and below this, different agglomerations are situated, where the height increases or decreases according to the *milieu*. As we shall see later on, in studying its influence on the organism in general, the height is perceptibly modified by the action of comfort and nutrition. Anthropology has not succeeded in dividing humanity on the ground of stature, and it can only offer us data of purely descriptive value. Its information is, moreover, confounded with that of hygiene and medical therapeutics, which supply us with certain recipes to gain physical vigour and health.

It teaches us that stature varies according to the health and the nourishment of peoples and individuals, that it will be greater in rich countries and in those where physical exercise and sports are cultivated with most ardour; that it often diminishes with the altitude, and that the female sex shews less height than the male. Nevertheless, the way of living and the physical exercises often succeed in neutralising the influence of sex. We notice, for example, that in the families of American multi-millionaires women begin to display a height sometimes equal to that of men, and sometimes even superior to it

This phenomenon is attributed to the special mode of life lived by young girls in the United States, who, exonerated from the occupations to which young men must apply themselves, live in the open air and spend their youth in playing lawn tennis and football.

The height varies according to age, and only attains its maximum towards the thirtieth year. According to Quetelet, man is 50 centimetres at the time of his birth ; about 1 metre at five years, 1m. 50 at fifteen, and at nineteen he lacks about 15 centimetres of his height which he gains in the eleven succeeding years.

Consequently, everything which produces a harmful effect on our health during the time of our growth reacts on the height. It is thus that children engaged from their tender age in mines and factories lose height and never attain their normal development.

It has been said, on the other hand, that nations, regarded as a whole, succeed under the influence of favourable conditions in augmenting their mean height. Let us add, moreover, that civilized humanity, far from being smaller, has, on the contrary, gained some centimetres in the course of centuries. According to palæontological data, modern man is of greater height than the man of neolithic times.

Has man degenerated in the course of ages, and from being a giant in prehistoric times, decreased to mediocre height in our day ? Mythologies and religious books teach it. Poets have sung it, and the people believe it.

The Bible speaks in several places of peoples of giants. The spies of Moses find them in the Promised Land, and the prophet Amos compares them with the oaks for strength, and with the cedars for height. According to *Deuteronomy*, Og, King of Bashan, was greater than Goliath, to whom the *Book of Samuel* attributes a height of over nine feet.

Homer and Hesiod lament the diminished height of their time as compared with that of illustrious ancestors. According to Plutarch, his contemporaries could only be compared with the new-born children of the ancients. The learned Pliny, in order to confirm all these beliefs, even speaks of human skeletons discovered in Crete the length of which attained 20 metres.

The epics of modern peoples are likewise influenced by this

belief, which is so deeply rooted in the popular conscience. The science of our great-grandfathers often tried to uphold this article of faith which was imbibed with their mothers' milk. We recall the curious theory of Henrion, who, in the beginning of the 18th century, offered to public credulity an exact plan of the lowering of the height since the time of Father Adam. The height of the latter, which was 18 metres, fell gradually to 9 metres in the case of Abraham, 3 metres in that of Hercules, and 2 metres in Alexander the Great.

Modern science, more exact and enlightened, has demonstrated how ill founded all these superstitions are. In submitting to exact measurements the human bones of the Quaternary epoch, it has succeeded in proving that human height has undergone no variations since the hundreds of thousands of years during which man has inhabited our planet. According to the measurements of M. Manouvrier and M. Rehon,[1] the man of Neanderthal (Quaternary Epoch) was only 1m. 613; the man of Spy, 1m. 610; the crushed man of Langeria, 1m. 669; the troglodyte of Chancelade, 1m. 612. This estimate, drawn from 429 male bones and 189 female, dating from the neolithic period, gives us the mean height of 1m. 475 for women and 1m. 525 for men !

When these prehistoric heights are compared with those of moderns, we perceive that the latter, far from being diminished, have rather increased during the course of centuries. The French, whom anthropologists class among the small heights, are shown to be in this respect superior to their gigantic ancestors.

It would be useless to dwell on the differences between centuries nearer to us and the modern age. What thousands of centuries have been impotent to accomplish, a few hundred years can still less do. The evidence furnished on this subject by M. Rehon demonstrates, however, in a concise manner that the height of Parisians has not varied during a dozen centuries. In the measurement and comparison of human bones discovered in the cemetery of Saint-Marcel (5th cent.) with those of the cemetery

[1] Let us remark at this point that, owing to the ingenious method discovered and applied by M. Manouvrier, we can easily reconstruct the height of the human body from certain of its parts.

of Saint-Germain-des-Prés (11th cent.), he has declared the mean height of 1m. 677 for men and 1m. 575 for women. There is, it is true, a little difference of about a centimetre among modern Parisians, but this perhaps is due to the quality of the bones preserved. We know that their duration depends often only on their hardness, and it is probable that among so many people buried in those cemeteries we have only the remains of the strongest individuals which have resisted the attacks of time.

It is possible, on the other hand, that the ancients knew individual cases of giants just as we come across them in our time. Only that we, better informed and far from seeing in it a special privilege of heaven, find in it a diseased state and a proof of perverse nutrition. Science only perceives in them dystrophic examples, infantile monstrosities and degenerate individuals, all suitable subjects for medical pathology.

Consequently there are no peoples of giants ! The Germanic barbarians therefore on this matter of height are thus found to be perceptibly equal. The small differences which anthropology reveals are reduced to a few centimetres, which the influence of *milieu* easily explains.

What has contributed to the belief in giants is, as we have said, the fact that from all time the bones of animal fossils have been confounded with those of prehistoric man.

Let us remember, as an example, the case quoted by Von Zittel. The molar tooth of a mammoth is venerated at Valencia as a relic of St. Christopher. Another tooth, also that of a fossil, was long borne at the head of processions imploring rain, as a relic of St. Vincent.

Buffon disclosed the fraud of which the savants and public of his day were victims, in identifying human bones with those of animals. "There was a time when warriors were interred with their warhorses, perhaps also with their war elephants, and it is the remains of these which are wrongly identified with the skeletons of our ancestors."

Nevertheless, in spite of the protestations of specialists, the fossil remains of animals, falsely attributed to men, continued and still continue to be venerated. According to M. Launois and M. Roy, there could be seen in 1872, under the

porch of the Chapel of the Castle of Cracow, a curious
collection of holy relics which were really only the skull of a
rhinoceros, a simple bone of a mastodon, and a half jaw of a
cetacean.

France was for a long time the scene of a very amusing
discussion on the subject of the bones of a giant who was of
the phenomenal length of 25 feet. They were attributed
to a King of the Teutons, named Teutobochus, vanquished
by Marius near Aix in 102 B.C. These bones were discovered
in 1613 in the neighbourhood of Romans, in Dauphiné.
Nearly all the savants of that period were of the above
opinion, which died hard, for it was only 220 years later that
Blainville succeeded in dissipating the misunderstanding
created round the pretended skeleton of Teutobochus. It
was really the remains of a mastodon similar to those found
in Ohio !

Under the influence of *milieu,* which for us comprises the
sum total of all the circumstances which act on man, the
heights of different peoples can naturally vary, but what is most
essential is that the relative periods of the increase of height
are everywhere subject to the same laws. The studies made on
this subject, by Bowditch, Gould, Roberts, Beneke, &c., among
others, demonstrate that the height increases everywhere, according to age and sex, relatively in the same way. Quetelet, in his
studies, *Homme* and *Anthropométrie,* has, however, thought it
possible to formulate into a special law the influence of well-
being, age and sex on the height.

It goes without saying that the mode of life should be added
the reactionary effect of which cannot be neglected. The
example mentioned above concerning rich young girls in the
United States is reproduced on a much larger scale in Japan.
E. Baelz, in his profound studies on Japan from an anthropological
point of view, notes the existence of two peoples, so to speak
who are quite distinct in point of stature and physical vigour
First, the descendants of rich classes, who, having abandoned
their life of ancient warfare, now devote themselves passionately
to studies and become more and more feeble and decrepit
then the children of the people, strong and well-built fellows
who seem to issue from quite another stock. In this way the

scions of ancient noble families, the *Kwazoku*, affected by all kinds of scrofulous maladies, diminish in height and strength. The education and the detestable mode of life of Japanese men have also contributed much to aggravate the evil.

Let us note that with the energy which characterises the Japanese, they have undertaken a number of measures to stamp out the evil. Gymnastics, once so much despised, now occupy a prominent place in the system of modern education.

When the many causes which influence height are regarded, it becomes impossible to adopt the opinion of Broca, Boudin, and so many other anthropologists who only look at height for a specific expression of race. We shall give numerous proofs later on which constitute almost a direct experiment on the influence which housing and nourishment exercise on the height. Let us merely confine ourselves to note the conclusion of the learned German, Otto Bollinger, who was the author of numerous books on human growth, viz. that the influence of race on stature is a negligible quantity in comparison with so many other factors, such as nourishment, the abuse of physical or psychical labour, maladies acquired or hereditary, &c.

The following is a significant example of the illusory influence of race on stature. We take it from American life according to measurements made there on the stature of the inhabitants. First, we mark that the three special varieties of its inhabitants—the Whites, Indians, and Blacks—have nearly the same stature. According to the measurements of Baxter, the Whites attain 1m. 73, as against the Indians (Gould) and Blacks, 1m. 70.

A still more curious detail which we owe to Gould is that the Irish who land young in the United States attain a proportionally higher stature than those who arrive after the age of 30, that is, the time of life when growth ceases.

The numerous observations collected in France corroborate in all points those made in the United States. Let us dwell particularly on the very careful data of Dr. Carlier.[1] With a patience worthy of all praise, he has for nineteen years (1872–1890) devoted himself to researches on the height, the

---

[1] See the *Annales d'Hygiène publique* (1892), where Dr. Carlier sums up his work.

race, and the different professions in the *arrondissement* of
Evreux. To work with greater certainty he has taken for
purpose of comparison the lists of those who have drawn lots
together with the descriptions of all the heights of those
recruited from each of the eleven cantons. The following are
his conclusions—

The individuals who may be regarded as having been brought
up, as their profession would suggest, in good hygienic conditions
and in the enjoyment of a certain leisure (students, teachers, agriculturists, gardeners, vinedressers, carpenters, clerks, merchants,
butchers, joiners, woodcutters) have generally a stature above
the average, whereas those who are ill-nourished, badly-clothed,
brought up in unfavourable surroundings (workers in iron
factories or cotton mills, nailmakers, ironmongers, founders,
moulders, turners, pastrycooks, &c.) are inferior to the others.

In proceeding with the same method, divers other observers
arrive at analogous conclusions. Let us note on this subject
the works of M. Chopinet on the Pyrenees, those of M.
Collignon on the Côtes-du-Nord, of M. Chervin on the Seine-
Inférieure.

We are asked to believe that stature is generally synonymous with distinction and noble origin. In starting from this
standpoint, the anthropo-psychologists place at the head of
humanity the fair-haired and tall dolichocephalic. But in
adopting the division of Topinard into four groups—(*a*) *high
stature* from 1m. 70 upwards; (*b*) *stature above the mean* from
1m. 65 to 1m. 70; (*c*) *below the mean* from 1m. 60 to 1m. 65; (*d*)
low stature below 1m. 60—we notice in the first place that high
stature is to be found especially among the Patagonians (1·781),
Polynesians (1·762), Iroquois Indians (1·735), Negroes, Kaffirs,
followed by the Scandinavians, English, Scotch, Eskimos, Irish,
Vadagas of India, &c., &c. The French (1·650) take a middle
place with the tribes of Eastern India (1·652), the natives of
the Caucasus (1·650) and the Algerian Negroes (1·645).

Let us add, however, that the figures given by the anthropologists are generally to be used with caution. It is enough
to recall the case of Humboldt with his measurements of the
Caribbeans of the Orinoco, whom he succeeded in passing as
giants (1·84), which was subsequently demonstrated to be

altogether erroneous.   An example no less characteristic is that of the Patagonians.   According to Magellan, who discovered them for the first time in 1519, they were 7½ feet in height; according to the Dutchman Sebald de Noort, 10 to 11 feet; according to Commerson, 5 feet 6 inches; according to the Commodore Byron, 7 feet, &c.   To-day we know that these pretended giants have a height equal to that of the Scandinavians or the Scots. We must in general make many reservations with regard to these measures, made by occasional travellers or by explorers who lack authority.

The weight of the body is related to the height.   Nevertheless the weight is not always in proportion to the height.   According to the figures brought forward by Gould, 1 centimetre of height corresponds in a Spaniard to a weight of 364 grams; in an Englishman, to 366; among the French, Belgians and Swiss to 372; in a North American, 374; in a German, 376; in a Scandinavian, 382 ; in a Negro and a Mulatto, 387; and in an Iroquois, 422, &c.   Even granting that these figures are quite true, it would be impossible to draw from them any conclusion whatsoever.   It appears, therefore, probable that the mode of occupation must play the chief *rôle* in determining the weight, besides other conditions of *milieu* such as nourishment, length of sleep and physical exercise in the open air.

II. *The Colour*

The colour of our skin strikes every observer at first glance. According to its shades humanity has been divided for all time into white, yellow and black.   Red skins were added as an after-thought.   This oldest of all human classifications is at the same time one of the most defective.   Its errors are obvious the moment the specific characteristics of each of the categories are considered. For while among the *whites* there are men whose skin is as black as ebony (the Bicharis or the black Moors of Senegal), there are among the *blacks* fair or yellow skins like the Bushmen. Whence is this difference of colour ?   The skin of the negro, the yellow and the white is identical as to that which concerns its composition, which comprises three essential parts, the derm, the mucous membrane and the epidermis. What varies is the colour of the cells of the mucous membrane; these are blackish brown in the negro, pale yellow in the fair-white, a yellow more or less brownish in the brown-white. But when this difference of colouring is examined closely, it must be acknowledged that the *milieu*, represented in particular in this case by the intensity of the solar rays, exercises a preponderant influence on it.

The melanism in fowls, which corresponds with the negro phenomenon among men, provides us with a curious illustration on this subject. We know that the " negro " fowls which are so frequently seen in the Cape de Verde islands, the Philippines and Bogota are descended from the European variety. But these fowls, which present in the winged world an equivalent to negroes[1] among men, do not differ in other respects from other fowl varieties. The black colouring appears here in an accidental way, and is perpetuated by heredity under the influence of the *milieu*. And another curious matter is that among black fowls all the mucous and all the fibrous and aponeurotic systems, and even the muscular membranes, become black. This change of colour is in this way much more pronounced and more intrinsic than among black men. Yet no one has taken it into his head to perceive in black fowls a race destined irrevocably to a sort of inferiority in the world of hens!

The colouring depends, in short, on the production and the distribution of colouring matter in the organism. The skin of the Scandinavian is white, almost colourless, or even rosy pink, owing to the transparence of the epidermis which allows the red colouring matter of the blood to be seen. When after an attack of anæmia the number of globules descends from 127 (normal) to 21, the lowest proportion, the teguments become pale and assume the colour of virgin wax.

The Antisians of Peru, who are distinguished by their white colour (d'Orbigny), dwell at the foot of pointed rocks under immense trees whose ramifications form a sort of roof impenetrable to the sun's rays. They live in a humid atmosphere plunged in dark shades. Their complexion is affected by this,

---

[1] Fowls, like men, show the three extreme colours seen in man : (1) Gaulish, white ; (2) Cochin China, yellowish ; and (3) black.

and the Antisians are much fairer than the tribes of the Aymaras or Moxos, who occupy shadeless plains or high plateaus in the same neighbourhood.

In studying the influence of the *milieu*, we shall see how much this affects the colour. In what concerns the negroes transported into the northern United States and even into those of the South, let us add that their complexion has singularly paled, while at the same time their features have become considerably modified. When a negro born in North America is compared with his congener in Africa, we are astonished at the physiological variations which a century has been able to effect in his constitution and in his external aspect.

" In the space of 150 years," so E. Reclus tells us, " the Negro has surmounted a good fourth of the distance which separates him from the Whites." What is more characteristic is that the Negro and the Yankee under climatic influence both approximate to the aboriginal type of the Red Skins. They will no doubt never resemble in all points the red tribes doomed for the time being to irremediable disappearance. The evolution of the Negroes and the Whites in the United States, working under conditions not identical, must naturally result in different effects. But both are evolving towards the type of the Red Skins. It is difficult to doubt it when we observe the physiological modifications realised in the United States by its present inhabitants.

Let us remember also that according to Giuseppe Sergi, Professor Brinton, &c., the white race, the ethnographical pride of Europe, is only the direct fruit of a negro race, the Euro-Africans, established in Europe from time immemorial and who came from North Africa! A certain consistency is given to this theory by the fact that a number of bones considered to be negroid have been discovered in different parts of Europe.

In studying the skeletons found in the Grotte des Enfants, near Mentone, M. Verneau arrived at the conclusion that they must be negroid. Their teeth (Albert Gaudry) showed a perceptible difference when compared with those of the Whites living to-day. In 1903 M. Hervé brought to notice two skulls which were also negroid. These were found in the peninsula of Quiberon. They belong, one to the neolithic age, and the other to the Gaulish period.

An analogous discovery has been made quite recently by M. Pittard in the Rhone valley.[1]

Whatever the truth may be concerning the settlement of negroid peoples in Neolithic Europe, it is nevertheless incontestable that under the influence of climate nearly all the traits which distinguish the negro type are modified. Where we fail to grasp the direct influence of external factors, their disappearance, appearance or modification takes place as the result of the law of the co-ordination of traits which governs the numerous organic changes whose cause escapes us.

We must not, however, trust to colour when it is a matter of the classification of human beings, as Linnæus has already affirmed. The differences of colour are reduced, in short, to a varied colouring of the pigment of the mucous membrane. Now this being modified by the influence of external conditions, gives to the skin a scale of tints varying between ebony black, red, yellow, the most pronounced white and half tints passing from one colour to the other.

All these distinct colourings are connected by an infinite variety of shadings. There are Makalolos with colour like café au lait, yellow grey Bushmen, Asiatics olive green or yellow like gingerbread, Obongos of a dirty yellow, Bisharis of red mahogany, Polynesians of a coppery cinnamon red, and Foulbes of rhubarb yellow.

In the matter of colour nothing is fixed or stable from the moment that the conditions of the milieu change. In this as in other physiological modifications one must count not by years but

---

[1] See on this subject the account given by the Académie des Sciences for June 13, 1904, also the studies of R. Verneau in l'Anthropologie, 1902, and G. Hervé's Crânes néolithiques armoricains de type négroïde (Bull. et Mém. Soc. d'Anthrop., 1903). Re the bones of M. Pittard, this is a curious passage from the memoir read before the Académie des Sciences : " Prognathism is facial and maxillary, not dental. A descending perpendicular from the nasal point on the alveo-condylian plan touches in front of the first true molar. The index of prognathism, obtained according to Flower's method, gives respectively, 106·86 and 102·78. The first of these numbers is altogether remarkable. Many of the skulls of negroes do not attain it. These two indices surpass considerably the mean or individual indices of the series from which they have been drawn. The skulls of Quiberon with M. Hervé had, as indices, 102 and 100. The nasal index of the two Valaisan negroid skulls show platyrhiny in both, as that of the two Breton skulls of M. Hervé."

by human generations. Certain traits are modified in the first generation. It is thus that among the Japanese the skin changes colour after twenty years' residence in Europe. After the second generation the peculiarity of the eye has also disappeared. The same applies to negroes, whose complexion becomes whiter in France.

We perceive that the *milieu* succeeds in modifying colour by the changes which it produces in the plumage of the fowl species. Thus in the South, white fowls imported from northern countries soon become yellow. In addition to the modification of plumage, we notice a change of pigment in the flesh itself. M. H. L. A. Blanchon attributes it to the influences exercised by food. " Who knows," he asks, "whether the feathers of brilliant colours which belong to tropical birds are not partly due to nourishment ? " We must not ignore the fact that under the influence of maize the yellow claws of fowls assume an intenser colour, whereas the plumage becomes yellow and takes a saffron tint if the fowl is white or of light colour. Consequently one avoids giving this grain to fowls of white plumage, whereas it is given to fowls which have no white in their plumage (the Hamburg, the Golden Padua, &c.). Iron also plays an important part in the colouring. In making them take a pinch of carbonate of iron daily *during the moulting period* the same experimenter affirms that the colours of the plumage, once the moulting period is over, are brighter, and the metallic reflections which certain fowls display are accentuated in a remarkable way. If carbonate of iron were mixed with the paste given to white fowls the appearance of a special pigment would be seen, giving to the white feathers a yellow colouring. In nourishing white fowls with cayenne pepper mixed with soaked bread and potatoes, M. Saermann obtained striking results. After the tenth day a young white cock had orange feathers. One had orange lines on its breast. In time the first had the breast and the comb quite red with the remainder of the body orange, whereas the second remained white with a red breast. There were, however, chickens on which this feeding seemed to exercise no influence at all. But then we must remember that this experiment had only been made on twelve examples during a year. It is also probable that this feeding influenced the plasmas, but to our great regret this breeder did not examine the descendants of the fowls subjected to this special treatment. For a long time the breeders of birds have had recourse to feeding considered as a dominant factor in colouring. With this object in view cloves are used, also the bark of quinine, the gum of kino, the roots of orchanet, madder-root, cayenne pepper, cashoo, saffron, &c., all of which have the property of modifying the light yellow colouring into red or dark yellow. Professor Wyman, astonished to see that all the pigs of a certain part of Virginia were black, sought and found the reason of it. He learnt that all these animals nourished themselves on the roots of *Lachnanthes tinctoria*, which colours their bones pink and causes the hoofs to fall off in the case of all pigs which are not black.

Who knows if the colouring of human beings is not often like that of animals and plants, in direct correlation with their chances of survival in certain surroundings? In Tarentin, Darwin tells us, the inhabitants only breed black sheep because the *Hypericum crispum* is there in abundance. This plant, which kills white sheep at the end of 15 days, has no effect whatever on black sheep. Even the sun itself appears to act differently according to the colour of the beings on which its rays shine. It kills certain plants and animals, and has a vivifying effect on others. Horticulturists teach us, for example, that certain pansies and pelargoniums profit by the sun, whilst others lose a great deal under its action. Red wheat, we are told, is much more vigorous in a northern climate than white wheat.

It has been proved many times that colour is in direct correlation with the action of parasites. Quatrefages tells us that the butterflies of the silkworms which produce white cocoons resist illness better than those which produce yellow cocoons. Darwin quotes this fact from the *Gardener's Chronicle* (1852, p. 435), that during the first period of the vine disease near Malaga, the white varieties were the most attacked, whereas the red and black, which grew in the midst of the diseased plants, suffered in no way from the malady. Among the different kinds of vervain, the white ones are particularly subject to blight.

Light-coloured animals suffer more, as a rule, than those of dark colour. It is thus that in the West Indies white cattle cannot be utilised because they are tormented by insects.

It is the same in the case of men. Certain white men cannot resist certain climates, whereas men of colour accommodate themselves easily to them. With the progress of bacteriological science, perhaps the causes which favour the acclimation of certain human varieties, and render it difficult to others, will be found. For the time being it is sufficient to state as an example that at equal latitudes the warm regions of the southern hemisphere are generally more favourable to the white races than those of the north. Boudin has also demonstrated that the average mortality of the English and French armies was about eleven times greater in our hemisphere than in the South. The negro everywhere suffers less from malarial fevers than the white.

It seems therefore probable that colour is often but an unconscious adaptation to the conditions of the *milieu.* It is under its influence, and doubtless as the result of selections which cover hundreds of generations, that men have acquired certain colours which are propitious to their evolution. If this explanation is true, nothing is more natural than the weakening and even the disappearance of this characteristic trait with the change of surroundings. When we examine closely the modifications undergone by the black race when transported to the United States, we shall find many proofs to confirm it.

Acclimation, that is to say, the physiological adaptation to the *milieu,* is a general fact the action of which is incontestable on living beings. In the same way as our domestic animals have become under the influence of other conditions of *milieu,* and without any intervention from the breeder, sheep with long or matted hair, hairless bulls, pigs covered with wool, dogs with the ears and skin of a fox, &c., so the Red Skins would change colour if transported from America to Australia as the Negroes of Africa are modified by long residence in Europe. Let us remember, on the other hand, that white men living in the United States begin after a few generations to show the prevailing traits of Red Skins, including the colour of their skin.

What facilitates the variations in the colour of our skin is that these are only of superficial importance. As stated by Virchow, who has made remarkable studies on human colour, the diverse colourings which are so perplexing to ordinary people are resolved under the microscope to a very simple expression. " There we have neither fair nor black nor blue; everything is brown. The skin of the negro under the microscope shows dark pigments, as also that of the fairest European. The blue of the iris of the eye shows also dark pigments under the microscope. European colouring is not made of milk and of blood, or of other colourless substances, not of *Ichor* like the gods of antiquity but of dark pigments. Differences of colour are reduced to differences of quantity and not of quality. Sometimes on the surface and sometimes deeper, these pigments in all cases form the essential element of differentiation."

Under these conditions it cannot be doubted that colour is the direct effect of the *milieu*. " A fair person (Virchow tells us) placed in a certain *milieu* becomes brown, and *vice versâ*." This fact was known long before Darwin, but its mode of action still remains inexplicable.

III. *The Hair*

The hair is in direct correlation with the colour of the skin. It is thus that with the dark skin of the Negro is seen their woolly hair, very short and frizzled. Bory de Saint Vincent thinks there are two principal qualities which distinguish human hair. In the case of some it is smooth (*leiotrichous*), with others it is woolly (*ulotrichous*). When the hair appears rectilinear in all its length, we consider it smooth. But when curved and like little ringlets interlacing each other like tufts of wool, we call it frizzled.

Nevertheless the hair, like the colour, varies from shade to shade. An attentive observer could even establish a sort of harmonious gradation which would comprise all varieties and render their successive transformations evident. According to Brown, the stem of a hair cut transversely allows us to recognise human races. In the Negro it is like an elongated ellipse, in the Red Skin like a circle, and in the Anglo-Saxon it is a form between these two.

Pruner Bey, in starting from the thickness of the hair's stem, points out three principal categories: hair with very narrow stem like the flat hair of the Bushmen or ordinary Negro, the intermediary hair of white races, and finally the hard hair, thick and round, belonging to Mongols, Chinese, Americans and Malays.[1]

But it is enough to study Negro hair among the representatives of this race in order to see how it changes with the *milieu*. It is thus that the Blacks living many generations in the United States tend to resemble other Americans such as Germans, Slavs or Anglo-Saxons.   Cross-breeding, even in the first degree, often radically changes the colour and the characteristic qualities of the hair.

Sorby (quoted by Virchow), in using sulphuric acid, succeeded in extracting various coloured substances from the hair.   All are reduced to four principal categories, pale red, dark red, yellow and black.   But experiment has proved that all these substances constitute a gradation, for they all proceed one from the other and in progressive transformation.

This fact is of first importance.   It confirms above all the theory that it is only a matter of different quantities and not of irreducible elements.   Let us mention, however, the existence of red colouring matter in all red hair, which varies from flaming red to dark red.   This matter represents the dark pigment of other hair.

The reds form in consequence a category apart, and there is no more difference here between fair hair, red or brown than between black and fair.   The bearing of this fact, however, must not be exaggerated, for, as we have seen above, all the colours which we succeed in extracting from our hair only form a successive gradation, proving their common composition and source.

In default of fundamental differences in the coloration, the attempt has been made to find a distinctive sign of racial differences in the quantity of the hair.   We know that in addition to the long single hairs which attain their development

---

[1] *Sur la chevelure comme caractéristique des races humaines*, &c.   Mém. Soc. d'Anthrop.   Vols. II. and III.

on the head, there are also stiff and short hairs to be observed on the eyelids, the eyebrows, nostrils, armpits, elbows
and the inner angle of the eye. All this constitutes what
is called the pilous system. But are there in the matter of
the hair's growth and abundance and of the pilous system
any essential differences among men? Excepting the Ainos,
well known for their excessive hairiness all over the body, and
also the Todas, very like them, there are no peoples or races
to be found distinguished in this particular.

Savants, however, have fallen back on the internal structure
of the hair, to find a solid basis on which to divide humanity.
Topinard,[1] for example, tells us that the spiral form gives us the
best characteristics for the distinction of racial types. The four
essential kinds of hair, viz. *straight, undulated, curled or frizzled*,
and *woolly*, are distributed among human beings as follows—the
yellow and American races are distinguished by their
rectilineal hair containing traces of undulation; the European
peoples, Semites and Berbers have wavy or undulated hair; the
Australians and Negroes mixed with Yellows and Whites are
distinguished by their frizzled hair, the spiral curves still
touching without perceptibly commingling, whereas in the negro
type of frizzled or woolly hair the spiral curves are so close that
they commingle. The hair of Negroes commingled and
interlaced is seen like cylinders several millimetres in diameter,
and massed together they appear on the surface of the head in
tufts often very distinct.

But here also, whilst admitting the exactness of this division,
we notice the imperceptible passing of the straight and pliant hair
to the undulated hair and then the curled and frizzled, to arrive
finally at the woolly hair. We insist on this odd progression,
which demonstrates that in this case evolution and progress
go from the yellow and white races to the Negro! His hair
becomes in this way the supreme expression of progress, the
goal towards which all the hair of the other peoples and races
ought to tend.

For in reality woolly hair, in serving as the usual basis for
the division of humanity into pariahs and privileged stocks,
establishes a kind of superiority for the Negroes. If man is

[1] *L'Homme dans la Nature.*

essentially more noble as the distance between him and anthropoid apes widens, it must not be forgotten that these monkeys only have straight and little undulated hair, resembling that of the yellow races and the American peoples, and perceptibly approaching Europeans, Berbers and Semites! The woolly hair of the Negroes, having nothing in common with that of the apes, procures for them in this way a decided advantage (?) over men of other colours and races!

We shall see, however, by what follows how very risky this gradation of humanity according to the accepted canon becomes. Very frequently the so-called inferior races show precisely the physiological properties which by reversing all preconceived methods of classification place them at the head of humanity!

IV. *The Brown and the Fair*

The colour of the skin and the hair is closely related to the question of the brown and the fair, which troubles the brains of many anthropologists and especially those of anthropo-psychologists. Connected especially with the structure of the skull, it gives birth to a class of privileged men who unite dolichocephaly with fair hair and fair complexions.

These "fair dolichocephalic" become a kind of auto-suggestion of race to most of the theorists. It often makes them lose the idea of reality and the respect due to the dignity of man. Later on we shall have occasion to show the inanity of this strange dogma, the cult of which can only be explained by those attacks of collective folly which seize with equal intensity both the multitudes and those whom they accept as leaders.

Intoxicated with the spectacle of certain fair peoples with long skulls, to whom with reason or without they attribute the merit of having guided human civilisation during centuries, certain savants have wished to erect this occasional circumstance into an inexorable law. To do this they have either forgotten or made themselves forget this indisputable historical fact, that the leadership of human thought has often changed hands in the course of time. Without taking the least account of the form of the skull or the colour of the skin or of the hair, we have seen human supremacy go now to the Ethiopians, Chinese, Greeks, and Romans, now to brown Celts or fair Teutons, people of all shades and of all craniological structures. What interests us particularly here is the fact that one can no longer divide humanity under this heading. Brown and fair, long and broad skulls are found intermingled in the same country, in the same district, and in the same family. How then can we succeed in differentiating them ?

In what particularly concerns the hair and the colour of the eyes, let us remember the imposing inquiry organised by the German Anthropological Society under the direction of R. Virchow. It bore on the colour of the hair, eyes and skin in the case of children of both sexes in the German schools. The success of this enterprise caused some successful imitations of it in Belgium, Switzerland and Austria. Anthropology has thus obtained the results of the examination of about ten millions of children. Germany procured 6,758,827 scholars, Austria 2,304,501, Belgium 608,698, and Switzerland 405,609. Now the number of fair-haired amounted to about a fourth without counting Belgium, that of the brown to a sixth, and the remainder, that is six out of ten millions, belonged to the mixed type. Germany, " the land of the fair-haired, " only showed 31 per cent. of fair-haired, 14 per cent. of brown and about 55 per cent. of mixed type !

Let us also mention the inquiries of Dr. Beddoe, the results of which were drawn up in a number of tables. We extract from them these significant figures : of 1,100 Scotch Highlanders, who as Celts ought to have been brown, 45 per cent. were fair-haired, 30 per cent. brown, and 25 per cent. mixed ; of 1,250 Viennese (a fair Germanic race) 32 per cent. were fair, 23 per cent. brown, and 45 per cent. mixed.

The attempts made in France to draw up the statistics of fair- and brown-haired gave identical results. Among ourselves, as elsewhere, the brown and the fair are extremely mixed and widely disseminated.

These numerous observations can be generalised under this commonplace—that Southern countries show a greater number of brown-haired, and those of the North a greater number of fair-haired.

CHAPTER IX

WE go on to notice several traits of physical ugliness concerning which many travellers have made a great stir. Denounced with some exaggeration as contributing to the deformation of many primitive peoples, they have excited the wild imagination of the Whites. We note in this connection steatopygy, the excessive length of the breasts and the "apron." When we perceive on the gluteal muscles of Hottentot, Bushmen, Kaffir or Somali women, masses of fat developed out of all measure and vibrating at the least movement like two bags attached to the waist, we say it is a case of steatopygy. Let us state in the first place that even among these tribes it is *not general* but only very frequent. Sometimes also, according to G. Fritsch, well-nourished boys and men display a tendency to acquire supplementary patches of fat on the same spot. According to Livingstone, certain Boer women, and therefore white, who have been settled for a long time in South Africa show an analogous agglomeration of fat on the buttocks.

If this information was exact, we would perhaps find a plausible explanation of this phenomenon, which, to say the least, is odd, in the conditions of that *milieu*. It would be interesting to make a counter experiment and to subject steatopygic women to the influence of another *milieu*. According to all probable previsions, this phenomenon would disappear after a few generations. The experiment not having been tried, it appears to us impossible to adopt the opinion of the anthropologists, several of whom, as circumspect as Topinard, want to see in steatopygy a profound anthropological division among races.

It would separate human beings in the same way as the dog and wolf, and the goat and lamb! Nothing but the rarity of this phenomenon makes this conclusion excessive. The example of Boer women, however, singularly weakens it, and the absolute want of any counter experiment in the sense mentioned above robs it of all scientific value. Let us add that it is only a matter of the augmentation of local fat varying in degree, and not the appearance of an irreducible organ or trait. It strikes our attention when seen in an excessive degree, but it nevertheless exists in an intermediary state among many white women. We remember that certain images found in the ruins of Pompeii show this kind of " growth " apparently as a sign of beauty !

Our æsthetic tastes, on the other hand, may be shocked at the leisurely sight of these floating balloons of fat, but those of the women on the spot would be in entire disagreement with us. These, indeed, find therein a trait of beauty, and exhibit it with the same pride as white women do their false hair and false breasts.

As to the exaggerated length of the breasts and the " apron," they are much more rarely found among these same Bushwomen. Travellers tell us, it is true, that there are women who can throw their breasts over their shoulders, as there are other women who have the little lips of their genital organ so elongated that they almost form an apron. These attain among certain Bushwomen from 15 to 18 centimetres.

Without desiring to dwell on this delicate subject, let us remark that these three phenomena are found in the same human type living in identical conditions of *milieu*. Nor are they found in a general and usual way, but sporadically. A more important matter is that, regarded from the point of view of the transition of human traits, they cannot be considered as the irreducible and exceptional characteristics of certain peoples and races.

The exaggerated elongation of the breasts is easily explained by the regrettable process of drawing them which is practised by certain women among the Bushmen and Hottentots. According to Ranke, certain country women of Northern Ireland, and also certain Dalmatian women, show for the same reason an excessive length of breasts.

Again, the " apron " is found more frequently than is supposed among young white girls.   A comparative study, sure to be made some day, holds in store some surprise for us on this subject.   We cannot for the moment restrain ourselves from stating that from the monkey point of view, considered by many anthropologists as a criterion of beauty, the existence of the " apron " constitutes a very enviable preference !   Among female gorillas, the little lips remain almost absolutely invisible. We ought logically to appreciate as a trait of superiority the striking spectacle which the " apron " offers us.

CHAPTER X

Physiological and Pathological Distinctions

I. *The Identity of Physiological Functions*

THE physiology of man is the same in the case of all his representatives. He who would speak of a special physiology of yellow men, or black men, would run the risk of making himself ridiculous. Far from seeking distinctions of all sorts under this heading, we find the completest harmony of all physiological functions among all the representatives of humanity whatever their race or colour. Their functions of breathing and digesting, the period of gestation and of growth through the successive phases of age, in one word the evolution of their physiological life between the two most solemn moments of their terrestrial existence, birth and death, undergo the same laws. Those differences which are met with in animals of the same species, with regard to gestation, are not found among human beings. The she-wolf carries a little over a hundred days, large dogs 63, and little dogs from 59 to 63. Among the different races of pigs, gestation lasts from 109 to 123 days (according to Nathusius, this period would in general be shorter among precocious races). According to the observations of Tessier, made on 1,131 cows, there was a difference of 81 days between the length of the shortest and longest gestation.

M. Lefour affirms that the period of gestation is longer among the tall German races than among the short. When we study the other domestic races in this particular, we also perceive that the period of gestation varies according to the races. The observations of Nathusius teach us that merino and

Southdown sheep living in identical conditions differ nevertheless as follows in the length of their gestation :—

Merinos . . . . 150·3 days
Southdowns . . . . 144·2 „
Crossbreeds of these two races . . . . . 146·3 „
Three-quarters Southdowns . . . . . . 145·5 „ &c.

Fecundity varies according to races. The number of litters in the year and the number of little ones in each litter varies according to animal races of the same species. Domestic animals outstrip wild animals in this respect. Whereas the wild sow bears twice yearly from four to eight little ones, the domestic sow bears from two to three times and has as many as ten little ones every time. The wild rabbit bears four times in the year, and every time from four to eight young ones. When domesticated it bears from six to seven times yearly, having each time on an average from eight to ten. In the works of Darwin [1] and Herbert Spencer [2] many enumerations are found of birds and other domesticated animals, whose fecundity varies according to race. The wild duck, for example, lays from five to ten eggs, the domesticated from eighty to one hundred in one year.

Is this the case with the different varieties of human beings ? Who would venture to maintain that white or yellow women, civilised or savage, are distinct from one another in the matter of length of gestation or the faculty of giving birth to children ? The number of births indeed often varies among different peoples, but no one would think of attributing this difference to the factor of race. All human varieties are sometimes prolific and sometimes relatively sterile. The reasons for a great or insignificant birth-rate are always to be found in transient sociological causes, comprising the habits or mode of life peculiar to the given population. The period of nursing varies, it is true, but here also the differences which we see are only the effects of custom and usage. It even changes considerably within the limits of the same country, province and district.

All the phases of sexual life are to be found equally regularly

[1] *De la Variation des Animaux.* Vol. II.
[2] *Principes de Biologie.* II.

among all human beings. It is true that the time of puberty varies, not because of a different physiological structure, but because of the influence of climate.

The circulation of the blood likewise is the same in all and follows the same laws. If the pulse of the radial artery, which is an accurate expression of the beatings of the heart, shows certain variations, they are due to the state of health, age, digestion, corpulence, or temperament of the individual, and not to a different physiological structure in races and peoples.

Respiration and digestion are sometimes bad and sometimes good according to the individuals and their general health. As to breathing, let us note the irritating ignorance which is met with on this matter both among savage and civilised peoples. It is only in these modern years that it has been seen that respiration must be learnt, and that left to themselves children breathe wrongly to the great prejudice of their health. Scientific respiration, as now taught, contributes to the enlarging of the lungs and to the strengthening of the digestive organs.

All attempts at dividing humanity according to faculty of speech, singing, good sight, good hearing or good smelling have completely failed.

All men are equal physiologically at their birth, and never cease to be so till they die. Death appears everywhere under the same conditions. The mean duration of human life varies, particularly owing to climate, comfort and hygiene, and not because of racial differences. It is our way of living, not our way of being born, which lengthens or shortens life. Longevity is sometimes hereditary, but the same phenomenon is found both among civilised and uncivilised. Health stored up by the parents often profits the children, but it is a capital which is not very secure, and one which a second generation may tamper with and squander. In discussing this question at greater length in my *Philosophie de la Longévité*, I have had occasion to demonstrate the absolute equality of human being in the presence of death.

As to diseases, they are generally common to men. They renew and multiply themselves with regrettable frequency Scarcely is one overcome before others appear on the horizon to make havoc of the human organism. Their novelty lie only in their names. With the progress of science, special pathological states are discovered which escaped the vigilance of our ancestors. But whether old or new, diseases are connected with *milieu*, and not with man. Several exceptions have been brought forward, upon which to erect the sorry privilege of race.

Reality, however, refuses to endorse these charters of exclusiveness. Without doubt certain infections attack white men more readily than Negroes in hot climates, but this fact is explained by the natives' special power of endurance, and their mode of life, which is more adapted to the conditions of the *milieu*. Malaria, which carries off certain populations on the outskirts of marshy districts, is as unrelenting to the natives as to all white, yellow, or black men who settle in these regions. When at length bacteriological science succeeded in finding the zoospore of this terrible malady, it profited all its erstwhile victims without distinction of colour or of cephalic index. From official documents relating to the death-rate in Sierra Leone from 1829 to 1836, it was seen that all maladies which swept away the population prevailed not only among the Whites, but also among the Blacks, who, it might be thought, would have been exempt from them. Both paid and still pay their frightful tribute to eruptive fevers as to paludal fevers, and to gastro-intestinal maladies as to those of the liver. "Dysentery and liver complaints prevail among Negroes as among Whites. Malignant fevers, which with these two last form the pathognomonic trilogy of Senegalese pathology, attack Europeans in preference, but the Blacks are far from being exempt" (Berchon).

The sleeping fever, the latest of epidemic fevers in Africa, attacks Whites and Blacks equally. Cholera and the Plague do not bow before racial considerations, but strike all human beings with the same cruelty. What varies is the power of resistance which individuals oppose to the attacks of new maladies. Every disease when carried into new countries by contagion begins by making relatively more victims. Afterwards, owing to a better organised resistance, and to a growing power of endurance, its deadly effects diminish to the habitual level. But it is ever a matter of changing conditions of *milieu* and not of irreducible and innate human qualities.

II. *The Beauty of the Human Body*

The study of man as well as the comparison of human beings
having been established and directed by white men, it follows
that all the traits observed in and among Whites are thereby
idealised and regarded as essentially superior. The idea of
beauty being essentially subjective, there is nothing astonishing in the fact that everywhere and always, whenever Whites
have been engaged in its definition, they should have borrowed
its essentials from their immediate surroundings. Starting from
this basis, they have declared all human types beautiful or
ugly which approximate or diverge from formulas established
by White artists and authors, from White exemplars.

From ancient times we see conventional rules known as
canons applied to the æsthetic estimate of human beings.
Throughout all these "norms of beauty," many of which are
to be found in Egypt, a master idea emerges to our view,
namely, the unity of the human type. It is only in Albert
Dürer that a diversity of specimens appears. It is he who first
shows us the drawing of a negro dissimilar from the white
type. All the same, it must not be forgotten that the canons
of antiquity, like those of modern times, carried convention to
the obvious contempt of reality.

The Egyptians employed a canon dividing the human figure
(if one may judge from the drawings found by Lepsius) into
nineteen horizontal parts without counting the coiffure. The
statue of Polycletus shows us the most popular canon in
Greece. Let us recall, among other canons, those of Vitruvius
(first centuries of Christianity), Alberti (Renaissance), Albert
Dürer and Jean Cousin (15th and 16th centuries), and in
more recent times those of Gerdy (1830), and of Quételet (1870).

The measurements of artists have preceded those of anthropologists by many centuries. Under their influence came the
conception of artistic beauty, which has not failed to leave its
traces on anthropological canons.

We are born with certain sentiments of plastic beauty,
engendered by tradition and the opinions of those who surround
us. The sheepish nature of man rarely revolts against admitted

ideas which often equal in force innate ideas. We find beautiful everything which those who are before us find beautiful, and especially the people called competent. This applies to women, pictures, and masterpieces of sculpture. Which of us has not admired the plastic beauty of Laocoon? Yet his right leg is much shorter than the left, whereas, obviously to keep him company, one of his children has, on the contrary, a "more pronounced" right leg.

G. Audran [1] makes this curious remark, that in the most beautiful figures of antiquity details are found which would be readily regarded as faults if found in the work of a modern. Apollo, for example, has the left leg too long by about nine lines; the Venus of Medici has the "curved" leg longer by about three lines than that on which she stands, &c.

According to the canon established by Audran, which had a certain vogue in the 17th century, the head is divided into four parts: (1) from below the chin to beneath the nose; (2) from beneath the nose to its top between the two eyebrows; (3) thence to the beginning of the hair on the forehead; (4) to the crown of the head. Each of these four parts is divided into twelve lines. If, then, according to the measures of Audran, the right leg of the tall son of Laocoon is too (?) long by nine lines, it is seen that this divergence demands attention!

It may be said, therefore, that the ancients paid little attention to anatomical exactitude. They also followed the opinions of the day and gave to great men large foreheads and voluminous heads, because the gods were considered to have them. Nevertheless, nothing can be more false than the foreheads of 90 to 100 degrees of Greek sculptors, which resemble hydrocephalic foreheads. The neck was thrown into relief and the limbs were made long and slender when nobility was to be indicated (Quételet). Wide shoulders expressed force, whilst narrow shoulders symbolised youth or an effeminate character. At certain epochs the face of some eminent personage who set the fashion of the day appears, and under its influence all artists worked. Persons who provoked sympathy were benefited by analogous traits, whilst, as far as possible, a

---

[1] *Les Proportions du Corps humain.* Paris, 1683.

different physiognomy was given to slaves and foreigners. When it was desired to make portraits of conquerors, a " divine stamp " was bestowed upon them, together with all the conventional traits which spelt force and superiority. The schools which succeeded the Renaissance were inspired by the same sentiments, according to Topinard. In Italy forms were elongated to give dignity; in Spain they were shortened to obtain delicacy; in Holland they were made stout for realistic purposes; whilst in France recently the head alone was exaggerated in order to draw all the attention.

When after having being fed with all these sensations of conventional beauty it is attempted to apply them to the variety of human types, we are unconsciously unjust with regard to those whose types are outside these limits.

Nature, which takes no account of our canons of beauty, nearly always diverges from them. Not willing to regard as false our particular conceptions as to the proportions of the different parts of the body, we declare those which diverge from them to be ugly or inferior.

For our modern canons, preached by all anthropologists, are all founded on the white man's observations. Among the best known we note those of Ch. Blanc and Gerdy. Both, however, are very similar to the anthropological canons. For Ch. Blanc, the length of the body equals 30 noses or $7\frac{1}{2}$ heads. For Gerdy, 32 noses and 8 heads.[1]

It is well understood that it is not a question here of speaking of any fixity. Since the height of the human body easily increases under the influence of conditions indicated above, it follows that the proportion of the different parts of the body can and must vary at the same time. Let us do justice to the more thoughtful anthropologists, who in face of

---

[1] This is the canon of Ch. Blanc (canon of the studios). Height, 100.

Head			
	The crown to the hair's limit, $\frac{1}{4}$-head . . . 3·3		
	Hair to root of nose . . . . . 3·3		13·2
	Root of nose to its base . . . . . 3·3		
	Base of nose to below chin, $\frac{1}{2}$-head . . . 3·3		
Neck	. . . . 6·6		
Trunk	. . . . 30·0		
Lower limbs	. . . . 50·0		

99·9

these changing characteristics are ready to acknowledge their small value. Topinard even welcomes the doubtful fixity of these characteristics, inasmuch as it favours transformation. It shows us in particular (he says) that under their apparent immobility, human types are in a state of perpetual decomposition and composition.

Bravo! But the satisfaction which the learned author of *l'Homme dans la Nature* feels does not prevent other anthropologists, as well as ignorant people, from drawing conclusions from these canons which are prejudicial to all those human beings who evolve outside these rules. In this way the arms and feet of Negroes, which are too long in proportion to their bodies, are deemed a mark of inferiority bringing them near to apes. But according to Weisbach and other naturalists the Whites resemble ourang-outangs much more than the Negroes in this respect. It must be stated that Negroes and Australians have relatively the shortest trunk, and that they are further removed from the monkeys than any race in the human scale owing to the length of their arms and feet. It is the same in what concerns the corpulence of Negroes. As we saw above, a centimetre of height corresponds in the Negroes with about 387 grams of weight as against 366 in the English (Gould). But here again the racial factor counts for nothing. From the researches of Majer among Germans, it follows that corpulence and relative weight depend especially on the kind of occupation in which individuals are engaged. According to him corpulence varies regularly with employment and goes from tailors, who are the lightest, to brewers, who are the heaviest. Next to these last come the carpenters, bakers, students, masons, locksmiths, weavers, bootmakers, &c., &c.

There have been legends of people resembling monkeys. All the attempts to discover among living beings a race forming an intermediary link between man and monkey have remained unfruitful. What we know on the contrary is that nowhere does a people exist who approximate monkeys *most* and *in all respects*, as there is no people who diverge from monkeys in an exceptional degree in regard to all their traits. The different human types now approximate and now diverge from monkeys, as the conquests made by the explorers of the ship *Novara* have proved. The Negroes, whom it is desired to place at the bottom of the human scale, are in many respects much more removed from monkeys than the purest Whites.

It is enough to confront human beings in their many aspects to perceive that nature does not recognise superior and inferior races. This gradation, which means nothing physiologically, is equally inadmissible æsthetically.

The fable which is current on the subject of the tail attributed to savage or primitive peoples can be turned against the whites themselves. This anomaly, due to troubles in embryonic evolution, is according to Bartels' studies especially frequent among the Whites, not that these are themselves "inferior," but simply because of the special care given to the deformed, who among primitive peoples perish so easily, left as they are to their own resources.

Negroes, who from all time have enjoyed the sorry privilege of passing as the race nearest the monkeys, have had the advantage among other things of a defect with which certain anthropologists lightly reproach them. For, as Burmeister and so many others tell us, not only have they very long arms, but these even exceed the length of their lower limbs. It will be understood that under these conditions they would only have to use their hands to walk like monkeys. Place their front limbs at right angles on the ground with fingers stretched out, and behold, animals with four feet! But this mirage of Negro-monkeys has vanished since impartial comparisons have been started. Let us remember first of all that the length of the arms surpassing that of the legs among Negroes is a pure myth, and, what is more important, that the differences between races measured in this respect never exceed 8·9 per cent., whereas they attain 13·8 among the representatives of different professions in the same country. And if one persists absolutely in making this trait a mark of monkey ugliness, we must acknowledge, what Ranke confirms, namely, that the French and Germans are in this matter nearer the monkeys than Negroes, Australians or Bushmen. The English and French are on the same level as Negroes, whereas much below Negroes and other primitive peoples must be counted the Chinese. Among other æsthetic differences we must note that of the *brasse* (the extreme length of the two extended arms from point to point). But it has been proved that the measures obtained in this way cannot provide us with any appreciable result. According to the calculations of Gould, G. Schults, &c., the variations depend entirely on the professions in which the individuals are engaged, and are in every case insignificant among the various human types. Thus certain peasants of Northern Europe approximate the Negroes more than do the educated classes in the United States.

Nor does the exact proportion between the arm and forearm give us any positive information. A simian sign has been seen wherever the arm is proportionably longer. But the results of comparative studies only show the fact that the whole human race resembles, in this respect, gorillas and mammifers.

The proportional length of the neck, which is deemed a sign of beauty, often varies among races. But still more does it vary among different social classes according to their daily occupations.

In general, as we study human beings in the matter of regularity and harmony of features, we perceive the great influence exercised by their daily occupations. Gould, in comparing bodily proportions among divers representatives of the American people, states that there are greater differences between sailors, agriculturists and men of culture than between Negroes, Redskins and Whites.

Bælz points out the same thing among the Japanese. Those of the upper classes are distinguished by length of arm, which is equivalent to 43·8 of the bodily height; among workmen it reaches 42·6, which confirms Gould's theory that length of arm depends on the occupation, and reaches its maximum among workmen.

G. d'Harcourt also brings forward a number of measurements made on Arabs which prove that they are much nearer civilised people than primitive Negroes. Their arm and forearm, like their legs, are much shorter than those of Negroes. Not without cause, for are not the Arabs nearer to us in the matter of culture?

Ranke[1] even thinks it possible to divide humanity into three categories, not according to colour or form of skull, but accord-

---

[1] *Der Mensch.* Vol. II.

ing to mode of life and occupation. In the first category there would be women, who generally evolve outside the usual occupations of men ; then people engaged in mechanical work and the unemployed; thirdly, those who only work with the brain. To these three divisions would correspond the relative lengths of the trunk, neck, arms, lower limbs, development of chest and muscular force, &c., &c.

Thus it is that nearly everywhere among the Whites and primitive men the woman's constitution is like that of a child rather than that of a full-grown man, and that among civilised peoples the intellectual classes, quite apart from the colour of skin, are distinguished by a relatively longer trunk, shorter extremities and more voluminous head. We see, according to results obtained by Weisbach in his measurements of the diverse peoples who comprise the Austrian Empire, how little racial origins influence the proportions of the different bodily limbs among peoples living in identical conditions of civilisation or comfort. The intellectual classes among the Magyars, the Uralo-Altaic peoples, the Slavs or the Germanic races, furnish us with identical measures of trunk, extremities, &c., whereas individuals of the same race differ considerably when once distinctly separated by their occupations.

Another no less curious fact is that the measurements of Austrian Jews correspond entirely with those which Gould mentions in the case of cultured persons in the United States. But, as we know, the Austrian Jews engage almost in no mechanical work, but are almost exclusively employed as usurers and small shopkeepers, or figure as lawyers and doctors. On the other hand, the Caucasian Jews (J. Tcherny's measurements) correspond in this respect with other inhabitants of Southern Russia, whose occupation they share.

The attempt has also been made to condemn Negroes for the exaggerated projection of their heels, and again this trait, which is considered typical, loses all its significance with the changing of the conditions of *milieu*. On the west coast of Africa we come across numerous negro tribes whose feet are analogous to ours in every respect. The same applies to numerous Negroes in the United States, where no trace of such heels is found. Flat feet also, with which so many Negroes are endowed, are brought forward as a sign of ugliness. But, strictly speaking, we only meet with this phenomenon among Negroes condemned from infancy to bear heavy burdens. Here also it is only a matter of a professional trait, for we find the same flat feet among Whites whose business compels them to bear crushing burdens with bare feet.

It even follows from Gould's tables, who examined several thousands of Black Americans, that the mean diameter of their feet is greater than that of agricultural labourers in the United States. These are the proportions furnished by Gould. In taking 100 as the dimension of the body, the curve of the feet in different American professions was : labourer, 3·83 ; Indian, 3·94; Negro, 4·04; the cultured, 4·09.

On the other hand, Negroes could boast their superior development of chest. According to our ideas of beauty, what contributes to enhance our æsthetic value is the difference of the diameters of chest, hips, and waist. Now in this respect numerous negro tribes surpass the English themselves.

We close our enumeration of æsthetic characteristics with the particular odour emitted by certain peoples and races. For a long time it was thought that white men were exempt from this, but now we have to admit a strong smell peculiar to white skins, a smell which the Japanese declare to be insupportable. There is something extremely funny in these mutual reproaches as to odour among human beings. The missionary Huc affirms that he could recognise the Tibetans, Chinese, Arabs, Hindoos, Negroes and Tartars by their smell. We can go further and state that every *milieu* gives a particular odour to those subjected to its influence. If the subtle differences of these odours escape us, they do not therefore cease to have a real existence.

Thus a specific odour accompanies each human agglomeration, or rather each individual. This odour being only the result of our mode of life, which comprises all external and internal influences, and includes our nourishment, varies naturally according to the change of our mode of life. African Negroes, whose pronounced odour produces nausea in many Europeans, lose this peculiarity when transplanted into other climates and submitted to the conditions of life which prevail among the Whites.

Americans no longer complain of odour among certain Negroes, not because they have lost the capacity of smelling it, but merely because the Negroes who surround them have entirely lost it.   They no doubt exhale another odour like that of their neighbours, for which reason these last are no longer affected by it.

CONCLUSION

WHEN, after comparing different human types æsthetically, we wish to draw any conclusions, we soon perceive their inanity. It would be vain, Broca tells us, to wish to establish a series of progressive types from the primitive or savage man to the White. Always and everywhere we see the same phenomenon. People are seen beautiful and ugly at the same time, or rather they are only beautiful and ugly according to our subjective ideas. What is more important is that humanity varies in particular according to degree of culture. In short, human beings could be divided into two leading types, civilised and primitive. Regarded in this way and studied with reference to the influence of *milieu*, individual modifications display their secret sources. Above all are they seen as the products of a mode of life and of a progressive mentality. The more our life is seen as logically related to the needs of our organism, the more does it evolve harmoniously and attain full development. But high intellectual culture is in no way synonymous with æsthetic beauty, for the abuse of intellectual work has on the contrary produced a deterioration of the physiological type among many civilised peoples. It is only a life wherein the needs of our body and the aspirations of our soul are well balanced which can procure for the human type that degree of perfectibility which is possible.

The radiant future, therefore, which opens out vast hopes for the humanity of to-morrow, summons humanity as a whole. It leaves out no single variety, for they are all equally dear to the eternal principle of things.

PART II

TOWARDS THE UNITY OF THE HUMAN TYPE

CHAPTER I

THE MILIEU AS A DOMINANT FACTOR IN HUMAN EVOLUTION

I

THE facts previously analysed have demonstrated that the differences established between human beings are only of secondary importance. We might describe them as a kind of alluvial soil which circumstances have carried down and which circumstances will carry away. Over and above all these modifications of lesser importance, which have appeared with time and owing to special influences, there always and everywhere breaks out the fundamental identity of man. All those who have been hypnotised by these distinctive traits, and who have confined themselves to contemplating them without ever rising to the idea of human unity, remind us somewhat of those visitors to the zoological gardens of whom the moralist speaks. They saw there all sorts of insects, but they did not see the kings and giants of the animal world, lions and elephants.

Man, like all organic beings, is subject to the influence of the *milieu*, the factor which dominates all the transformations which take place in nature. Besides this force, acting slowly during an interminable number of centuries by way of modification, there is another which seems to modify its influence in working by way of preservation.

This second force is heredity, owing to which acquired characteristics tend to persist in the rising generations. In these two influences, centrifugal and centripetal, are condensed the principal elements in the evolution of living matter. We have seen in the theoretical part of this work that, according to the neo-Darwinians, there is a special cause,

apart from these factors, which revolutionises beings and occasions the birth of new genera or races, and species, namely,
sudden varieties. These, which play so important a part in the
animal and vegetable world, do not manifest themselves among
human beings. If monstrous and exceptional forms do appear
among them, they are only found in isolated cases, and disappear
with those who unfortunately possess them.

We shall see later on what conclusions we may draw from it.
But whatever may be the influence of this new factor, which
seems to triumph in evolutionary science, it is incontestable
that even sudden variety, as well as heredity, undergoes the
dominating influence of the *milieu*, which is the trunk of the
tree, the other influences being only the branches. In order
that the *milieu* should exercise its manifold action, which works
in every direction, it is necessary above everything else that the
definitions of it should cover a vast field of action. For us it
includes the sum total of the conditions which accompany the
conception and earthly existence of a being, and which end
only with its death.

It is thus that the climateric conditions, the composition of
the soil, the social, political and intellectual life, and the
material comforts, play a distinct part in the definite expression
of the *milieu*. At the risk of changing the nature of its real
influence, we must not exclude from it any one of the thousands
of factors which compose it, just as it is impossible to banish its
action at the time of the germination and evolution of the
embryo. As we ascend in the scale of living beings, the *milieu*,
which reacts on their existence, becomes more and more complex.
That of an entozoon does not go outside the body of the animal
in which it lives. That of a water plant is virtually confined to
its native ditch.[1] The beings who live at the bottom of the sea
act under the influence of a much more restricted *milieu* than
that of beings found on the surface of the earth, for, to use
Spencer's expression, they are affected by a smaller number of
co-existences and of sequences than earthly beings. The
acalepha carried by running water, compared with the caterpillar
obliged to struggle against the force of gravity, shows clearly the

[1] Herbert Spencer, *Principes de Biologie* (French translation. Paris, Félix
Alcan).

narrowness of the *milieu* in the case of the one when compared with that in which the other moves. Compare again the life of insects with that of birds, the latter with that of animals and men, and we shall see how complicated the *milieu* becomes with the evolution of beings. The progress of external causes which fashion the individual, evolve thus in a sort of mathematical progression. It is enough to consider the life of a man in order to see that the *milieu*, or rather the number of *milieux* on which he depends, attains a fabulous figure. The complete physiological life is above everything else the result of incalculable causes, and its processes of nutrition and respiration alone involve thousands of millions of causes and influences. Let us add the social, moral, and political *milieu*, which, when analysed, represent by themselves unimaginable numbers of elements.

The *milieu* acts also on the intra-uterine or intra-ovarian existence, just as much as in the case of an individual already formed. In changing the *milieu*, the nature itself of certain beings is radically changed. Let us remember on this subject the convincing experiments of M. A. Chauveau. He succeeded in rendering the carbon bacteria inoffensive. In other words, this experimenter succeeded in depriving it of all its virulent properties by submitting it to the influence of hyper-oxygen-ation, that is to say, by modifying the *milieu* of its natural evolution. It has even been possible to fix these new charac-teristics so as to produce a distinct race. These character-istics, thus acquired, become permanent, and by ordinary culture continue to exist in successive generations. After having deprived the microbe of its virulence, M. A. Chauveau succeeded afterwards in revivifying the same virulence by the addition of blood to bouillon culture.[1] With the modification of the *milieu*, success is in this way achieved in artificial trans-formation in pathogenetic microbiology. In a further extension of the action of cultures under hyper-oxygenation, one might perhaps succeed in creating species radically distinct from B. carbon. Thanks to micro-biology and artificial cultures, we can utilize this influence of the *milieu* in a very striking way. It is especially manifest in cryptogamia, which show a prodigious facility in the multiplication and succession of generations.

[1] A. Chauveau, *Arch. de Méd. expériment. et d'anatomie pathologique.* 1889.

M. Laurent[1] has shown that the *Cladosporum herbarum* mushroom can, according to the manner in which it is cultivated, show seven different conditions.

Flourens succeeded in giving a red colour to the bones of a female mammifer's fœtus by mixing madder-root with its food. Costé caused certain trout to be born which had lost the characteristic coloration of their race, by placing the spawn of a salmon trout in water which only nourished white trout.

Examples of this influence abound in all spheres of organic life, and we shall never be able to quote enough. M. Decaisne, after having cultivated in the Museum of Natural History at Paris seven divers forms of plantain, considered to be good species, found them after a few generations changed into a single form. It is enough to compare the action of argillo-silicious and argillo-calcareous soils in order to see the influence which these exercise on seeds. Whereas the first, cold and rich in silicates, only produces insipid plants and mediocre herbs, the other, owing to the calcareous elements which prevail there, favours great fecundity and gives beautiful and vigorous plants.

In France, for the same reason, when one goes from Normandy to Maine, from the plains of Poitou to the hills of Limousin, from Causse of Rodez to Segala, from Burgundy to Morvan, from the banks of the Loire to the land crossed by the Clayette and Chauffailles, we see rich cultivation disappear, sometimes almost suddenly.[2] The same phenomenon is to be seen in the animal world. Often in the same valley, divided by a little river, where on one side there is silicious soil and on the other calcareous, the cattle, horses, and sheep seem to be from different lands and of different origin. On one side big, fat, and strong animals, and on the other feeble and small.

[1] *Annales de l'Institut Pasteur.* 1888.
[2] Prof. Magne, *Traité pratique d'Agriculture.*

II

In the living matter of plants we only find the inanimate, that is, mineral elements, for the vegetable matter is only a mass of inorganic composites. If inorganic matter furnishes plants with the principal sources of alimentation (Liebig), it is the same also in animal and man. This fact has been ignored for centuries, but it begins to triumph even in what concerns human beings. We note, for example, that in the department of l'Aveyron the inhabitants as well as the domestic animals are divided into two clearly marked types which correspond with the two great geological divisions of the district, silicious and calcareous. In the first, man and sheep are of small stature and frail bones, whilst in the second both are of greater height and of massive skeleton.

With these geological differences of habitat correspond also equally marked contrasts as to the formation and soundness of the teeth, the moral character of the people, and even the pronunciation of the native idiom.

Whereas the Aveyronian from the country of sterile soil, rye, chestnuts and cider has bad teeth, slender and sometimes frail form and very low stature, the inhabitant of Causse, a calcareous country, is remarkably well developed and has teeth lasting generally as long as the individual himself.

Delpon[1] tells us that in the ward of Figeac (department of Lot), whereas the inhabitants of the calcareous and fertile plateau of the canton of Livernon are strong, vigorous, and have a mean height of 1 metre 632, those of the mountainous canton of Latronquière, with a granite and sterile soil producing only rye, buckwheat, potatoes, and chestnuts, are remarkable for their narrow shoulders, tight chests, and lymphatic temperament, and attain their maximum height only at twenty-two or three, which height is on an average about 1m. 599, decreasing to 1m. 579 in the commune of Montet. Lagneaux has shown that in granitic countries which lack phosphate, animals, plants and men do not attain their normal height.

[1] *Stat. du Dep. du Lot.*   Vol. 1.

Costa[1] states that defect of stature is particularly common in poor cantons like Salice, Bocognano, Omessa, Serra, &c.

When we ascend very high mountains we perceive that plants, animals and men become less and less strong and robust. The most important organs are often attacked. The number of the sepals, petals and stamens even, is often reduced (Gubler), and the disposition of the veins of leaves is modified. Thus it is that the composition of the soil and especially its mineralisation influence the form and vitality of living beings. If man contains relatively less mineral than animals in the same way as these last contain less than plants, he is nevertheless strongly mineralised. According to the calculations of M. J. Gaube,[2] the human body, representing a weight of 68 kilograms, is composed as follows : water, 44·66 kg. ; organic matters, 21·30 kg. ; mineral matter, 2·04 kg., which gives about 3 per cent. of minerals. We thus understand the importance of lime, soda, iron and potash for living organisms.

Take the example quoted by Gaube of a female hare submitted to a nourishment which was poor in mineral matters. The birth lasts a very long time, the little ones only attain half or a third of their habitual size, their skin is glabrous or gelatinous, their limbs scarcely set, their upper and lower incisive teeth are lacking, and their mortality shows a very high percentage.

If potassium plays a preponderant *rôle* in plants, the same applies in the case of sodium for man. He needs every day at least one decigram for every kilogram of his weight. This explains the importance of salt in the human organism. Vegetarians who nourish themselves with food containing relatively little, are obliged to add it to their nourishment in a more palpable form. To perceive the importance of sodium, it is sufficient to note the jeopardy in which the health of a man or animal deprived of it is placed. Here, as elsewhere, nature opens an account with us, and we must at whatever cost balance our debit and credit side at the risk of compromising our health for ever. If every European loses annually on an average ten kilograms of sodium, he makes it good by absorbing twelve kilograms of sea salt or chloride of sodium. But potassium is

---

[1] *Rec. de med. mil.* Vol. XXIX. *Recrut. de la Corse.*
[2] *Cours de minéralogie biologique.* 4 vols.

also very useful to us. It is indispensable for the economy of our blood, for it is favourable to oxidations in renewing the hemoglobine. Certain ferments like the pancreatic diastasis, which we know to be most important to human life, depend on it directly.

The importance of iron is no less great. It would be enough to eliminate the few grams of iron which the organism contains in order to arrest its development and cause death. The blood, which is too much impoverished by the excessive diminution of this mineral matter, becomes deficient and death ensues. The same applies to manganese and sulphur, &c. In one word, minerals play a considerable part in the life of organic beings. They exercise their influence before birth, and never cease afterwards to traverse the vital functions of the organism in every sense and in all directions.

The following is a curious observation contributed by a French agriculturist, M. J. Bonhomme. If from a stable on the mountain of Guiole or Aubrac (basaltic soil), he tells us, twelve bulls of thirty months are taken which resemble one another as much as possible, and if they are divided into three lots, one of which remains on the mountain, another on the Causse (calcareous), and the third on the Levezeu (gneissic), three years afterwards the three lots coming together again would be found so different that they would seem to belong to three distinct varieties. Those which remain on the mountain are short, their limbs and head of medium thickness, and they are altogether of good proportion. The lot on the Causse are larger with strong bones. The lot of Levezeu have acquired height and length with fine head and remarkably small limbs and feet.

The plant *Hypericum crispum* of Sicily is only poisonous when it grows in marshes (Lecce), where in consequence its roots are nourished in a special way.

Now the causes which occasion the variability of living beings act on the adult organism, the embryo, and probably also on the sexual elements before fecundation.[1] Let us remember on this subject that mice, naturally prolific, become completely sterile when nourished on elements lacking in magnesia.

[1] Darwin, *De la variation des animaux et des plantes*.

The importance of mineral matters for our organism appears from this fact that since we are perpetually losing them, the organic equilibrium necessitates their being replaced. They pass off especially by the kidneys (urine), but also by the hair, nails, nasal mucus, tears, &c. The hair is very rich in minerals. In its composition are found sulphur, lime, potash, silica, magnesia, iron, soda, silver, arsenic and even copper.

According to the calculations of J. Gaube, the nearly 14 millions of adult women in France carry in their hair about 630,000 kilograms of mineral matters. According to this author, the mean quantity of hair weighs 300 grams. Now of these 300 grams, each woman loses about 10 centigrams every day, which makes 511,000 kilograms for the sum total of women during a year. This half-million of kilograms, if we admit that the hair contains 15 per cent. of its weight in minerals, restores thus to the earth annually 75,000 kilograms of mineral matter.

If the mineral which we lose through the nails is not as considerable, it nevertheless counts for something in the economy of the organism. According to the estimate of the same savant, each one of us in cutting the nails gives back to the soil every year 64 centigrams of minerals.

The influence of mineral matters is closely connected with that of alimentation in general. Inasmuch as the fertility of the soil depends especially on its mineral composition, the difficulty of separating these two factors is easily understood. We have seen how the mineral composition of the soil reacts on the height and health of animals and persons. This susceptibility of living beings who are affected by the influence of external elements is still more manifest when we consider the influence effected by nutrition. The vigour of vegetation and the abundance of herbaceous nourishment in the miocene epoch had no doubt much to do with the large number of colossal forms which are found among the herbivorous animals (Cornevin). Nathusius, who on this matter has studied the pig, shows that abundance of food radically transforms the body of this animal and causes the enlargement of its head and face.

Nutrition also influences the essential peculiarities of

animals and plants. According to Wallace, the natives of the Amazon feed the ordinary green parrot with the fat of big Siluroid fish, with the result that it becomes streaked with yellow and red feathers.

Darwin affirms that bullfinches and certain other birds fed with hempseed become black, whilst caterpillars nourished on different kinds of food produce butterflies of different colours.

III

As the different parts of our organism are compactly knit together, it is difficult to study the influence of *milieu* on any particular organ. On the other hand, the *milieu* is not only very complex, but its constitutive elements are intermixed, and operate at one time with very regular harmony and logical sequence, and at another time, and that most often, simultaneously.

Thus the mineral composition of the soil reacts on alimentation just as this last depends on climate, heat, the degree of electricity with which the air is impregnated, and the geological constitution of the district, which all react fatally on the productivity of agriculture. Alimentation, the salubrity of a country and the health of inhabitants are in their turn closely connected with agricultural progress.

Wherefore instead of stopping at the partial influence of any particular cause in the *milieu*, let us rather study its action on the organism as a whole. The examples which we propose to quote somewhat abundantly will render evident one of the truths which we shall afterwards summon to the aid of our leading idea.

Climate acts directly on man and animals. Let us borrow a number of curious facts from Darwin, Quatrefages, and many other of the most circumspect naturalists. It has been shown that bulldogs, introduced into India, lose at the end of a few generations, not only their ferocity and vigour, but also the characteristic development of their lower jaw. Their snout also becomes more pointed and their body lighter. On the coast of Guinea, dogs, according to Basman, undergo strange modifications. Their ears become long and stiff like those of a

fox, and after three or four litters the barking disappears for a
kind of howl.   According to Pallas, the Kirghiz sheep changes
after a few generations in Russia, its mass of fat gradually
diminishing.   The degree of heat of the temperature affects
the wool of sheep to such an extent that those taken from
Europe into the West Indies lose all their wool except that on
the loins, in the third generation.   The exceedingly rich variations of races and species in the animal and vegetable world
are especially the result of climatic influences.   At Saint
Dominic wild dogs are as large as greyhounds (Col. Hans
Smith), whilst at Cuba dogs which have returned to a wild
state are nearly all of mouse colour.

Living in islands is not favourable to height.   In the island
of Gomèra (Canary Isles) there are found cattle which, though
of the same race as that of the other islands of this archipelago,
are smaller.   The horses of this islet, though of the Andalusian
type, are only as high as ponies.[1]

At Malta a fossil elephant was discovered, the height of
which at the adult age was not over 75 centimetres.   Strabo
relates that in this island was formed the famous dwarf dog so
popular among Romans.

We find in Cornevin's works numerous proofs of this
immediate climatic influence on the height of animals.

In Corsica, he tells us, horses and cattle are of very small
height.   Stags also are smaller here than anywhere else, so
that mammalogists have made a special species of them, viz.
Cervus corsicanus.   It is a descendant, however, of the *Cervus
elaphus* of Europe, since there did not exist, according to the
testimony of Polybius, any stags in Corsica two centuries before
our era.

In 1764 Spanish horses were taken into the Falkland Islands,
and their descendants have so much degenerated as to have
become unfit to ride.

The *milieu* with its atmospheric conditions also reacts on the
colour of animals.   Marshall, in his curious study on *the coloration of animals*,[2] says that light is the chief stimulant in
exciting the development of colouring matter.   Let us note on

[1] See the studies of Verneau in the *Revue d'Anthrop.*   1887.
[2] *Revue Scientifique.*   1885.

this subject the experiments of Paul Bert on the larvæ of the axolotl. They are pale when emerging from the egg and become coloured by the deposit of pigment under the influence of light, whereas in darkness or in a red light the pigment is not developed.

If this phenomenon is more closely examined, it must be acknowledged that the least refrangible rays of the spectrum have no influence on the production of pigment. By the rapidity, therefore, and not by the extent of the vibrations, does light act on the fermentation of colouring matter. It has been proved, among other things, that the proximity of the sea has the effect of darkening. In Switzerland it is generally believed that the colour of cattle pales through permanent stabling or through sojourning in the lowlands. If, on the other hand, the cattle are made to sojourn at certain altitudes, their colour becomes darker. The same remarks apply to France. The brown beasts of the Righi pale at the end of a few years' sojourn in the valley of the Saône. The mammifers brought from the Asiatic steppes by Prjevalsky had a fawn or pale yellow tint, which was the result of the solar rays which had decoloured their hair, owing in particular to the absence of trees which would have mitigated the intense heat of the sun.

In Java there lives in thick and semi-dark jungles a black panther (d'Abbadie). In Angora, not only the goats but also the sheepdogs and cats have fine and woolly hair. In the West Indies the sheep change their fleece at the end of three generations. Among several species of birds, the colour, size of body and beak, and also the length of tail differ from north to south. Weismann has observed the same phenomenon among butterflies. Wasserzug has shown that under the influence of heat the nature of certain bacilli can be radically changed. They can be given a permanent form different from their original form. Let us take, for example, the *micrococcum cyanogenum*, the bacillus of skimmed milk. Normally, the first cultivation in veal broth is a micrococcus. When submitted for five minutes to a temperature of 50° and a small quantity is taken after cooling and put in a suitable broth slightly alkaline, development begins. Let this second culture and the succeeding ones be also submitted to a temperature of 50°, and at the end of a certain number of generations the micrococcic form will have disappeared for a bacillary one, the solidity of which is relative to the number of cultures so treated.

Beaton states that he obtained by seed during six years at Shrubland, 20,000 plants of *Pelargonium Punch* without observing a single instance of streaked leaves, whereas at Surbiton, in Surrey, more than a third of the plants of the same variety had streaked leaves. The root of the *Aconitum napellus* becomes inoffensive in very cold climates. The *Pistacia lentiscus* gives no resin in the south of France. Hemp in England does not produce that resinous matter which it does in the Indies, and which is used for the making of narcotic substances. Dr. Falconez saw an apple tree of English variety, a Himalayan oak, a plum tree, and a pear tree assume the appearance of a pyramid or tiara in the hottest parts of India. The *Rhododendron ciliatum* cultivated in Kew Gardens, near London, produces much larger and paler flowers than those which it produces in the Himalayan mountains, where it is indigenous. Certain species of planted vines vary in different countries as regards the colour of the fruit and period of maturity, &c.

IV

The decisive influence of the *milieu* on the coloration of plants and animals has been stated and proved. If science does not often give us the key to the enigma, that is to say, the wherefore of certain effects of coloration, it is because the *milieu* is very complex, and that apart from the sun there are other innumerable factors which contribute to the result. Electricity with which the atmosphere is charged, the heat and humidity of the air and nutriment, are so many elements which often act simultaneously and whose particular parts are difficult to distinguish and define. The important point for us is to prove beyond dispute the violent modification of colouring under the action of outside factors. It was pretended that Wagner had succeeded by the aid of electric currents in changing the colour and the disposition of the pigment in the wings of certain butterflies just as many American physicians have succeeded (so we are told) in modifying by electricity the colour of the negro skin. These facts appear very doubtful, but what is certain is that we soon succeed in colouring in a very vivid way the fry of ordinary red fish which originate in China, by placing the aquariums which hold them in overheated rooms (Lortet). The effects of the European climate on American varieties of plants are very remarkable (Darwin). Metzger has sown and cultivated in Germany grains of maize from various parts of America, and the following among others are the changes observed in one of the tall variety (*Zea altissima*), which comes from one of the hottest parts of the New World. During the first year the plants attain the height of 12 feet but only produce a small number of ripe grains. The lower grains of the ear preserve their proper form, but the upper grains show certain changes. In the second generation the plants produce more ripe grains but do not exceed in height 8 or 9 feet. The depression in the outer part of the grains disappears, and their colour, originally pure white, becomes somewhat tarnished. In the third generation they hardly resemble the original and very distinct form of the American maize. Finally, in the sixth generation, this maize is the same as the European variety.

The pine of Scotland has few varieties in its native country, but it suffices to cultivate it elsewhere for a few generations in order to see how modified it becomes in appearance, foliage, form, thickness, and even in the colour of its cones. The pollen dust of petunias, collected before its complete maturity and isolated or simply heated, communicates to the flowers which have issued from the plants which it has fecundated, colorations which the original stock does not possess.

The brilliant coloration of certain animals living at great depths in the sea seems in appearance to contradict the influence of the sun and the light. But even *in this case*, where the *milieu* does not lose its rights, we must admit with Marshall that light exercises its influence in spite of this apparent contradiction, for water stops, it is true, the least refringent light, but it allows blue light to pass. Now the red rays are useless for the development of colouring matter. As for very great depths, it is possible that the obscure rays of ultra-violet, perhaps even those of violet and blue, succeed in acting on the development of colouring matter, being of great efficacy by reason of the rapidity of their vibrations.

But let us pass on to the examples furnished more particularly by man.

As the same laws govern the evolution of organic beings, man also is subject to the influences of *milieu*. Under its action man varies like animals and plants, and if this action remains uniform and stable, the changes thus acquired remain permanent.

According to Virchow, the *milieu* wherein a person lives makes him brown or fair. Pruner[1] has shown that Europeans dwelling in Egypt become darker at the end of a certain time; in Abyssinia they develop a bronze tint; in the highlands of Syria a reddish tint, &c.

According to Waitz,[2] the colour of the skin is especially due to heat, nourishment, atmospheric humidity, the abundance or scarcity of forests, and also geographical latitude. The Negroes of Bongo have skins nearly red from the colour of the soil of their country, which is impregnated with iron ore. According to Livingstone, the humid heat deepens the coloration of the Negro populations of Africa, and Simpson[3] affirms the same as to the Jews, whose complexion varies from the white of Caucasian races to the black of Negroes.

D'Abbadie affirms that in Abyssinia the colour of the populations darkens as one ascends the plateaus and pales towards the plains.

Escayrac de Lauture maintains that the Arabs of light skin, whom we meet in places which enjoy a temperate climate, assume at Mecca a dark yellow shade, and even lose their aquiline nose and the characteristic traits which distinguish the Bedouins. At Yemen, on the other hand, their noses regain the plastic beauty of Greek noses. In the south of Damascus they become short in stature and are marked by a scanty head of hair. In Nubia Arabs are found who are quite black though they never mix in marriage with the Negroes of the place.[4]

G. Pouchet[5] attributes to sunburn a preponderant influence in the coloration of the skin.

But then the sunburn is not in direct relationship with the

---

[1] *Die Krankheiten des Orients.*
[2] *Anthropologie der Naturvölker.*
[3] *Narrative of a Journey round the World.*
[4] Prichard, *Natural History of Man*, 4th vol.
[5] *Des colorations de l'epiderme.*

intensity of the sun's rays, for, according to this author, the sun
burns as strongly in Central Europe in March and April as in
July and August. These peculiarities of climate are also
noticeable in the island of Réunion, the atmosphere of which
makes fair instead of dark, so that many creoles are very fair
in this place.

The differences among the Yakoutes living in diverse countries, Waitz tells us, are altogether striking. They vary in
height, colour of skin, and even in form of skull. The same
applies to the Tchouktchi.

It is ordinarily admitted that the Bushmen are descended from
the Hottentots, as indeed their language shows. But the differences which separate them are considerable. The Bushmen are
in the first place much darker than the Hottentots, and remind
us of the Guinean Negroes. But whereas the first live in woods,
the Hottentots are nomadic shepherds, and live in steppes. From
this manner of living, including difference of nourishment and
habitations and occupations, a number of dissimilarities which
radically separate the two peoples originates. People have
wished to see in Bushmen a race quite apart, the most monstrous
and almost the intermediary link between men and monkeys.
Their excessive thinness and the remarkable smallness of their
height involve no ineluctable fatality. It is all explained by
hunger! The Laplanders, likewise famished, resemble the
unfortunate Bushmen in height and thinness, for the chronic
insufficiency of food produces quite a number of analogous
phenomena between these two human types, who live, however,
in countries so diverse. Virchow, in speaking of these races,
which he regards as pathological, undermined and ravaged by
hunger, places them both in the same category. It is enough
to observe the rare specimens of Bushmen at the Cape, who,
being well nourished, are changed in aspect and stature, to see
what a single element, viz. nourishment, can effect in the
appearance of man.

The *milieu* sometimes reacts suddenly on the physiological
characteristics of man, as Quatrefages proves. After eight years
of slavery among the Yucatanians, whose costume and mode of
life he had been constrained to adopt, Jerome d'Aguilar, the
interpreter of Cortez, could no longer be distinguished from the
natives. Langsdorf found at Noukahiva an English sailor whom

the sojourn of many years in that island had made entirely like
a Polynesian.

In the case of Negroes brought into Europe, the colour becomes
fairer.

V

Under our eyes we behold a new human variety called the
Anglo- or rather the Europeo-American [1] race. As race it is as
distinct and as well characterised as any other human race
whatsoever.

Todds [2] tells us that the true Yankee is to be distinguished
from the Englishman by the pointed and angular cut of his face.
He approaches the aborigines of America, and is also marked by
this characteristic trait that the lower part of his face is almost
square, as opposed to the oval form of the Englishman. Knox
has noticed among the Yankees the diminution of the adipose
tissue and the glandular apparatus, whilst Desor mentions a
lengthening of the neck.

Pruner-Bey states that the Anglo-American shows from the
second generation characteristics of the Indian type which
bring him near to the Lenni-Lenapes, Iroquois and Cherokees.
Later on the glandular system is reduced to the minimum of its
normal development. The skin becomes dry like leather,
losing its glow of complexion and redness of cheek, which are
replaced by a muddy tint and among women by an insipid
pallor. The head becomes smaller and rounder or pointed,
being covered with hair, smooth and dark in colour. The neck
lengthens. There is observed a large development of the
zygomatic bones. The eyes sink deeply into the sockets and
are somewhat close to each other. The iris is dark. The bones
become particularly elongated at their upper extremity, so much
so that France and England manufacture a peculiar kind of
glove for North America, the fingers of which are exceptionally
long.

The pelvis of the woman becomes like that of the man. And
whilst Jarrold recognises this influence of *milieu* even in their

---

[1] A. Murray, *The Geographical Distribution of Mammals.*
[2] *Cycl. of Anat. and Physiol.* IV.

unmelodious voice,[1] Kriegk [2] dwells on their thinness and pallor and also on their precocious development physically and intellectually.

The same phenomenon of the transformation of a people under the influence of *milieu* is observable much nearer home, in Paris and among the Parisians. Manouvrier [3] and Topinard [4] state that in general the youths of the poor quarters are of lower average height than the youths of the rich quarters.

Boudin, Gratiolet and Champouillon notice this fact, that the descendants of Parisians die out after a few generations. Not only is a notable lowering of stature to be seen among them,[5] but also signs of scrofula, frequent deformations of the spine, limbs and skeleton of face, especially the upper jaw bone. In spite of the multiplicity and the persistence of his researches, this author has never been able to find, or only as the rarest exception, Parisians of the fifth generation; he is careful to add that even these do not reproduce themselves but die young.

Let us imagine for an instant the city of Paris abandoned to its own resources of existence from the point of view of the quality of the population. We shall then witness the degeneration of a people which we do not fail to regard as a separate race, and all the more so in that so many external qualities distinguish it radically from other Frenchmen.

But then let us add that even Parisians transferred into the provinces easily succeed in regaining their height, health and longevity.

VI

According to the experiments made by H. V. Hoeslin in the Pathological Institute of Munich on two dogs descended from the same parents, which at the beginning of the experiment weighed the same, viz. 3·1 and 3·2 kilograms, one, well nourished, weighed after a year 29·5 kilograms, whilst the other, which had

---

[1] *Anthropology ; or, On the Form and Colour of Man.*
[2] *Lüddes Zeit. für Erdkunde.* I. 484.
[3] *Sur la Taille des Parisiens.* Bull. de la Soc. d'Anthrop. 3rd series, vol. XI.
[4] *Statistique de la Ville de Paris.* Revue d'Anthrop. 2nd series, vol. IV.
[5] Champouillon, *Revue des Mémoires de Médecine militaire.* Vol. XXII.

received only an insufficient nourishment (a third of what the first dog had), only weighed 9·1. As to their height it was in the proportion of 100 to 83. Explorers have shown an analogous phenomenon among primitive or savage peoples. Generally the families of the chiefs who are fed to satiety are superior in height to their neighbours. O. Bollinger attributes with reason the height of English and German nobles to similar causes of comfort, which im~lies principally a more abundant nourishment.

The poor Jews of Roumania, Slav countries and Germany, who, as we know, are insufficiently nourished, are generally much smaller than their neighbours, but placed in other circumstances they increase in stature. Thus the descendants of the same Russian, Polish, German or Roumanian Jews attain at the end of the second generation the height of their English or French fellow-citizens.

Let us not forget that, owing to the law of co-ordination, the other parts of their bodies undergo at the same time other modifications, which assimilate them physiologically to their immediate entourage.

The alimentary regime also acts on our physiological nature and on the aspirations of our soul. Flesh nourishment, more or less exclusive, Armand Gautier tells us, is, in a higher degree than race, one of the factors in a gentle or violent individual disposition. According to Liebig the irascibility of pigs may be so far excited by feeding them on flesh as to provoke them to attack men. The vegetarian regime is considered to soften habits and to induce passivity in human beings, for which reason no doubt all the founders of religion prescribe it to the faithful.

The quantity of food necessary to sustain human life varies according to conditions of *milieu* and occupation. According to M. Maurel,[1] man of intertropical countries needs for his azotised nourishment five-sixths of the quantity needed in temperate climates, that is, he needs 1 gram for every kilogram of his weight as against 1·2 gram in temperate

---

[1] See his curious works published in the *Archives de la médecine navale*, Vol. LXXXIV and LXXXV., under the heading *Influence des climats et des saisons sur les depenses de l'organisme chez l'homme.*

climes. This quantity should be augmented for those who work hard and should be diminished in hot seasons. It depends in addition on the age and health of individuals. The science of alimentation has become to-day so vast and exact that we cannot here sum up its complex teaching. It is enough to quote this truth that defective or insufficient nutrition contributes to the physiological degeneracy of peoples and individuals.

Nutrition plays a chief part in what concerns the variations aimed at. According to Darwin, who occupied himself entirely with plants and animals, excess of nourishment is the most effective exciting cause. But the same statement is made with regard to human beings.

According to Collignon,[1] whatever may be the nature of the soil, whether granitic or calcareous, flat or undulating, one thing alone always regulates variations and that is nourishment. If this is good, favoured either by wealth or by a soil sufficiently productive to nourish well those who occupy it, the race, whatever it may be, will be fine and will attain the most complete development compatible with its proper nature. If there be added the accumulative action of selection, which of necessity only allows those to exist who are more or less hardy and capable of living on little, we naturally expect to find small races comprising many sickly and infirm in all poor regions. This author quotes, in order to bear out his theory, numerous observations made by him in Limousin, Perigord, Brittany and Normandy. Leaving on one side what is excessive in this estimate of the factor of nourishment, which is so difficult to detach from the other elements composing the *milieu*, we must acknowledge that its rôle is one of the most significant.

It is enough to examine the African tribes condemned to misery, who, though sprung from the same stock, differentiate to such an extent as to form races which are most distinct. They need only be compared with their well-nourished brethren in order to see the importance of nourishment in the history of the evolution of races.

Travellers in Australia nearly always insist on this fact, that

[1] See his profound researches on the French population from the point of view of its recruitment for military service.

individuals of small height are generally badly nourished and badly clothed, whereas tall stature is general among the natives of the interior who enjoy some comfort. The attempt has been made to prove the influence of nourishment on species. It has been thought in particular that it was confined only to individuals and that it had no possibility of modifying races, which is a matter inconceivable and inadmissible. For, as Magne justly says, if it be admitted that the male and female have been modified in their conformation and temperament, they must necessarily give birth to individuals who resemble them.

Experience, however, has demonstrated that characteristics which are the result of an alimentary régime, are transmitted by generation.

Collignon, mentioned above, has shown by abundant proofs taken from the department of Gard how much nourishment influences the height of recruits.[1] The inhabitants of more or less fertile plains show a mean height of 1m. 640; those of the mountains 1m. 585. The marshy districts furnish the largest proportion of those invalided on the ground of illness (217 per 1,000). In three cantons, Plens, Linvallon and Quentin, whose clay soil, damp and sterile, gives little corn, the inhabitants are very poor and are in height 1m. 544. The same applies to the ward of Mont-de-Marsan, where men feed miserably on *escoton* (boiled flour of millet).

Does the *milieu* go so far as to make an impression on the craniological conformation? Durand (de Gros) quotes this singular fact that brachycephaly is general in the rural population of the wards of Rodez, d'Espalion and Milhau. But it is quite different with the urban population, among whom the heads are much larger, sometimes very large, and show numerous examples of pronounced frontal dolichocephaly. The same author mentions this fact also, which is no less characteristic, that this cranial type, so distinct in form and volume from that which prevails without exception in the country, is observable among citizens whose parents and grandparents were simple peasants of the neighbourhood.

These facts cannot be sufficiently insisted on and we do not

[1] *Mém. de la Soc. d'Anthrop.*, 3rd series. Vol. I,

think it useless to multiply their number. The laws of the influence of the *milieu* are not yet clearly established. What is especially lacking is the adjustment of the partial influences of the numerous factors which compose it. In the impossibility which we experience in formulating in a precise way the action of external causes on the physical and intellectual values of human beings, we are forced to register incontestable and uncontested observations as they come quite promiscuously. It is from these as a whole that the explanation of the genesis of the formation of human varieties emerges, however contradictory they may appear at first sight.

The moral causes, such as the liberty which people enjoy, the consideration of which they are assured, the wholesome sentiment of equality before the law and the respect of human dignity, the instruction which is given them, the national system of taxation which contributes to their comfort, the facility of internal and external communications, the way in which the State exercises its privileges and monopolies, justice which respects all the legitimate aspirations of citizens, and as many other conditions of a healthy development of a country, have all likewise their counter effect on the physiological formation of human beings.

Here are certain striking examples.

Norton[1] assures us that in the country studied by him the Negro children born in liberty have more beautiful eyes, a more elegant appearance, and an easier bearing like that of Europeans, than in the countries where they are ill treated. The same remark has been made by Lewis and d'Orbigny. Day[2] improves on this fact, and states that Negroes who hold higher situations are distinguished by their features, which resemble those of the Caucasian races, and are not unlike those of very dark Jews.

Lyell, in his account of his second voyage to the United States, tells us that Negroes who have had continual relations for a long time with Europeans become like these last physiologically. According to Dr. Hancock, the civilised Negroes of Guinea show tendencies to become like their white

[1] *A Residence at Sierra Leone.*
[2] *On the Causes of the Variety of Complexion and Figure.*

neighbours physiologically, and he insists on the fact that even their encephalon undergoes similar changes.

Stanhope Smith[1] maintains that negro slave merchants are distinguishable from Negroes in a striking way.   Whereas those sold continue to keep all their characteristic traits, the vendors lose after the second and third generation their woolly kind of hair, and the characteristic negro smell. With the change in their material and moral situation, Negroes have altered considerably during the last two centuries (Stephen Ward).[2] The thickness of their lips has diminished, and also the very accentuated lower jaw.

Dr. Warren[3] states this fact that the skulls of Negroes of past times found in New York have a cerebral capacity much less than those of modern Negroes.

Let us add that the climatic situation of a country reacts on the appearance and persistence of certain diseases, and so produces many physiological modifications.   In Peru the population are only affected by *veruga* at an altitude between 600 and 1,600 metres, whereas yellow fever in Mexico never goes above the altitude of 924 metres.[4]   On the other hand, various diseases often become severe or slight, affecting the organism profoundly or disappearing without leaving traces, according to the latitude or the physical conformation of the country.

[1] *Five Years' Residence in the West Indies.*
[2] *The Natural History of Mankind.*
[3] *Quarterly Review*, June, 1851.
[4] Darwin, *Voyage d'un naturaliste.*

CHAPTER II

CROSSING OF RACES

I

WE have seen how human types evolve under the influence of their *milieu*. Climate and mode of life, in the widest meaning of these terms, succeed in counterbalancing hereditary influences. The skull and all the other parts of our organism undergo in this way essential changes, and yet, while undergoing modification, never cross the limit which separates mankind from other animal species.

Mixture, otherwise called crossing of blood, among human varieties causes by itself almost as many changes as the innumerable factors of *milieu*. It has been practised unconsciously ever since man's appearance on the earth. Owing to it, intermediary races exist whereby the over-violent contradictions which the *milieu* left to itself might have engendered are softened and equalised. This phenomenon is, in short, as old as humanity itself, and what has contributed to its appearance, extension and duration is the fact that the human species has been divided only by the barriers of *milieu*. No special instinct has ever prevented the varieties from interblending, whilst the conformation of their sexual organs has never placed any obstacles in its way. To-day, as in neolithic times, the highest and lowest in the human scale have been able to contract fruitful marriages.

Moreover it is possibly owing to this crossing from time immemorial that our distinctive traits are so far from being as irreducible as certain anthropologists would have us believe.

It is with men as with animals. Darwin tells us that in uncivilised or very little civilised countries, where herds cannot be separated, there rarely exists, if ever, more than one race of the same species. The example of North America is one of the most characteristic, where for a long time there was no distinct breed of sheep, for they were always mixed. Again, animals of the same race enclosed in a park have characteristics which distinguish them from others penned up in another park. In this way do races evolve and are even lost under the action of this most important factor. It has been shown for instance that varieties of cats taken into new countries lose their peculiar characteristics owing to their vagabond nature. When the domestic cat becomes wild again in some countries, it assumes for a similar reason uniform characteristics with the wild.

Now man has from all time lived under the influence of unconscious cross-breeding.

II

The word "cross-breeding" may be applied both to men and animals, but the results obtained from it bear different names. The progeny of crossed human varieties are called *halfbreeds* and those of plants or animals, hybrids. Crossing acts in two ways. In mixing different types without preconceived ideas, it produces an intermediary type, whilst in working purposely towards a well-defined end, it brings about the appearance of new races with well-marked characteristics of their own. The first applies in particular to men and animals living in liberty, whereas the second applies to domesticated animals and plants, and is known as "artificial selection." Breeders and cultivators, who, conscious of the end they are pursuing, succeed by crossing animals and plants of the same species in obtaining individuals of a certain type, are making an artificial selection, to which indeed we owe the appearance of so many animal and vegetable varieties.

The breeder, in short, takes advantage of the circumstances of *milieu*, nourishment, and other factors. In bringing together two types marked by qualities which particularly interest him, he causes the birth of a new variety. In reality he creates nothing but only stamps his own desire on nature's work. When he directs this selection methodically for a certain number of generations he arrives at the formation of a special and thoroughly marked race which is distinguishable from the others by certain specific and hereditary qualities. In this way it has become possible to create a number of bovine races, goat races, dogs, horses, rabbits, and pigeons. The hundreds of races of pigeons, so different in their aptitudes and structures, are all descended from the *Columba livia*. In working with the object of obtaining certain desired characteristics among animals, breeders preside at their couplings and completely divert the evolution of their species.

Man has never been " selectionised " according to a preconceived method. Crossing between his different samples has encountered no obstacles except those resulting from social prejudices or from natural barriers. The faculty which he possesses of moving from one place to another and of being easily acclimatised, surmounts these obstacles, so that crossing between the most diverse representatives is seen as a general rule in his history.

Far from strengthening the divergences produced by the differences of *milieu*, the possibility of crossing, powerfully aided by the intellectual factor which draws all human beings together, has only modified the distinctive traits and created passing phases which link together all the unities of the great human cluster.

III

The new blood which crossing is reputed to bring into the organism, produces the most complex phenomena in it. Nathusius in his standard work on the skulls of pigs (*Schweineschaedel*) maintains that it suffices to introduce into a race of the type *Sus Scrofa*, $\frac{1}{64}$th of the blood of the *Sus Indicus*, in order to modify the skull of the former. To the influence of crossing, the same author also attributes the monstrous pig of Japan, which, with its very large snout, very short head and special traits, is so different from the rest of its species.

Together with the skull, the modifications bear on the period of gestation, length of limbs, the force and resistance of the animal, number of molars, and even the pulse which, as Youatt says, varies according to the height of certain animals. The distinction thus obtained among the individuals of the same species is altogether surprising. The brain of certain dogs is low, long and narrow in the anterior part; with others it is high and arched and shows perceptible differences in weight. Their height also varies in the extreme. According to Geoffroy Saint-Hilaire some dogs are six times as long as others, without counting the tail.

The number of generations which is necessary to obtain a new variety varies according to circumstances. It is generally thought that from three to six is sufficient to obtain certain characteristic traits in plants. In the animal kingdom their number appears to be much more considerable. The mixture of the representatives of the two varieties does not always mean an equal influence on the part of the two parents. Their blood in crossing seems to struggle in the procreated organism. The characteristics of the newly born depend accordingly on the preponderance of one of the two individuals crossed. Moreover some varieties show traits of much greater persistence. Account must also be taken of that unexpected element called atavism, which is the tendency to revert and which often paralyses the regular action of the new type's success.

Cross-breeding, which biologically touches the most mysterious depths of a being, cheats human investigation in many respects. In the animal and vegetable kingdoms, breeders and cultivators meet with frequent surprises which the present state of science fails to explain. We are speaking in particular of certain impenetrable affinities between the representatives of the two sexes crossed. The reason of the greater or lesser fertility of some and the sterility of others frequently escapes us. The best explanation bearing on the differences of species is far from being satisfactory. In default of special laws it is experience and concrete results which guide breeders. Broca, without attempting to give the key to the enigma, endeavoured to classify all the cases in what concerns the results of crossing. He notes, to begin with, two leading categories, viz. *heterogenesis,* which comprises all cases of sexual connections where no fecundation takes place, and *homogenesis,* with different degrees of fecundation.

Fecundation is *abortive* when the fœtus is born before its time ; *agenesic* when fecundation is relative in the sense that the progeny remain sterile among themselves or with individuals of one or the other of the parent races; *dysgenesic* when the hybrids, although mutually sterile, are fecund when crossed with an individual of one or the other of the parent races ; *paragenesic* when the results are fecund among themselves, but only for two or three generations ; and *eugenesic* when the progeny are normally fertile.

To form varieties or new races, this last case is the most interesting as there is no impediment to the evolution of the new forms which are created by the mixture of the two crossed parents.

The number of conditions, however, is so great that it is impossible to formulate any rules whatever. Moreover, we have to consider the new characteristic which we desire to have produced. The *milieu,* on the other hand, with its innumerable factors, never loses its rights, acting both on the parents, and on the product of their crossing. It is thus almost impossible to overlook its simultaneous action and to speak only of crossing. We know, for instance, how conditions of life affect the reproductive system before and after fecundation. The *milieu* in this case acts directly and in its way contributes to the sterility or fecundity of crossings as also to the quality of their results. Cross-breeding, from its first application, causes profound changes in an organism.

The relative sterility of cross-breeding is a question on which naturalists have been very much divided. Let us note, however, that sterility is due almost exclusively to differences of sexual constitution, especially noticeable among different species.

In general, when it is a case of coupling two individuals *belonging to the same race,* fecundity is the rule. Wherever the pairing has no results, some naturalists have even wanted to see different species.

This circumstance is of prime importance in the case of crossing among human beings.

Whereas among *species*, even the most closely related, sterility is the rule, it never occurs even when the most divergent *races* pair among birds of the farmyard, pigs, horses, and dogs. Not only do all domestic races couple thus with success in the matter of fecundity, but also their hybrid progeny are observed to be quite fecund.

It has also been shown that varieties of organised beings need to be crossed in order to augment their vitality. Left to themselves they become weak and display a tendency to diminish and disappear. The progeny thus crossed are generally considered to be much stronger than their parents.

IV

As applied to man, cross-breeding, modified by the special conditions of his life, generally presents the same advantages as in the animal kingdom. Fire, left to itself, burns itself out, so Herbert Spencer tells us. Vital forces, in like manner, always tend to a state of equipoise. To preserve their vigour it is necessary to excite and restore them by submitting them to the action of other forces. Man did not wait to commingle with his species until science should tell him to do so. With him cross-breeding has been facilitated by the complete fecundity of halfbreeds and the sexual concord between representatives the furthest removed from one another. Since the first migrations of peoples, this phenomenon has taken place. In the blood of modern white Europeans flows that of Negroes who lived on our continent at the end of the Quaternary epoch.

Cross-breeding among the most differentiated races, far from being sterile, adds to their fecundity. According to Le Vaillant, Hottentot women, who generally give birth to three or four children, have as many as twelve when united to white men or Negroes. The crossing of Negroes with white women or of white men with Negro women produces similar results.

A similar statement is made as to Russians and their unions with the indigenous populations of Asiatic Russia.

Later on we shall examine the composition of French blood, and shall see that it is only a mixture obtained by the union of innumerable human varieties. All peoples and races resemble one another in this respect. If any race is deemed pure from all mixture, it is only because we are unable to disentangle its constituent elements.

As means of communication dévélop and the march of progress continues, crossing becomes more common. This not only increases in the middle of Old Europe but also among all the inhabitants of every part of the Old and New Worlds. If the word halfbreed was strictly applied to the progeny which has really issued from a mixture of varieties, it would be necessary to include under this denomination all human beings with rare exceptions. Moreover war and conquest always involved mixture of blood. The Whites, whose ethnical origin is far from being pure, have in their turn founded a new stock in the New World by commingling with its aborigines. Mexico in particular is peopled by halfbreeds, the progeny of Spaniards and local peoples. The United States is a vast crucible wherein for centuries an indescribable mixture of peoples and races has been going on. In Brazil, Argentina, Chili, as in the other republics of Central and South America, halfbreeds abound. In Peru there are more than twenty names to define the various products of crossing between Peruvians, Negroes and Portuguese.

In Africa we find that the Zulu Kaffirs, regarded as the purest of the pure, are the result of mixtures, difficult to disentangle and define. If in some respects they resemble the Whites, they often show many traits of the Negro. In many places in Africa the influence is seen of the so-called Hamitic blood, which is of Asiatic and European origin. According to some anthropologists, Hamites mixed with Negroes were the origin of the Ethiopians, the fundamental ethnical basis of ancient Egypt. Cultured Negroes in the United States maintain, perhaps not without reason, that their real ancestors were the Ethiopians, creators of a much older civilisation than that of the Whites in Europe. In addition to the Ethiopians, the Himyarites (Southern Semites) passed over in far back times from the opposite shores of the Red Sea and mixed with Negroes, Ethiopians and Berbers.

What shall we say of the Arabs (Northern Semites), who for

about fifteen centuries have continued their invasions into the African continent and who were followed in the 18th century by Europeans whose blood is being more and more mixed with that of Africans ? We meet with Kouchito-Khamites, that is Ethiopians, in all the N.E. of Africa, and it is especially from among them that the people of Abyssinia (the Agaou) are recruited. The Foulah-Sandé, a term adopted by J. Deniker to define the mass of the populations living in Africa on a strip of 5 to 6 degrees in breadth from east to west, are only a mixture of Ethiopians with Soudanese Negroes (the Nigritians). Their number includes the Mangbattou, the Niam-Niam, the Ndris, the Bandziri, the Poul-Bé, &c., &c.

The numerous Nigritian peoples are also strongly mixed with Arabs and Ethiopians. The zone of their habitat is from the Atlantic to the basin of the Upper Nile and comprises the Soudanese, Senegalese, Guineans, &c.

As for the Bantus, whose name covers innumerable Negro tribes of Central and Southern Africa, they are strongly mixed with the Ethiopians. Those on the coast between Cape Delgado and the port Durnford, where Swahili is now the most widely spread of local dialects, are also much mixed with Arabs. The Zulus are not exempt from Ethiopian blood.

The Hottentots, having crossed with the Dutch and other Europeans, have given birth to numerous *Bastards*.

The Ethiopians, who have so largely influenced the formation of Negro races, are merely half-breeds of Negroes and Hamites. Their reaction on the ethnical composition of the Whites is indisputable, which fact opens out new horizons for savants who will one day wish to explore the many links of relationship uniting the Negroes with European peoples and, through these white intermediaries, with all humanity !

The crossings between the inhabitants of Europe and Asia are much more apparent and less discussed. Nearly all the principal races considered as Asiatic, are found mixed with other peoples and races, in other parts of the globe. On this matter, let us note the Semitic and Mongol races, the Negritos, Eskimos, Turko-Tartars, &c.

It is not our intention to study the origins and affiliations of the principal races of the world, but only to indicate in a summary way the mutual interpenetration of diverse peoples, which renders almost illusory the search for an absolutely pure race.

In the present state of science the place of honour assigned to pure races could only be claimed by certain savage or primitive peoples whose history is buried in oblivion.

But can one as a matter of fact still speak of pure races and peoples after considering the permanent effects which two or three cross-breedings produce? Breeders furnish us on this subject with proofs altogether surprising. Let us note for instance that quoted by Fleischmann. The primitive German breed of sheep, which provides ordinary wool, produces 5,500 fibres of wool per square inch. After three or four crossings with Merinos, they produce 8,000 and after the twentieth crossing 27,000.

Who will ever estimate the quantity of blood of all origins which flows in the veins of a white, yellow or black man?

The history of human varieties may be reduced to these most simple facts, viz. that primary races formed under the influence of the *milieu* have never ceased mixing among themselves on the occasions when they meet, especially during the migrations of peoples. The consecutive crossings which have taken place under the influence of *milieu* acting incessantly everywhere, have given birth to a number of intermediary types which serve as links uniting humanity. It is cross-breeding which finally levels all the types created by the *milieu*.

V

What is the value of cross-breeding? Opinions have been divided for a long time on this subject. In their inordinate pride, the Whites have never been willing to admit that women of other races, and especially those of so-called inferior ones, are able to give birth to children equal in value to purely white progeny. People have quibbled for years on the absolute value of crossed products without being ready to take into consideration the special circumstances which have contributed to their intellectual and physiological formation. Arguing from examples of American mulattoes they have endeavoured to cast opprobrium on all human crossbreeds, which is an illogical attempt, for are not all human beings crossbreeds ?

Moreover, are these mulattoes such deplorable specimens as one would have us believe ? It is sufficient to recall the circumstances which accompanied their birth, the conditions of their youth, and the bitterness of their life, in order to understand that white men placed in similar circumstances would perhaps be worth still less. The white man who seduced a negress nearly always abandoned her when she became a mother, and the child coming into the world as the product of debauchery, badly nourished and exceedingly despised, grew up generally in conditions which are not to be mentioned. The white stamp which he had received at birth predestined him in his own eyes to a much more glorious and brilliant future than that of his black brethren. He entered life full of pride and scorn for his entourage, advancing with confidence towards white men, whom he was pleased to consider as his equals. But from this approach disappointments without number awaited him. Despised and hated, he was violently ejected from white society ; white prejudices against people of colour were particularly stirred against these halfbreeds, whose resemblance to the whites demonstrated so clearly the stupidity of racial superstition. The nearer the Blacks approached the Whites physically, the more did the Whites repulse them with passionate hatred, driven by the blind instinct of their own interests. Bewildered and unclassed, the mulattoes entered the only *milieu* open to receive them and this was the *milieu* of crime. With the work of negro regeneration which has followed the mulattoes' clearer vision of their surroundings, they have recovered their dreams of social equality with the Whites by hard work and a life as honest as that of their negro or white entourage. The impartial witnesses of their regeneration in the United States bestow upon their efforts the praises which they deserve and rank the mulattoes themselves on the same level as other peoples and races.

Those who, like Gobineau, Lapouge, Ammon, and other anthropo-sociologists, would have us believe that " crossbreeds " are physiologically and psychologically inferior to their "*races courantes*" (Ammon), appear to forget the lessons of history. We find ourselves, moreover, forcibly placed in a dilemma. Humanity, we are told, progresses without ceasing. Biologically speaking, it surpasses in worth its forerunners of the dark ages. But it is evident, as shewn above, that the crossing of human beings is a permanent fact. If then crossing results in decadence, man should have disappeared long since from the planet and should have fallen to the level of the protozoa.

Concrete observations from life, however, confirm the inanity of all these deductions. Cross-breeding has in no sense the sorry privilege of physical degeneracy, nor that of bringing people to final ruin, so writers on demography and impartial explorers assure us. Where did Tylor find the most beautiful women in the world ? At Tristan da Cunha (a little island between the Cape and South America), among the descendants of Whites and Negroes.

"Its inhabitants (he tells us) are mulattoes, well built but not very dark. Nearly all are of European type, much more so than the Negro. Among the young girls were some with such entirely beautiful heads and bodies, that I never remember having seen anything so splendid. And yet I am familiar with all the strands of the earth, Bali and its Malays, Havannah and its creoles, Tahiti and its nymphs, the United States and its most distinguished women."

It is pleasant to see that the crossbreeds of Java are superior to the Malays and that the Brazilians of the province of St. Paul, who are the progeny of Portuguese and indigenous tribes, viz., the Cerigos and the Gaynazes, excel physiologically, intellectually and morally. A detail worthy of notice is that longevity counts among these crossbreeds its most striking examples.[1]

The Griquas, mixed products of Hottentots and Dutch, or the Cafusos are quite equal to pure Whites, just as the crossbreeds of Indian and Spanish are at least as good as the Spaniards themselves.

If it is desired to question fertility of crossing, facts give the lie direct to all such pessimists ! Let us note first of all that crossing between aristocratic and common classes of White

[1] See my *Philosophie de la Longévité*.

society is recognised as a necessary factor in their continuation. Broca also insists on this fact, that the population of France has increased since the Revolution caused the two classes to mingle which originally represented conquerors and conquered.

When for any reason certain aristocracies refuse to mix with other social classes, they wither away and perish. The Spartans, Dumont tells us, numbered 9,000 in the time of Lycurgus. In 480, they had diminished to 8,000; in 420, to 6,000; in Aristotle's time, to 1,000; and in 230, to 700. In order to preserve the patrician order in Rome, it was absolutely necessary to ennoble whole masses of plebeians. We remember amongst other things that in 179 the Roman Senate only numbered 88 Patricians for 212 Plebeians. A number of Emperors were obliged to continue raising new nobles in order to preserve the Senate from disappearing. Galton tells us that among the oldest English families there are only five who seem to go back to the fifteenth century in the direct male line. According to Benoiton de Châteauneuf, the existence of noble French families never exceeds three centuries. The great historical names have long since become extinct. Surviving only in the female line, they have been revived by pure usurpation and often by special grants bestowed by the Kings and afterwards by the Empire. This phenomenon has also occurred in other countries. If we trace closely the evolution of the reigning families of Europe, we see first the usual degeneracy and then the disappearance of the stock. Those which persist, as for example, the Russian dynasty, owe their persistence only to a strong mixture of foreign blood. The rich middle class, which follows the example of the aristocracy in confining itself within a restricted circle, suffers the same mournful fate. According to the curious examples furnished by Hansen, there were 118 patrician families in Nuremberg in 1390; more than 50 per cent. had disappeared by 1490. There were at Augsburg, in 1368, fifty-one senatorial families; in 1538, only eight remained. From 1583 to 1684, 487 families were admitted into the bourgeoisie of Berne, but by 1783 only 108 remained. At Lubeck (the same author tells us) in 1848 the last scion of the patrician families died. Falling lower and lower in the social scale, he had been forced to become a simple office-boy.

In a general way aristocratic families, including those of reigning families, suffer the same fate as the Julia dynasty which has been so melodramatically described by Jacoby.[1] Degeneracy, premature death, folly, debauchery, alcoholism and sterility are the common lot of all these favourites of fortune. From the time of Edward II., who mounted the throne in 1307, up to the time of George I. (of Hanover), England exhausted six dynasties : the Plantagenets, Lancasters, Yorks, Tudors, Stuarts and Oranges.

All those who study the history of the European nobility without prejudice perceive very soon that wherever it has not undergone the beneficent influence of crossing with plebeian classes, it has soon degenerated or disappeared. What Benoiton de Châteauneuf has noticed in the case of France, Doubleday [2] states for England. About the year 1858, 272 English lords out of 394 dated only from 1760. Of 1527 titles of baronet, created in 1611, only 30 remained by 1819. The same phenomenon is also seen in the case of the frank-burghers of Newcastle. Once a rich and independent class enjoying many privileges, it gradually decreased in number and was only physically revived from the time it lost its prestige and mixed with the people.

What takes place on a small scale among the aristocratic classes of Europe is seen on a vast scale in the rule of castes in India. There a huge country, in which people are counted by the hundred million, falls so low as to become the prey of a few thousand audacious adventurers. And yet here in particular flourished and still flourishes the cult of blood, so piously maintained.

When the same problem is studied inversely, that is to say, in studying the origins of superior individuals in every country, one notices with astonishment that nearly all are the result of crossed marriages. Havelock Ellis affirms, for example, that the best American writers and thinkers, like Edgar Allan Poe, Whitman, Lowell, Bret Harte, Mark Twain, Longfellow, and many others, are descended from mixed families. The best known American inventor, Edison, is found in this class. This same phenomenon is seen in England. There also the

---

[1] *Études sur la Sélection chez l'Homme.* 2nd ed. (Paris : F. Alcan.)
[2] *The Law of Population.*

representative types of its insular genius are far from being pure English, as, for example, Tennyson, Swinburne, Rossetti, Browning, Ouida, Corelli, Romilly, Lewes, Millais, Disraeli, &c. To show how much European progress is indebted to mixed types would need many volumes. Let us confine ourselves to naming as they come, in France, men like Sainte-Beuve, Dumas father and son, Taine, de Maistre, Montalembert, Mérimée, and even Victor Hugo. The illustrious Kant, regarded as an incarnation of German genius, was far from being a pure German. The most typical poets among the Russian people, Pushkin, Lermontoff, and the creator of the Russian drama, von Vizine, were of mixed origin. In the veins of Ibsen there flows a mixture of Scotch and Norwegian blood. These examples might be multiplied to infinity.

VI

Thus the renewing of blood nearly always gives excellent results. Experience does in no way prove its sterility. Stokes furnishes us with conclusive proofs that even marriages between Europeans and Australian or Tasmanian women have very good results as regards the birth-rate.

Some English seal-hunters in the Bass Straits had in the beginning of the nineteenth century carried away a number of native women. Stokes tells us that in 1846 numerous and excellent seal-hunters were to be seen in this neighbourhood recruited from the descendants of these Tasmanian and Australian women crossed with the English.

In Indo-China the commingling of Annamite blood with that of Europeans has resulted in excellent mixtures (Morice).

Waitz [1] insists with reason on the constant amelioration of the inferior type by the superior type through crossing. According to this author, four generations suffice to make a mulatto white and five to make him black again through an uninterrupted return.

The American nation proves by the unceasing progress which it has realised in so short a time, the indisputable advantages of cross-breeding practised on an extensive scale. To grasp the whole extent of this mixture of peoples which goes on in

[1] *Anthropologie der Naturvölker.*

the United States under our eyes, it is enough to consider the quality and origin of the immigrants who arrive there annually. Let us take for purposes of comparison the year 1903.[1] The number of immigrants without counting those of Mexico and Canada amounted to 803,272 !   Austria sent in round numbers 30,000 Slovaks and Croats, 23,000 Magyars, 32,500 Poles, 13,000 Jews, without reckoning Roumanians, Lithuanians, Dalmatians, Czecks, Bosnians, &c.   Of the 109,721 Russians, 33,859 were Poles, 13,854 Finns, 37,846 Jews, 11,629 Lithuanians ; of Italians, 27,620 came from the north and 152,915 from the south (Neapolitans, Sicilians, &c.).   Also 55,780 Scandinavians, 29,001 Irish, 14,455 Japanese, 14,942 English, 70,000 Germans, 15,000 Greeks, &c., &c.   This constant stream of peoples, who have spread themselves over the United States for so many years, ends by forming a special race of North Americans whom the old peoples of Europe are pleased to recognise as a superior type.

We have seen above how under the influence of the *milieu* all these heterogeneous elements are transformed in the United States into a new and clearly marked ethnical type which is quite distinct from the people sent out from Europe and Asia. Even intellectually the United States has succeeded in dissolving the separate traits of these immigrants.   A kind of moral unity takes place among these descendants of many peoples. According to the last census, there are in the United States less people ignorant of English than there are people in the German Empire ignorant of German.   The number of journals published in foreign languages diminishes every year, whereas that of English journals increases perpetually.   In 1900 the round number of these English journals was sixteen times greater than that of all the journals published in other languages, viz. in German, Polish, Italian, Chinese, Hungarian, Danish, &c.

It is enough (so Americans tell us) for one or two generations at most to make of this European overflow a remarkably stable, intelligent and enterprising people !

Wherever crossing takes place under normal conditions, inferior types become better without causing any degeneration

---

[1] The year counts from April, so that in this case the numbers are for twelve months, from April, 1902, to the end of March, 1903.

whatever of the race or of the so-called superior classes. The pessimistic assertions of the detractors of cross-breeding are disproved by the mere fact of the constant progress realised by humanity, whose representatives have done nothing but mix among themselves in every way. On the other hand, the disastrous effects produced by purity of blood show us how frail is the foundation on which the theory of pure races is based.

Modern science, moreover, offers a plausible explanation of the deterioration of a social class condemned to live entirely on its own reserve of blood, force and health. It would be unjust to explain the degeneracy of all the privileged classes as due to idleness or debauchery. The German and Swiss bourgeoisie, as also certain groups of the old nobility, are particularly distinguished for their domestic virtues, their economy, and an hygienic life free from all excess. A condemnation of principle weighs nevertheless on their posterity. Fed on political and social prejudices, the representatives of privileged classes will only marry within the restricted circle of their ethnical group, living in most cases under the influences of the same morbid factors. But all psychical anomalies, as Moreau (of Tours) shows, are closely related. They form a sort of sympathetic chain the links of which are attached to each other. The appearance of a morbid case in one generation can only increase in intensity from the moment when through union another member of the same family introduces his quota. Morbid cases, far from diminishing or disappearing, increase in this manner in a *milieu* particularly favourable to them. Psychical anomalies are found also in frequent and direct correlation with certain organic maladies like scrofula, defects in the organs of the senses, deformities of the skeleton, and the like.

We may readily see the devastations which marriages among people resembling one another in the same constitutional or psychical defects can produce in a centre stamped with disease. But the danger does not stop here. The psychopathic anomalies in passing from generation to generation are transformed and assume the most varied and serious aspects. In face of this phenomenon of morbid heredity we can easily explain the degeneracy and disappearance of families condemned to marry into their own defects and vices.

Modern peoples living under the influence of the same climatic and intellectual factors need also to renew their blood by additions from the outside. In their crossings on a large scale are to be seen the same advantages which are apparent in the union of the diverse social classes living in the same country. The example of the French and American peoples, these two great products of so many comminglings of peoples and races, bears eloquent testimony to the advantage of their unlimited crossings.

CHAPTER III

THE different parts of our organism form a whole connected by all sorts of links. A wound inflicted on one part of our body affects the whole. The weakening of one of our organs reacts more or less on the whole of our organism. Goethe and Geoffroy Saint-Hilaire had already mentioned it simultaneously and had endeavoured to express it in terms of a general law. The law of the budget of our organism, as Goethe said, or the compensation of crossing, as it had been defined by Geoffroy Saint-Hilaire, became with Darwin the law of correlative variability.

"I call balancing of organs (Geoffroy Saint-Hilaire says) that law of animate nature in virtue of which a normal or pathological organ never acquires extraordinary prosperity without another of its system or of its relations being modified in the same degree."

This co-ordinating force was familiar among the ancients under the name of *nisus formativus*. To this mysterious force numerous phenomena of organic regeneration were attributed.

Whatever may be the definition of the law, the facts which lie at its root are incontestable. When we work our muscles and so cause an increase in their size, we simultaneously develop the blood vessels, ligaments, nerves, and even the bones themselves. When we succeed in lengthening or shortening a bird's beak, the correlative parts of its organism tend towards corresponding changes. When the length of the body of " thick throats " pigeons is developed out of all proportion, the number of vertebræ increase and their ribs become enlarged.

Very often a single changed trait involves a number of other modifications which are its crowning or logical complement. It is thus that breeders in confining their efforts solely to the modification of a single member cause the change of many.

When the beak of a pigeon is lengthened, the length of the tongue usually profits by it. In examining several races of domestic pigeons like the rock-dove, the tumbler, &c., we perceive a great difference between them in the bend of the lower jaw. In these cases there is noticeable a corresponding difference in the bend of the upper jaw. Among short-faced tumblers the wings shorten proportionately to the reduced stature of this race. There is in like manner a very apparent correlation between the length of the claws and that of the beak (Darwin). The great Irish stag having acquired antlers weighing as much as a hundred pounds,[1] it follows that other changes will have taken place in its organism. We notice in it a thicker skull to bear the antlers, a strengthening of the cervical vertebræ and their ligaments, an enlargement of the dorsal vertebræ to support the neck, more powerful hind legs, &c.

In the domain of craniology we see a number of analogous phenomena. The development of the anterior lobe of the brain causes the forcing back of the occipital aperture behind. A skull which lengthens becomes higher, and on the other hand, as brachycephaly augments, the skull lowers. The complete flattening of the face, including the cheekbones, is accompanied by phenomena which are logically co-ordinate with the principal change. The *glabelle* becomes effaced and the root of the nose crushed.

In closely studying the vegetable kingdom, the same phenomena are observed. Sometimes the colour of flowers or leaves undergoes similar variations, and sometimes that of fruit, grain and leaves changes simultaneously. In the serpent melon, whose thin and tortuous fruit attain as much as a metre in length, the stalk of the plant, the pedicle of the female plant and the median lobe of the leaf are all elongated in a remarkable manner.

It may be said that the more the organism is developed, the more this co-ordination of characteristics becomes manifest. What is this compensation, correlation or harmonisation of variations undergone by an organism? For the moment

[1] H. Spencer, *Principes de Biologie* (French translation, Paris, F. Alcan).

their inner nature remains quite inexplicable, and in the majority of cases we can only state their successive or simultaneous appearance.

Is nature in this way anxious to maintain harmony among her creations in counterbalancing one modification by another which complements it ? Her designs remain obscure to us, and so much the more so in that this science of the co-ordination of characteristics has only just begun. Why do young white pigeons which, when grown up, are yellow, dove-colour or silvery blue, come from the shell almost naked, whereas all other pigeons whose feathers are differently coloured are when born covered with down ? What can be the correlation between the down and the dove-colour or yellow which prevents their co-existence ? Why are the skulls of certain gallinaceous races, on the heads of which are thick tufts of feathers, perforated with so many holes ? Why do white rabbits often have dark marks on the ends of their ears and feet ? Why is the period of gestation longer among large breeds of cattle than among small ? So many questions, so many enigmas, which no doubt will only remain so for a time. We must hope that science will some day reveal the majority of these mysteries and reduce them all to a comprehensive law. In the meanwhile it looks as if nearly all these phenomena depend on some kind of organic co-ordination. The terms " balancing " and " harmony," which appear to affirm a premature fact, seem to us improper. All that we know reduces itself to this, that we observe a number of co-ordinated phenomena which appear simultaneously or successively. We do not transgress the limits of experience in stating that there is " a law of organic co-ordination " the significance and causality of which escape us.

Everything which we have stated above regarding animals and plants is equally applicable to man. Why does fair hair generally accompany blue eyes ? Are the organs of sight and hearing generally affected simultaneously ? Isidore Geoffroy notes this fact, that additional digits appear in man simultaneously not only on the two hands, but also on the feet. It has been observed that Daltonism (colour blindness) goes with an incapacity of being swayed by musical sounds and of differentiating between them.

Certain observations tend to give credit to the opinion that the muscles of the leg undergo variations analogous to those undergone by the muscles of the arms.

The face is in immediate harmony with the skull. The enlarging of the base of the nose, and of the inner orifice of the nostrils in the skeleton, coincides with the flattening of all the nasal parts, bone and cartilage (Topinard). Cases of prognathism are generally accompanied with very thick lips.

In spite of the incalculable number of these correlations or co-ordinations, it is impossible to affirm that there exists a relationship of cause and effect. This kind of coincidence, as Claude Bernard remarked with reason, constitutes one of the gravest dangers which the experimental method meets with in all complex sciences, and especially in biology. It would be necessary, in order to establish a relationship of cause and effect, to be able to proceed to a kind of counter-proof, that is, to suppress a supposed cause, and see whether the effect still persists. Experimental science can only admit an explanation obtained from such exact conditions of counter-proof. When a chemist desires to prove the truth of his analysis, he only proves it by way of synthesis. In wishing to show that his theory is well founded, he submits it to analysis. Only after obtaining results which are altogether in concord can we express an opinion on the soundness of the given proposition.

But now in the matter of plants and animals, to apply this counter-proof is most difficult. The *milieu* which produces certain modifications is so vast in the number of causes brought together that it is almost impossible to submit artificially to the test the mass of these causes minus one.

The more the organism is perfected, the less chance has this counter-proving of being successful. In the case of man it becomes impossible, because of his psychical life, which reacts on all physiological manifestations, and takes an active part in them. Now it is difficult to leave out this important element, or to include it in the method of counter-proof.

Nevertheless, the reality of the phenomena of co-ordination, joined with the direct and equally incontestable influence of *milieu* on individuals, makes evident the changes which man

has undergone owing to external conditions. Thus we have
noticed one after another nearly all the prominent parts of the
human organism. All are susceptible to impression by the
conditions of the *milieu* and undergo modification under its
influence. The *ensemble* of these modifications, which distinguish
human beings from one another and suffer us to divide them
into different varieties, constitute what we have decided to call
the human races. In beginning with the skull and ending
with the colour of the skin, the stature, the hair, the forms of face
and nose, the mouth, the ears and the skeleton in general, we see
them all bending before the full action of the *milieu*. Where
the direct action is not sufficient to explain in detail the changes
which have been wrought, co-ordination of traits comes in as a
supplementary explanation.

It is in virtue of this law of equilibrium, correlation or co-
ordination, that wherever one part of our organism varies, there
takes place a parallel modification of other parts.

From the moment the *milieu* begins to act as a cause of
modification, it may be logically admitted that the moment
the cause ceases to act the effect likewise disappears. But
there is another side to the question which is not so self-
evident. When we place a man in a given *milieu* who has
acquired a certain anthropological type in another place, how
will this new influence operate? Will it merely graft itself
on the old type and so cause the rise of fresh characteristics
radically opposed to those already created? In order to confirm such a solution, it would be first of all necessary to admit
a sort of hereditary and age-long inflexibility of acquired
characteristics. But there is nothing to guarantee that this
supposition is well founded. The acquired characteristics or
modifications which have taken place in the living organism
remind us of the movements of a pendulum which makes a
number of more or less extended oscillations. The distance of
removal from the centre is greater for plants and animals than
for men. In every case the starting-point, that is, the original
form, maintains the equilibrium of movement and prevents its
going off at a tangent.

Thus under the influence of the *milieu* we obtain plants
which are all but new species. This is more difficult in the

case of animals, and absolutely impossible in the case of men. In comparing the most disparate varieties, such as a white fair-haired dolichocephal, deemed the most noble representative of mankind, and a Bushman of a tawny yellow colour, and lozenge face and very pronounced cheek bones, less variations are found between them than, for example, between Kirghiz sheep and the wild sheep (*Ovis montana*) which live in the mountainous parts of North America.

Between the men of the Cro-Magnon race, with their tall stature, platycnemic tibia, prognathic face, &c., &c., and those of our time, the differences are far from being as considerable as between the skeletons of *Bos* found in a fossil state in the late tertiary deposits of Europe and the skeletons of modern cattle.

The more we study the transformations of man down the ages the more we perceive that the *milieu* has changed the surface of his biological organisation without ever succeeding in changing its essential character.

Man evolves like all organised beings, but his evolution takes an ideal and mental form rather than a concrete and physiological one. Nothing is more natural! Man from the time of his appearance on the earth appears to be distinct from other living beings in the fact of a more intense mentality which has played and still continues to play a preponderant part in his march through life, and which will go on acting in the future. This it is which has enabled him to raise himself more and more in the animal scale, and to subject other organic beings to his will and to serve his purposes. If he varies down the ages, these modifications bear in particular on his intellectual faculties, and on the vast domain of their conquests, that is to say, his social, moral and intellectual life.

In comparing that same White with the Bushman, we easily perceive that the distinction between their mentalities and the consequences which follow on this distinction are much more considerable than all the variations established between their cephalic indices, or the construction of their skeletons. With this difference so formulated, it is evident that the gulf which separates human beings is particularly deep on the intellectual and moral side.

The evolution of man has never resulted in irremediable
or insuperable deviations in the matter of encephalon. In
reviewing all the craniological scales and in studying all the
foundations whereon is based the division of humanity, nowhere
have we met with an *organic condemnation* of any race
whatever on the ground of its intellectual faculties. Man,
however backward he may be found in the matter of his
intellectual development, never loses the right of aspiring to
elevate himself above his surroundings. Twenty years of intellectual work has often proved sufficient for a representative
of the Maori, Zulu, Red Skin or Negro races to win back in his
individual self the centuries of mental arrest or mental sleep
experienced by his congeners. This property common to all
human beings provides them at once with a trait of ineffaceable
equality. One might speak of these faculties as the common
foundations whereon the circumstances of physiological and
physical life construct all kinds of buildings.

But this common primordial property, the soul, the conscience,
the mentality—for the name matters little—also makes impressions on the physiological life of man by leaps. Owing to psychic
force, man has been able to overcome all the obstacles of nature
and to transplant himself to all geographical latitudes. Owing
to it he has been able to make himself master of the world.
And this property common to man has given him everywhere
a uniform stamp. It has prevented human varieties from
varying too far from the common trunk which is the primordial
regulator of their life and acts. And if man owes to it all the
benefits of his moral and intellectual existence, he owes to it
first of all his unity.

Human mentality shows numerous gradations. Between the
Toupi-Guarani with other cannibals and the modern French,
there is a whole world of separation with regard to their
manner of living, feeling and thinking. Nevertheless it would
be enough for one or two human generations of Toupi living
on the basis of European civilisation to fill up the moral
and mental lacunæ which separate them from an ordinary
Frenchman.

All the condemnations of peoples and races in virtue of an
innate superiority or inferiority have in reality failed. Life has

taught us to be more circumspect in our judgments. A savant who presumes to pronounce a verdict of eternal barbarism against any people deserves to be laughed at.

Civilisation indeed has had some singular experiences during a century. Let us remember, for example, that in the time of the Encyclopædists, savants like d'Alembert and even Diderot refused to concede to the Russians the possibility of becoming civilised after the European manner.

The following century was destined to give them the lie, for it gave to this people consigned to barbarity thinkers and writers who are accounted among the guiding spirits of modern humanity. If the Russian nation shall arrive some day at enjoying that liberty whereby it may develop unimpeded its moral and intellectual faculties, the cause of progress shall have counted a hundred million workers more !

This possibility of developing the faculty of thinking implies at the same time the faculty of benefiting by its age-long conquests. It is thus that the peoples who approach tardily towards civilisation succeed in easily regaining the time lost throughout their period of barbarism. The complex world of culture opens out at once before a people who begin to draw from its source. Together with European thought they appropriate its social and political advantages, its discoveries and inventions. They enter thus abruptly within the space of a generation into the great civilised family, and benefit by its institutions which were formed after centuries of persevering toil.

The Negroes, for example, whom it is desired to class among the most inferior races, astonish, as we shall see later on, all those who study their history without prejudice by their progress, which is altogether amazing. Fifty years ago those of the Southern States did not possess a hundred hectares of land. To-day the number of negro landed proprietors exceeds 130,000 and represents a value of 1,500,000,000 francs, whereas they all are worth more than four thousand millions. The balance sheet of the last fifty years of this race's existence, which race was believed to be predestined to " eternal servitude " under men of ivory or brown colour, is a fact which should make the experts of human inequality pause and ponder.

Community of life also fashions the physiological qualities of man. We thus find ourselves in a vicious circle, in a continual come and go of influences which tend towards human unity.

Above the one and the same layer of intellectual and psychical life which is common to all men, other layers are superimposed, formed by the ambient *milieu*. When this last varies, the acquired characteristics also vary. And if there are some modifications which appear more durable or ineffaceable, we must not forget that it is necessary to judge their persistence less by the number of years than by that of human generations.

Regarded from this point of view, the characteristic traits of races show a very moderate persistency. When we reflect that civilisation benefits humanity by an innumerable number of analogous influences, it may be easily understood that these tend more and more towards unification. At the spectacle of the approximation of types which is thus manifested in humanity, the anthropologists who are most inclined to divide it are driven to admit that the time is near when Race-anthropologists may be compelled to seek their proofs and materials exclusively among the history of extinct peoples and tribes!

Part III

ANTHROPO-PSYCHOLOGY AND ANTHROPO-SOCIOLOGY

CHAPTER I

THE FAILURE OF THE PSYCHOLOGY OF PEOPLES

I

Is it possible to enclose in a logical formula the very character and hopes of a people or race ? This question goes far beyond its theoretical bearing. Parallel to the exclusive doctrines of races which are based on anthropological data, we see the rise of a new branch of psychology, which also, leaning on anthropology, endeavours to link together the past, present, and even the future of great human agglomerations in exact definitions. One people is designated as possessing a bilious temperament, proud and cruel, feeble in will power, lacking tenderness and goodness, and non-moral, though strongly religious. Another people adds to its sanguine temperament a realistic and practical genius, a lust of conquest, an unscrupulous spirit, criminal aspirations. To one pertain all the virtues, to another all the vices. Some are endowed with every quality which can create admirable peoples and individuals. Others are charged with all the sins of Israel. Were it only a matter of an innocent arrangement of grandiloquent words, one might make fun of this new science (?), which deduces its laws from the imagination and, what is worse, from the passions of its creators. But this new scientific plaything aspires to higher things. It is especially used as a weapon in the relations between one people and another. Certain sociologists, and these not the least, even see in its teaching positive indications for the guidance of public affairs. Certain peoples are thus mistrusted, their unhappy representatives kept well at arm's length, whilst others are accepted and regarded as choice friends and desirable allies.

This doctrine has already to its account many wholesale condemnations, forcing on our attention numerous apologies for "superior" and much contempt for "inferior" nations.

All the more illimitable in that it soars outside concrete facts, the psychology of peoples includes all and touches all. Morality, science, philosophy, economic and social life, criminality, alcoholism, politics, religion, everything, in short, serves as matter for discussion and dogmatic conclusion. Not content with occupying its attention with the present, it summons the past before its tribunal and formulates previsions for the future.

Let us take one of its most circumspect, luminous and at the same time most impartial representatives, M. Alfred Fouillée. Optimistic by nature and even touched with scepticism as regards anthropological exaggerations, he brings his reserves and scruples where his co-religionists have only condemnations or wholesale benedictions to pronounce. Nevertheless it is sufficient to examine his *Psychologie du Peuple français*; his *Tempérament et Caractère* or the *Esquisse psychologique des Peuples européens* in order to show how far the aberrations of this new quasi-science can extend. Carried away by his subject, he also sets himself to distribute his rewards and modified censures on the mysterious aspirations of the peoples and their innate or hereditary virtues or vices.

Looked at from this point of view the psychology of peoples descends to the level of the psychology of novels. It treats national or racial groups as good or bad, base or noble, virtuous or vicious, modest or arrogant, just as the novel presents us with good or bad individuals, base or noble, virtuous or vicious, modest or arrogant. As the individual has created the Deity after his own image, he has created the collective soul after the fashion of his own individual soul. M. Gumplowicz even says that if it is difficult for us to foresee what the individual will do in a given case, we can predict exactly with regard to ethnical or social groups, viz. tribes, peoples, social or professional classes. Starting from such a point, sociologists like G. Le Bon, Stewart Chamberlain, Lapouge or G. Sergi threaten us with the decay of the Latin races just as so many others threaten us with the inevitable hegemony of the Germanic races, Slavs and Anglo-Saxons.

This psychology, however, is always invented after the event. It consecrates and glorifies success and breathes disdain on defeat. One people which is fortunate and prosperous in its economic and social life is pronounced superior. Another which is the victim of the complex circumstances which influence the life of every community is regarded as essentially inferior. Germany after the victorious war of 1870 has in this way been raised on a pinnacle as summing up all the virtues. Yet when we think of the events of this unfortunate war, the chances of which could so easily have been favourable to France (see on this subject the studies of Bleibtreu and Commandant Picard), we tremble on account of the superior qualities of Germany which at the same stroke would have become inferior.

What value can we attribute to the psychology of peoples living in the full force of evolution and transformation if it has failed in the case of peoples and races which have disappeared ?

What people, for example, has been more studied than the ancient Greeks ? The literature on this subject is the most extensive and the best supported. The number of volumes which tell of Greece is much superior to the number of its inhabitants under Pericles. Yet in spite of all the sides of its life thus opened to our gaze, we are unable to furnish an exact definition of its soul. According to Renan, the Greeks were the least religious people in the world. According to Fustel de Coulanges, the Greek life incarnates the religious life *par excellence*.

II

As a typical example of the invincible difficulties which bar the way to savants of this class we will consider the Celtic case, a case which is all the more important in that on its elucidation depends the fate of the psychology of the principal civilised peoples, French, English, German and Italian. As long as the balance sheet of the Celtic heritage is not drawn up, it becomes impossible to discuss the aspirations and contents of the modern soul. Ethnical psychology has so well understood this that far from considering the present state of the Celtic question which prevents all generalisation, it merely leans on a Celtic science designed for its own special use. Every psychologist has recourse in this way to his own " personal " science, and paints the Celts according to the needs of his own temperament and cause.

Among learned Celticists, Renan belongs to the most authoritative, he himself being the most finished and representative Celtic type. He tried from his childhood to penetrate the Celtic soul, and he continued to study it throughout his life. But this ingenious and delicate psychologist, instead of giving us the Celtic portrait, only provided us with his own. All the words and all the phrases which Renan uses to describe the soul of his race furnish us, in short, with that exclusive and exquisite soul of Renan himself. " Grace of imagination, the ideal of gentleness and beauty made the supreme object of existence, charming modesty, feminism," &c., are so many gifts which distinguish the subtle savant himself. At the time when Renan was painting idyllic pictures of the life of the Celts, the works of Gaidoz, Loth, d'Arbois de Jubainville, Le Braz, Dottin, &c., had not yet appeared. The little, however, which we have learnt since about them proves that these supposed Celts with the souls of women, tender and delicate, enamoured of beauty and dreams, were merely rude barbarians passionately enamoured of fighting. The few epics preserved in Irish manuscripts of the twelfth century only breathe war and action. They are all *Cath* (fights), *Orgain* (massacres), *Togail* (storming of strongholds), *Tain* (cattle-lifting) and *Aithed* (stealing of women). All these poems only sing of barbarism and a society founded on the principle of war. They tear one another on all occasions, and the chiefs of the people fight like simple individuals. The battle finished in this world continues in the other, and the poet himself is taken up to chant the exploits of war. War everywhere and always. The Druids only play a part because of their magical formulas which tell against the enemy; by means of their chants they excite *courage* and *bravery*. The king of the dead, Labraid, is only venerated by the Celts as vanquisher of warriors and "a quick handler of the sword."

> The bravest of warriors, prouder than the seas!
> He looks for carnage and is exceedingly beautiful!
> O thou who attackest warriors, greet Labraid.[1]

The Renanist conceptions on the ideal love of Celts for women have undergone the same overthrow. When in the light of recent discoveries we study the inner life of the Celts, we are surprised at their contempt for women and at their sensual inclinations. The wife is merely a tool for the procreation of male infants who are necessary for war. The woman is sold and passes from hand to hand at the customary price of three horned cattle.

And consider what follows as exemplifying the melancholy, languid and dreamy soul of Celtic women! In the heart of the lovely Derdriu, divine love awakes at the sight of a calf skinned in the snow, the blood of which a raven comes to drink. When she chooses her lover Naoisë, she yields to his wishes because she desires a lusty young lover such as he is!

M. Fouillée, altogether devoted to the old theories, still continues to speak of the Celts as peaceful *par excellence*. In taking his stand on this essential quality of their temperament he regales us with some delicious pages whose only fault is that they are terribly fantastical![2]

"The Celt as a rule supplements this insufficiency of his voluntary activity with passive resistance. He is a gentle obstinate. Moreover, not feeling very strong alone, he has an instinctive tendency to seek strength in union. . . . For the same reason he is peaceful by nature. Wounds and knocks are not to his liking."

"They do not feel the need of traversing the globe, to shoot arrows into the sky or to fight against the sea. . . . They love their native soil and are attached to their families," &c.

But here a few pages further on in M. Fouillée's book we find a quotation from Grant Allen which he appears to adopt on his own account, to the effect that "the Celt has an *indomitable passion for danger and adventure*"!

[1] H. d'Arbois de Jubainville, *l'Epopée celtique en Irlande.*
[2] *Psychologie du Peuple français.*

Again, when it is a matter of discussing the value of the warlike spirit, M. Fouillée defends his beloved Celts and says that they also have in their favour " *great invasions and great conquests.*"

The reader, thus bewildered, asks himself whether after all the Celts were peaceful or warlike. Were they distinguished by their love of the fireside or their thirst for adventure ?

We are still more bewildered in face of the deductions drawn from Celtic psychology, relative to the modern French. They tell us without flinching that " the will among the French people has preserved the explosive, centrifugal and rectilineal characteristic which it had already among the Gauls." " Like our ancestors (we are also told), we often push courage even to temerity "!

Learned anthropo-psychologists proceed in this way to enlarge on this Celto-Gaulish subject in volume after volume. Now the person who wishes to take the opposite side can do so without running the risk of offending the truth, for the simple reason that we know almost nothing about the life of the Celts. " Of their gods we know almost nothing. In the ancient period we only know the assimilations made by Greek and Latin writers, which are no doubt superficial. In the Romano-Gallic period, some Celtic surnames of local divinities reveal to us a Gaulish pantheon very different from that which the authors of antiquity have described." [1]

What is the contribution of the Gauls to the cults of stones, fire or water which existed in Gaul long before their arrival ? We shall never know, for, according to the statement of the same author, in this cemetery of past religions " the inscriptions are worn, the tombs empty and the graves in disorder." They teach us nothing save that we walk on the dust of the dead.

Refuge has been sought among the Bretons. According to many linguists and anthropologists, these are true Celts left to us by the past in order to furnish us with the solution of all the problems concerning the Gauls. Nevertheless, modern Bretonists tell us without circumlocution that the door is equally closed on this side and that, in the fifth century of our era, Roman Brittany was inhabited by a Romano-Gallic

[1] G. Dottin, *La Religion des Celtes.*

population like the rest of Gaul.   It is true that, later on, Celts much less Romanised came from Great Britain, but this stream of immigration ceased towards the tenth century.   The Breton population was much reduced as the result of incessant warfare, their language retreated and Brittany passed under French influence.

Where then is the Celtic soul to be found ?   Is it in their much praised drama, which has already cost us such hard study ?   " Where we looked for a national drama, nourished with the ingenious fictions and the heroic passions of the race," so speaks A. Le Braz,[1] " Ireland, unhappy Ireland, comes empty-handed, Wales and Cornwall show us some dull Anglo-Norman imitations, and our motherly Brittany bends her shoulders under a load of French mystery-plays."

" That which we improperly call Breton originality (the same author tells us elsewhere) is in the last analysis only a remnant of mediæval times which only appears as original in Brittany because elsewhere it has been abolished for some five centuries."[1]

Is it in those megalithic monuments (dolmens, menhirs, cromlechs) with which Brittany so abounds ?   But archæology has refused to see in them the work of Celts, and this simply because they are not to be met with in other countries peopled by Celts, like Bavaria, Bohemia, and Upper Italy.   Moreover, their existence in countries where there were no Celts such as Algeria, Western Sweden, and Denmark, is established,   Consequently we have here a mysterious people who preceded the Celts and of whom we are as entirely ignorant as we are of their name.

Lastly, we have recourse to the language of the ancient Celts.   Alfred Holder, in his *Altceltischer Sprachsatz*, still unfinished, has collected more than 30,000 words.   But this treasury must not astound us !   " The proper names are in enormous proportion, and as for the others we can only explain—150."[2]

Again, it is necessary to state that all the words handed down

---

[1] *Essai sur l'Histoire du Théâtre Celtique.*

[2] Dottin, *La Langue des Anciens Celtes.*

Let us state that the University of Rennes has the honour of counting among its professors several Celticists of high repute, including the celebrated grammarian, M. G. Dottin, MM. A. Le Braz, Loth, &c.   The work, *La Langue des Anciens Celtes,* has not yet appeared.   But the author has kindly allowed me to see the proofs.

by the authors of antiquity which are neither Greek nor Latin
are made to appear in Celtic vocabularies. They may just as
well be Ligurian, Iberian or Germanic as Celtic.

As for the words which the writers of the Middle Ages give
us as Gaulish, they clearly belong to the vulgar language
spoken in Gaul which had not at that time a Celtic dialect.

Let us not be discouraged. Is there no Breton literature ?
Yes, it exists, but its texts only date from the fifteenth century after Christ. What is more amusing is that they are
borrowed for the most part, like the Breton drama, from French
literature.

A last source remains, the popular Breton songs (*gwerz*)
which La Villemarqué wished to ascribe almost to prehistoric
times. But to-day we are forced to admit, owing to the conscientious collections of Luzel, that the *gwerz* are decidedly
modern and that there are none dating from before the
seventeenth century !

The provoking Bretonists of Rennes allow us nothing. Have
they not proved that the famous Breton pantaloons (*bragou-braz*)
have nothing Celtic about them !

Thus as we draw nearer to the Celtic race, its "mirage"
vanishes. A mystery inherent in this people envelops all its
existence, its wanderings, its thought, its life. We know very
few things for certain about it saving perhaps that it existed
without our being able to locate its origins or its frontiers. So
the collective psychology of the Celt, which can only be based
on concrete and positive knowledge, becomes in this way an
almost impossible creation. Nevertheless it attracts and
seduces thousands of historians, philosophers and sociologists.
Let us quote a few haphazard.

When Mommsen speaks of the Celts, be certain that he will
know how to astonish us in the same way as his illustrious
predecessors. He carefully ascribes to them all the virtues and
all the vices which Germans are generally pleased to bestow on
the modern French ! According to this great historian, the latter
being only vulgar Celts must already in the past have borne
their moral impress. In our days Heinrich Driessmann only
sees in European history the antagonism between two dominant
races, the Celtic and the Germanic. For him this is the key to all

the catastrophes of the past.   It goes without saying that the Teutons enjoy all his tenderness and the Celts all his hard words.   The Celts are the amusers of the world and its revolutionaries; the Teutons, its thinkers.   The English Revolution was caused by the upheaval of the Teutons against the Celts; that of France by that of the Celts against the Teutons. This is why in England all goes well whilst in France everything goes helter-skelter !

The essays of this kind of psychology are very often reduced to a most insipid verbiage.   It may be said that this pseudo-science is only composed of a number of stereotyped phrases which experts are ever manipulating as it serves their fancy. We notice, for example, that when Giesebrecht, the celebrated German historian, wished to describe the ancient Germanic peoples, he had recourse to the same stock in trade of panegyrics which Thierry had used to exalt the Gauls !

III

The life of peoples and the mass of their aspirations are so complex that in the impossibility of embracing them all, every observer attaches himself in particular to the sides which most strike his imagination.   In the sympathetic or unsympathetic portrait of a people, it is the individuality of the artist rather than that of his models which appears to view.   When hatred or infatuation, entering into party spirit, darken the clear vision of the author we have before us only false or caricatured images.   What increases the difficulties is the incredible quantity of data which this science has to make use of in giving more or less hazardous verdicts.   Its conclusions touch all spheres of the abstract and concrete life of a people, so that the person who formulates them must have an "innumerable heart" and in his brain an unfathomable spring of knowledge.   In beginning with the mathematical sciences and ending with history, linguistics and literature, he must be familiar with everything.   Inasmuch as the soul of a people manifests itself as much in its actions as in its ideal aspirations, he who would judge it must know how to hear and comprehend the least perceptible beatings of its heart.

He must know its intellectual treasures, its arts and its poetry; its crimes and its virtues; the visible actions of its politics and its invisible tendencies; its social and private ethics; the extent of its altruistic sentiments and also the force of its egoism. Moreover, it would be enough to let a few errors slip into this vast work in order to derange its mechanism and annul its value.

The coryphées of this fatalistic psychology console themselves with the thought that their large frescoes are so much the more true to life in that " they leave many details in semi-obscurity, in order to place the essential traits in full light." But they appear to forget that the essential traits are only the result of these manifold details. Before fixing a label on the soul of a people, one must know exactly the machinery of its working. Here, as in a chemical analysis, there are no negligible constituent principles. The traits which differentiate souls are often only shadowy. When it is a matter of analysing the logical significance of a phrase, it is necessary to explain the number, nature and composition of all the propositions, in order to distinguish and determine the different forms. If we leave out one or some propositions our work is faulty at the base and inexact.

The disadvantage becomes still greater when it is a question of the very complex and, at the same time, very delicate analysis of the mysterious motives of our actions. The most conscientious among the doctrinaires of collective souls remind us of those metaphysicians who, in studying the phenomena of the beyond, always console themselves with the thought that they only lack the little bridge to connect the things of the earth with those of the invisible world. Nevertheless, this " little bridge " was never created nor discovered, so that ontology has ended in bankruptcy!

Let us see, for example, how the most authoritative among the sociologists justify their collective psychology of peoples. The problem, however difficult it may be, does not appear to them insoluble, for this simple reason, that " the natural character pertains to the temperament and the constitution, which themselves pertain to the race and the physical *milieu*. Thus the component traits of races *begin* to become known. We can tell in a very general way how the physical and also the psychical constitutions of Teuton and Celt, Slav and Iberian,[1] are distinguished." It is enough to examine these justifying arguments in order to reject the theory altogether.

As many foundations, so many great unknown! How can this quantity of X furnish us with the desired solution? If the character pertains to the temperament, this last itself remains fluent and indefinite. It varies in particular, according to the individual, and it is as impossible to erect a psychological structure on this principle as to erect a monument on the flowing water of a river. A more important matter is that all these constructors fasten on racial origin as their principal foundation. But nothing is more chaotic and uncertain than the genealogical descent of any people whatsoever. The ethnical influences are everywhere intermingled, and the majority of the European peoples, to mention only these, show a most varied commingling of blood. When we consider more closely the ethnical history of peoples we perceive the impossibility of gauging their blood.

Let us admit, however, that some day we shall succeed (?) in defining exactly the racial composition of the nations and in pointing out the approximate percentage of Celts, Teutons, Slavs, Negroes and Mongols, contributing to their formation. There then remains to be shown what is the relative influence of each of these elements! It is outside all possibility that the formation of the collective soul can be considered as a simple alloy!

The small quantity of Normans who invaded England exercised a much greater influence on it than the more numerous Teutons who preceded them. The French refugees, after the revocation of the Edict of Nantes, profoundly influenced the Germanic soul and civilisation in spite of their small number. The advent of Bernadotte and his few followers in Sweden left imperishable traits in the evolution of the collective life of that country. After having thus analysed the composition of blood quantitatively, we still cannot say anything in what concerns the moral changes which must ensue. Thus after having proved that the Celts

---

[1] Fouillée, *Esquisse psychologique des Peuples européens.* Preface. (Paris : F. Alcan.)

have furnished the French people with one-third or nine-tenths of its blood, we can infer from this nothing positive as regards their character.

Moreover, we only know a number of contradictory things on the collective soul of these constituent elements, namely, Celts, Teutons, Slavs and Hungarians. How then can we construct anything with this fluent matter which slips between our fingers!

We have pointed out above the flagrant contradictions which exist between the definitions given of the Celts in the matter of moral factors as serious as their sexual and social life. Nevertheless this is one of the most studied of European races. Even now after being confronted with thousands of volumes which deal with their past in all its forms, we are unable to say whether the Celts were not Germanic people under another name! And even those who are agreed to differentiate between them are not at one on the places where they sojourned. According to d'Arbois de Jubainville, it is France which was especially peopled by Germanic peoples and Germany by the Gauls, that is, by the Celts!

Whereas we believe that the Celts were settled in Gaul and elsewhere from time immemorial, we only find them mentioned for the first time in the fifth century by Hecataeus of Miletus (died in 475 before Christ). He does it in a very vague and uncertain fashion. In speaking of Marseilles, he notices it as a town of the Ligures (Liguria) near the Celtic.

If we consider the Ligures and the Iberians, who have likewise contributed towards fashioning the soul of the European peoples, our data are still poorer and uncertain.

The light of history, generally uncertain, is singularly obscure on the subject of the mysterious origins of peoples. Their ethnical composition is a matter of indifference to the chroniclers of the past. Anthropology, on the other hand, is one of Science's youngest children.

When it came into the world, it was only able to relieve the absence of sure and positive information by means of philosophical speculations and hypotheses more or less plausible.

In order to fill the lacunæ, they had recourse to archæology which was within the bounds of possibility, and to protohistory or prehistory (*palethnology*) which was within the bounds of impossibility. But all such data brought together, as we have shown elsewhere, are most problematic.

So much for the history and the composition of races in the past. The analysis of their blood is beyond our powers, so that the gauging of their constituent elements becomes in this way altogether impracticable.

Supposing we admit that science, older by a few centuries, will succeed some day in deciphering the impenetrable mysteries of the origin of races. Still we shall not for that be much more advanced. There would still remain for definition the character and the qualities of soul of the "constituents."

But it is sufficient to have read a certain number of the collective psychologies of the same people—what am I saying ? —to have studied one isolated and striking manifestation of its intellectual and social activity, in order to see the difficulty of the task.

IV

Taine may be regarded as one of the savants who have done most for this new science. Furnished with a sure erudition and gifted with a genial critical spirit, he applied himself to making those syntheses or "*tableaux d'ensemble*" which enjoy so exceptional a notoriety among the anthropo-psychologists. One loves to quote his judgments on the English, Germans, Italians and French. To him is currently attributed the merit of having been able to decipher their souls and of having supplied us with a photographic image of them. It is sufficient, however, for one grain of Pascalian sand to enter into a vast brain in order to derange all its machinery. Stirred by the noble desire of showing himself to be courageous to excess and independent in thought, even at the expense of his own country, he unconsciously glided as far as to apologise for it in his psychology of the German people. The French nation thereby descended by several degrees lower than the conventional estimate. We thus read in Taine [1] enthusiastic praises lavished on the Germans, on their

---

[1] *Histoire de la Littérature anglaise.* Vol. I.

inventive, original and quick spirit, their native culture, created and grown on the soil itself. Germany, according to Taine, created all the ideas of the nineteenth century. France merely dished them up.

German genius at the end of the eighteenth century gave birth to new metaphysics, a new theology, a new poetry, a new literature, which is a somewhat large order !

The conception of original ideas is, according to Taine, the dominant faculty of the German people.

But at this very period France gloried in possessing men of genius like Laplace, Lavoisier, Lamarck, Bichat, Cuvier, to mention but a few.

France, however, has endorsed this fantastical judgment of Taine !

But Zeller, the justly reputed Alsatian historian, tries to demonstrate exactly the contrary. With the same stroke he demolished both this collective psychology of the German and the erroneous historical comments which served to support it, as being false from one end to the other.

We see before us the same facts, but the way of presenting them changes their aspect completely. The Germans, as original thinkers and creators of a special culture, are for Zeller pure imitators. As a civilised land, so this historian tells us, Germany is only the child of Gaul and of Rome. She has received everything *from the outside*—chivalry, civic liberty, the idea of Empire, her letters and her sciences, her universities (copied from those of Paris), her Gothic art (originally from France), even to her religious toleration, a thing little known in Germany. Zeller states that from Cæsar and Tacitus up till Charlemagne, Germania presents the rare spectacle in history of a civilisation absolutely stationary, absolutely barbaric, and that for eight centuries. Germany, he tells us elsewhere, has never made progress—*she has simply submitted to it !*

Mommsen, on the other hand, who ignores the fact that Germany is more Celtic than Germanic, stamps with disdain on the Celtic race as good for nothing, incapable in politics, without originality or depth, and exalts the Germanic peoples as a superior race, intellectually and morally.

It is enough to place side by side the opinions expressed by the most eminent writers on the same people, or, still better, on any trait whatsoever regarded as dominant in its character, in order to perceive the impossibility of arriving at a weighty opinion worthy of the attention of all impartial observers.

Every description of a psychological and collective quality, even when this quality forms the essential trait of a people or race, meets with insurmountable difficulties. What is to be said then of a definition of a mass of qualities, a kind of crystallisation of a hundred of these characteristic traits each of which is beyond our investigation ? Let us consider a concrete instance.

In order to have a plausible psychology of the French people, it is naturally necessary to make the French mind and genius enter into it. All the world seems to be at one on this, that what distinguishes the French nation intellectually and morally from all other nations is chiefly the quality of its mind and genius. But what is this French mind ? What are its essential qualities ? Wherein is it to be distinguished from the mind and genius of the German, Russian or English ? Can a foreigner assimilate it to such a degree that he can be no longer distinguished from a Frenchman ?

V

With the aid of certain savants and writers, the most representative of French thought that could well be found, I tried to elucidate this question in 1898. About thirty psychologists, novelists, poets, philosophers and professors were kind enough to send me, in reply to my inquiries on this subject, profound and luminous pages which demonstrate in their effect the absolute impossibility of a precise definition of the French mind.[1] According to M. Paul Bourget, we ought to question even the reality of these very popular formulas, the French mind, the Anglo-Saxon mind, &c. They are labels which disguise abstractions, and " to confine myself to France and its literature (he writes) what common definition is there which could apply to

[1] All the articles appeared in *La Revue* (formerly *Revue des Revues*), July st, 1898. This number is completely exhausted, and is no longer procurable.

Pascal and Voltaire, to Rabelais and Boileau, to Montesquieu and Hugo, to Racine and Balzac? These are all, however French geniuses." According to M. Jules Claretie, "what is clear, luminous and generous is altogether French, but this clearness does not exclude depth. Add also, horror of all affectation and cheap pedantry."

M. François Coppée tells us "that it is only in France that one knows how to be strong without being heavy, and deep without becoming obscure."

M. Michel Bréal does not think that the qualities "amiable and strong, brilliant and sensible, spiritual and enthusiastic are exclusively vested in the French, but are only to be found here more frequently than elsewhere. M. Anatole France however, distinguishes "a certain spirit of order, of measure, of clarity which is not to be found elsewhere, although all great writers in all languages have clarity, measure and order. But it is another order, another measure, another clarity." According to M. Urbain Gohier, "it is truly rash to take as characteristics of the French mind qualities which are in our literature the note *par excellence* of many foreigners. In the generally accepted sense, there were never writers more French than the English Hamilton, the Swiss Rousseau, the Italian de Maistre the German Heine and the Mulatto Dumas." And this supposed "measure" and "clarity," which apparently constitute the most incontestable heritage of the French mind, are ground to powder by M. Rémy de Gourmont, who tells us that "neither Ronsard nor Rabelais nor Corneille nor Michelet nor Hugo possess measure taste and clarity."

M. G. Larroumet, on the other hand, characterises the French mind as "the tendency to general ideas, the love of social life a prevailing capacity for eloquence and the drama, the desire for clarity and the passion of the intellect." According to Camille Mauclair, all this twaddle must be put on one side, for what characterises the French mind "is criticism which is the French race itself. Its imagination may be a deformation of the truth but never an invention."

M. Marcel Prévost considers the French mind to be clear, synthetic, loving and respectful of rules; to sum up, "clearness taste for ideas and general methods, classical spirit."

M. E. Rod hesitates before the difficulty of a definition, but he believes that this mind exists, and that "it is not that of other peoples." Georges Rodenbach makes pleasant fun of this pretention to a monopoly of clarity and taste. "Every writer who writes in French is a *French writer*. . . . The language in which he writes classifies him, and not his civil state. . . . In truth *those who are of French nationality often feel themselves to be more different from one another than from a foreigner writing in French*."

Francisque Sarcey tells us bluntly that "every book which is logically arranged and clear is for that very reason French." It is on this ground that " Rousseau and Dumas are excellent Frenchmen."

M. Sully Prudhomme affirms, on the contrary, that there is a clearly marked French mind. "If we consider writers of different nationalities, we are obliged to recognise that they can still less assimilate mutually their respective styles, even when nothing is said of their personal qualities, for they differ in their very essence through the stable and irreducible characteristics of their respective nationalities."

M. de Vogüé thinks the solution of this question well-nigh impossible, for "into the domain of intellectuality there enter, besides human liberty, many unforeseen variations which this liberty allows, as well as numerous cases of individual acclimation."

Emile Zola sees the Latins in the French, and "this is the great family to oppose to the families of the North."

We pass over a dozen other writers whose opinions only increase the above cacophony. The comparison, however, of all these divergent ideas furnishes us with lessons of wide bearing.

This is the "mark" of nationality which appears to be the best known, viz. " the French mind." Is it not deemed to be the fundamental and inseparable quality of the mentality of all French writers and thinkers? We find this term repeated *ad infinitum* in books and discourses. The learned and vulgar use it in and out of season. In its cult, we are told, all the people in the world participate !

When, however, we try to know what there is behind this

magical term, "French mind or genius," we perceive not only that it becomes impossible to define it, but also—a matter which is more important—that every writer understands it in his own way. According to some it is in reality the exclusive prerogative of the French. According to others, it is only more frequently met with in France, whilst certain other writers tell us that the qualities which we attribute to it are purely human, and are likewise found outside the geographical and ethnical frontiers of France !

In analysing the essential traits of this "mind or genius," each ascribes special qualities to it according to his own temperament and the qualities of his own soul.

A capacity, however, for analysing and determining the views of this brilliant group of thinkers and writers goes for nothing. They have not succeeded in their task for this simple reason, that they had no means of succeeding. In claiming for the French mind or genius certain exclusive qualities, they were foredoomed to sterile efforts. Our morals, our intellectuality, the aspirations of our soul pertain to a certain degree of our civilisation, to a certain mode of being and living. They apply to individuals, but not to peoples and races.

The mind of the majority of *modern* Frenchmen shows a dominant note. But this is not irreducible or eternal. It changes and will change with the profound modifications which our national life will undergo.

VI

The lack of method which characterises all these generalisations is seen when applying them to concrete facts, and to individual psychology.

According to Stewart Chamberlain, Byron was thoroughly Germanic, but Driessmann tells us that he was only a vulgar Celt.

His romantic adventures, "so essentially Germanic," which appeal to Chamberlain, repel the conscience of Driessmann. Did not Byron visit courtesans at Venice, and is not this trait pre-eminently Celtic ? [1]

---

[1] *Keltentum in der Europäischen Blutmischung.*

Cervantes was a great Aryan, so Chamberlain declares with emphasis. He was only a Celto-Iberian, so Driessmann replies. And whereas Chamberlain sees in the German social democrats Jewish types, and Driessmann Celto-Mongols, Woltmann, also an anthropo-psychologist of repute, goes into ecstasies over them as the most authoritative representatives of the Germanic blood and temperament.[1]

Immanuel Kant, the most representative type of German thought, is condemned by Otto Wilmann as a bad cosmopolitan, who excites himself sometimes on behalf of the English and sometimes on behalf of the French!

Again, what is to be said of anthropo-psychologists of the second order who have not the decency even to give a varnish of impartiality to their highly fantastical pictures! Without logic and without scruples they contradict themselves, and at the same time contradict reality.

When we come across such audacious psychology as the collective kind of Gobineau and Chamberlain, to mention only these two authors, whose influence on the contemporary mind is considerable, we are stupefied at the calmness with which they never cease modifying their opinion in the course of the same book. The same trait of inferiority shown in a certain people becomes a proof of superiority when met with in another. Dolichocephaly, considered as a first-class virtue in the Whites, does not count when found amongst the Blacks. In idealising a people or race, they impute to it all the virtues, even those which are not of its country or time.

Thus Houston Stewart Chamberlain [2] teaches us that the Aryans were never familiar with temples or divinities, and that they showed an ideal tolerance. Never, says he, did the Indo-Germanic people, that is the Aryans, have recourse to a violent propaganda of their beliefs, and to religious persecutions.

In order to enhance the civilising virtues of the Germans,

[1] *Politische Anthropologie.*
[2] *Die Grundlagen des XIX Jahrhunderts* (Vol. II., 5th ed.). This work enjoys very great popularity in all German States, and the Emperor William thinks it useful to show publicly his admiration for the author and the theories (most contradictory, however) maintained in these volumes.

he describes in very sombre colours the decay of Rome which
naturally followed "the chaotic mixture of the blood of races,"
and depicts the Germanic invasion as a veritable salvation
for humanity.   According to this strange savant, mixture of
races constitutes a real calamity.   The Jews have degenerated
precisely because of the same process which cost Rome her independence.   All the races throughout history which undergo
this infusion of blood from the outside, fall for this cause into
the rank of the degenerate and the inferior.   Chamberlain does
not fail to draw very sorry conclusions from this for—the Slavs.
But in the case of the Prussians, who are only the result of a mixture wherein the Slav blood predominates, he forgets his beautiful
theory and gratifies us with enthusiastic pæans in honour of
this exceptional race.

It must be remarked that Germany, so dear to Gobineau,
Lapouge and Chamberlain, is equally guilty of the great crime
which should consummate her ruin.   Has she not mingled her
original (?) blood with that of Slav races like the Obotrites
(Mecklenburg) ; Sorbes or Serbes (Brandenburg) ; Welatabs or
Wiltz (Pomerania), and the Wends, to say nothing of numerous
Celtic races like the Helvetii, the Tectosages, the Ambrons,
&c., &c.?

The following is a still more typical example.   The psychology
of the German people, as Chamberlain understood it, had need
of certain special adornments in order to please the powerful of
his day.   He wanted to demonstrate that the Teuton had always
been faithful to his sovereign and to his oath of service   The
author, throwing Germanic history overboard, gravely declares,
that from all time loyalty and fidelity to kings had been the
chief characteristic (*der bedeutendste Zug*) of the German character !

In order to justify this theory he quotes a few anecdotes,
negligently disregarding in the meantime the numerous facts
which proclaimed aloud how monstrous it was.   Germanic
loyalty was, at the very beginning, severely criticised by almost
all Roman writers.   The conduct of Arminius, the conqueror of
Varus, was deemed even by the ancients a revolting crime in
inter-racial relations.

"The Franks (and therefore Teutons)," so Vopiscus tells us, "smilingly break their promises." [1]

In looking through the history of Germany during the Middle Ages and even in modern times, we find numerous instances of the violation of oaths of fidelity. If their repeated attempts at rising did not end in delivering the German people from their sovereigns, who were only adored intermittently, it was doubtless not because of lack of will.

In what particularly concerns Prussia, the Knights of the Cross, the real founders of the kingdom, would laugh in their graves to think of the loyalty and the fidelity with which they are credited after their exploits against Poland. And what conspiracies against its king has not Germany to its account, beginning with that against Charlemagne !

The Burgundians in this respect are equal to the Longobards, and these last are equal to the Thuringians. "Revolts, regicides and treacheries, such is the balance-sheet of the activity of German princes" (Dahn).

It is enough to read the subterfuges to which Chamberlain resorts when he would prove, now that Jesus was not Semitic and now that his thought was nevertheless Semitic, in order to have a clear idea of the scientific processes used by representatives of the "psychological fatality" of peoples and races.

If there is any fatality at all, it is this insurmountable propensity to preach nonsense which we meet with among the majority of anthropo-psychologists. One might say that the condemnation of the Lord weighs on their faculty of reasoning. Thinkers who are so prudent in other spheres fall in this matter into stupefying generalisations.

De Candolle, in order to explain the superiority of fair-haired folk, ventures on a theory which would be unworthy of a child. The brown-haired, he tells us, have a much greater vitality than the fair-haired. These last, in order not to succumb in the struggle, are forced to make greater efforts and to become more "spiritualised."

---

[1] Numerous arguments may be found against this false assertion of Chamberlain, among others, in the work of Fr. Herz, *Moderne Rassentheorien*, specially written to combat the errors of Chamberlain's doctrine.

To see the humour of this imaginary struggle, let us remember that the fair-haired and the brown-haired are disseminated not only throughout the same races but also the same provinces, wards, communes and even in the bosom of the same family! Many brown-haired are found among peoples who are emphatically fair, such as the Eskimos; we also meet with fair Negroes. Th. Poesche[1] dwells on the fact that even in the fairest part of Germany the Browns are in the majority.

Fair-haired people are found in Asia, and Vambéry states that these constitute the majority among the Turkomans. According to Galen and Hippocrates, the Scythians even were fair-haired. They are found among the Berbers of Morocco as among the Afghans, in short wherever there are brown-haired.

Driessmann, moreover, tells us that the decay of the fair-haired in Germany is only the result of women's bad taste, which generally prefers the Browns to the Fairs.[2]

Benjamin Kidd in his psychology, starting from the point of view that France is essentially Celtic, continues the use of the old stereotyped phrases which served to idealise the Gaulish soul and civilisation. This distinguished sociologist, who is persuaded that an impassable wall separates the Celts from the Teutons, states that the ethical sense exceeds the æsthetic among the Teutons! What is particularly lacking in them is the idealism of the French mind. Although a sincere admirer of France, he supposes nevertheless that the Teutonic races have qualities which, without being in themselves intellectual, contribute more to social power and the domination of the world. Naturally a number of other psychologists, on the contrary, oppose German idealism to the practical "bon sens" of the French! Whilst Driessmann says that exact science, which he does not appear to appreciate very much, is the work of Celts, Chamberlain ascribes it to the Teutons. Starting from this they proceed to depict in an entirely different way the scientific aspirations of the repre-

---

[1] *Die Arier.*

[2] Beddoe, of Clifton, it is true, reproaches Englishmen for the same thing. The number of fair women diminishes because English gentlemen prefer brown-haired women. Of 100 women, he tells us, with dark, dark brown, light brown, fair and red hair, the proportions of the married were 79, 69, 60, 55, and 67 (?) (*Anthrop. Review*, Vol. I., 1864). Thus, with the aid of selection, the fair with their virtues and superiority over the brown disappear from the earth!

sentative individuals of the two races. Nothing is more "anti-Germanic," says Chamberlain, than " universalism," for which reason the French Revolution and the work of Napoleon could only have been engendered by the Celts ! The Papacy was only the daughter of Catholicism, which again is essentially Celtic. Woltmann, on the contrary, finds that tendencies to universality characterise the Germanic mind and that the Papacy, "Napoleonism" and the French Revolution were the work of the Teutons !

VII

Is it astonishing that collective psychology should tremble on its foundations, when the simple narrations and the descriptions of travellers are often so contradictory ?

The same peoples who are noble and generous according to some are cowardly and degraded according to others.

The modern Japanese are for some travellers proud and war-like, for others peaceful, simple and amiable.

The Schilluks, whom Schweinfurth ranks among the noblest races of Central Africa, are considered by many others as not above the level of the monkey. The French, described as im-moral and frivolous by many psychologists, are exalted to the skies by others, owing to their spirit of economy and the high morality of their family life. Statistics also lend themselves to misunderstanding and erroneous judgments.

England, considered by some to be at the height of its glory and prosperity, is declared to be decadent by others. A very rich country, some say ; in full decrepitude, say others.

According to some, the Germans, since 1870, have progressed morally as well as socially. According to others, they have deteriorated from a humane point of view. Some proclaim Russia and the Russians young and vigorous ; others only see in the Empire of the Tsars a country exhausted and old before its time.

The same peoples are thus judged differently on the same data. The apotheosis of some is the anathema of others. When we consider all these disparate verdicts we can only place very little confidence in anthropo-psychology and its theorists. Their phrases, bandied about without rhyme or reason, remind us of those games of chance in which cards are arranged in a fantastic way. There could be applied to some of these judgments the reserve which is generally used in matters of taste. One must abstain from discussing them. Seeing the complexity of their constituent elements and the varieties of ways of looking at them, all the conclusions drawn from them can be both maintained and disputed.

VIII

Nevertheless it would be unjust to deny the capital importance which the psychology of peoples *might have had*. If it were possible, says Kant, to penetrate sufficiently into the character of a man or of a people, if all the circumstances which act on individual and collective wills were known, we could then calculate exactly what the conduct of a man or a people would be as we calculate an eclipse of the sun or moon. Unfortunately, this desire somewhat resembles the pretensions of the possessor of a rather more than modest fortune in making himself pass for a millionaire.

The soul wishes to go to Paradise, but its sins detain it on the earth, says a Slav proverb. The attempts to erect anthropo-psychology on strictly scientific foundations fail precisely because of the excessive frailty and inextricable complexity of the materials of construction. What would we say of an architect who was obliged to use thousands of elements of whose solidity and capacity for resistance he was ignorant? Even if after laborious efforts he succeeded in building up his modest structure, a gust of wind might be enough to throw it over. Now these are heavy storms which blow on the anthropo-psychological edifice. As its windows remain open on all the phases of the life of peoples, very strong currents of air come from all sides. Sometimes drawing conclusions from the form of government to which a people submits, they say that it thirsts for authority and only sees its salvation in governmental tutelage. But we have the French who have emigrated to Canada accommodating themselves admirably to English self-government, and prospering under principles diametrically opposed!

The English, on the other hand, we are told, are distinguished in an important way from the French. They are as individualistic as the others are socialistic. (G. Le Bon.)

Neo-Latin savants like Ferrero and Sergi, followed in this by Demoulins and many others, write on this subject volumes, ominous for the French, Spanish and Italian future. But the same English in Australia and New Zealand have become State socialists, who strikingly resemble the *Kathedersocialisten* of Germany. There follows, according to C. H. Pearson,[1] an essential modification of characteristics. English individualism becomes transformed and gives way to a sort of personal heedlessness, sheltering itself under the beneficent protection of the State.

This fundamental trait, therefore, of the Anglo-Saxons only has its origin in the ensemble of civic and economic conditions which govern them. The failure of this supposed essential quality of the English soul involves, however, the continued mystery of many other characteristics in its collective and hereditary psychology.

The majority of the theorists of this school depict the Spanish character as full of hardness and cruelty. Their judgments, based on the historic past of this people and among other things on the Inquisition and on the exploitation of its colonies, have no doubt their *raison d'être*. But historians show us that English administration in the Indies has only been one uninterrupted act of age-long cruelty, and that their attitude towards the Irish was not without hardness and injustice.

Nearly everywhere where the English have planted themselves they have only been able to destroy or exploit. Let us recall the following fact mentioned by Boutmy.[2] When the news of the bombardment of Alexandria was made public in the House of Commons, this declaration was received with a spontaneous and resounding ringing cheer, such as one might expect from schoolboys, and not from an assembly of intelligent men, and of Christians, to whom it had just been announced that a town of 200,000 souls had been wantonly bombarded and fired at with grape-shot !

---

[1] *National Life and Character.*
[2] *Psychologie politique du Peuple anglais au XIX siècle.*

The conduct of the French among the Hovas or in Algeria has given rise to reproaches which offend our humanitarian sentiments,[1] so true is it, as had already been stated by Montesquieu, that all races in certain circumstances show themselves to be unjust and cruel. The Americans of the Southern States, both before and after the War of Secession, acted in a barbarous way towards the Negroes. Those of the North added crime to crime in their work of extermination of the Indians. Under our eyes the Prussians act with a revolting cruelty towards the German Poles; the Russians do the same with regard to the Finlander, Jew and Armenian; whilst the Turks in their anti-Armenian policy, carried on with the tacit consent of several civilised governments, leave far behind the Spanish atrocities in the Philippines or in Cuba.

The cruelty and hardness of the Spanish cease to be exclusive. In observing the numerous cases where nations considered to be the most sociable and humane act in the same way, must we not conclude that a certain savage ferocity sleeps at the bottom of the conscience of all peoples? The nations recognised as gentle and just only owe their reputation to a co-operation of favourable circumstances in their historical evolution. The past, which has spared them the necessity of inhuman actions, might have turned in another direction, and might have made this in-humanity necessary to their interests. For it is the opportunity which makes the thief. It is vain to pretend that the moral and intellectual characteristics which constitute a national type are as stable as the anatomical characteristics which determine species (G. Le Bon), an affirmation which makes us smile in the presence of the incessant modifications which take place under our very eyes.

The Irish who have emigrated to the United States change their mentality and their state of soul after fifteen years. The Prussians at the beginning of the nineteenth century, as described by travellers and historians, do not resemble those of our day. The Negroes before the War of Secession and those of our day who have received a superior instruction, form a marked contrast in character and aspirations. With the dignity of man which has been inculcated, the vices

[1] See on this subject the studies of Vigné d'Octon.

which are considered as instinctive in them have almost completely disappeared. The Maoris of New Zealand having passed through English schools and having adopted the liberal professions, have finished by assimilating English morals and mentality.

The soul of the Nippon of 1905 is not that of the Nippon of the Samuraï. Whatever may be the issue of the struggle with Russia we may be certain that it will contribute still further to his essential modification. The fact is so true that already all the old definitions of the Japanese soul are shown to be false and obsolete. All the demographs so far (1905) are unanimous in representing them as an imitative people incapable of inventing or creating anything. Accustomed to see them slavishly adopting our civilisation and our discoveries, we thought them condemned for ever to borrow the results of our intellectual efforts. But civilisation has only acted with regard to them as it does with regard to other peoples, white, red or black. After a period of digestion of received ideas and of facts ascertained, follows a period of incubation and of creation. The faculty of creating is the property of individuals and not of ethnical groups. It is thus that the Japanese at the end of forty years of intellectual borrowings try in their turn to enrich the treasure of a common civilisation.

On this subject let us recall the scientific discoveries of the last years and among others those of Dr. Kitasato, who first cultivated the bacillus of tetanus and applied serotherapy to diphtheria long before Dr. Roux; of Shiza (serum against dysentery), of Takamine (glands), Drs. Miura and Yamagniwa (the Kakké or béri-béri), &c.

The studies of Professor Nagaoka on the relations between magnetization and torsion (magneto-striction) have become classical, in the same way as those of Professor Sekiya and his successor, Omori, mark an epoch in seismology.

If, as the Americans believe, the letters patent taken out in a country bear testimony to the creative faculty of its people, the Japanese have the right to hold their own among Europeans. Though the law of patents only dates from 1885, the Japanese have already succeeded in obtaining 6121 certificates for genuine inventions. The progress realised in this respect is most

astonishing. From 99 in 1885 the number of patents in a yea
went up to 205 ; in 1891 to 605 ; in 1902 to 871 ; and in 190?
to 1024. The Japanese author, Tomita Tanadori, fron
whom we have borrowed these data, points out the ver
regrettable indifference of his compatriots with regard to
inventions realised. He tells us that very often they allow
them to fall into oblivion, and allow themselves to be outdon
by strangers who take out patents in their name.

"The Japanese, though all insular, have not, like the Englisl
appetites of conquest and expansion" (Vacher de Lapouge
But the Chinese war occurs, and the Japanese show us that the
appetites yield in nothing to those of European peoples. A fe
years later they will throw themselves into a formidable war fo
the domination of Corea and Manchuria !

Nearer home, the Hungarians have long since lost th
characteristic traits of Mongols, and are on all points like th
so-called Aryans. The Swiss were once known as soldiers ; i
their quality of mercenaries they swarmed in all States. T
day these typical warriors have become skilled hotel-keeper
The Norwegians, who are now so peaceful, were noted
the Middle Ages for their adventurous spirit. Nearly a
the historians of Poland have attributed the dismemberme
and fall of this country to Slav indolence and passivity, to th
lack of political feeling, and to the frivolity of its manners. B
other Slavs, like the Czecks, afflicted therefore with the san
faults, have accomplished a series of heroic acts, and ha
furnished an example of exceptional perseverance in the
efforts towards emancipation. On the other hand, these sar
Poles, having grown in the school of sorrow, far from disappeari
in the midst of their three age-long enemies, develop in
prodigious way, and justify their faith in their certa
resurrection.

The Jews, who are to-day regarded as the pacific people *p*
excellence, detesting and fearing war, possessed in times gone
a warlike temperament. The name "Israel" means God
battle. The poem of Deborah, one of the most ancient mor
ments of Hebrew literature, is only a song of war. "Jehoval
is represented in certain Jewish songs as descending to t
earth to take part in the battles. The Book of Judges is full

the heroic exploits of the Jews, whilst the history of David fighting against Goliath, or that of Samson killing six hundred of his enemies with a large bone, suffice to point out how great was the cult of courage and strength.

There even was a time (towards the 2nd or 1st century B.C.) when the Jews played the part of mercenaries like the Swiss in later times. In this capacity they were distinguished for their courage and fidelity.[1]

The same Jews, according to ethnical psychologists, possess the power of being able to resist all climates. But this pathological peculiarity, which is always mentioned in descriptions of them, is only due to the special hygienic conditions of their life. Their religion, their customs, their isolation, their persecution, their temperate habits and so many other conditions of their existence help them to resist diseases which are deadly to other peoples owing to intemperance and improvidence. Neufville, Legoy, Dieterici, &c., dwell on the regularity of their lives and the care given to the sick, which singularly reduces the mortality of their children and increases their health.

It has been shown elsewhere that the Israelites who have experienced the influence of the surrounding *milieu* morally and intellectually, and who have adopted the manners of their environment, lose at once the benefit of this exceptional virtue and enter into the common law.

IX

Not only does the psychology of masses contain cruel deceptions for us, but even that easier psychology of certain concrete qualities of our intellectual and moral life. The clearness and attraction of the literary form which it is desired at any cost to present as the exclusive privilege of French writers and savants, are very often not to be found in their writings, but are on the contrary found among foreign writers. Count Gobineau attributes the first failure of his work to their defective form. It was necessary for him to have the powerful friendship of Wagner in order to rise out of oblivion and attract the attention of the German public.

[1] Stade : *Geschichte des Volkes Israël.*

Constant Prévost forestalled Charles Lyell on all points. It is he who is the true founder of the "realist school." On the ruins of the "cataclysm" of Cuvier he successfully established the theory of slow evolution. And whereas Sir C. Lyell became popular owing to his clear and persuasive style, Prévost, because of the obscurity of his writings, has always been ignored, together with his works.

How is Lamarck's way of writing superior to that of Darwin ? Literary history furnishes us with thousands of examples of the same kind. Heine and Boerne exhibit the most brilliant French qualities in their writings. The same can be said of many German novelists and dramatists of our day. We even notice that the crude style so much objected to in German writers and savants becomes more and more modified and approximates to the clearer and more exact manner of the representatives of French and English thought. Moreover, what we have been accustomed to consider as the organic fault of mentality is often only the fault of the instrument of thought, that is the language.

Thus many strangers shine in "*l'esprit parisien*" when they set themselves to write in French. M. Barrès, a writer profoundly imbued with all our national prejudices, tells us a still more curious thing, that one of the greatest French poets of our time is a Roumanian woman (Mme. de Noailles, *née* Brancovan), so that even the charms of poetry which are so impenetrable, and wherein the mysteries of the soul of the country are reflected, give way before instruction and education ! Strangers can also possess them as they can any vulgar data of theoretic or applied science. What is there left, therefore, of the impenetrable and the unassimilable in the domain of feeling and thought ?

X

The illogical nature of the pretended psychological fatality of races and of peoples does not fail to be visible on every occasion when their "composite" descriptions are applied to real life. For if races no longer live in a pure state, neither do peoples any longer correspond with any racial definition. Composed of individuals belonging to different races and showing various mixtures of blood, they ought to be fatally divided as to the character and the aspirations of the unities which compose them. Moreover, every country comprises provinces and districts where the quality of races and their proportion vary. But the addition of several numbers of varying quantities must naturally involve different results. Once we admit a sort of psychological and hereditary fatality, there is no further need to "generalise." It is rather a matter of "singularising" and of confining oneself to the psychology of families or rather to that of individuals, since each part of the population is marked by its "fatalistic" and inevitable aspirations.

A Breton does not resemble a Norman, nor does the latter resemble a Gascon; a Gascon is to be distinguished from a Parisian and the latter from a Marseillais, whilst neither of these is like an Alsacian. In the case of Germans, it is difficult to place Bavarians, Prussians, Swabians, Pomeranians and Badenese in the same category. In studying the provinces apart, we perceive there also differences which exceed conventional limits. Races are no more fixed by country, which is a political conception of the present, than they are by province, a political conception of the past. Their irregular immigration has followed illimitable directions. Let us take, for example, the department of Ain. Ethnically we find there, from the time of the Huns to that of the Cossacks, nearly all the peoples and races which have traversed France. In *certain parts* of Rousillon, Languedoc, Béarn and Provence, we meet with Saracens, whom we would look for in vain elsewhere. In *certain parts* of the north-west coast of the Mediterranean, we recognise traces of Phocœans, Rhodians and other Greeks. In studying Belle-Isle (Morbihan) we should not forget the Acadian families who settled there after the Canadian war, nor the Scotch of Saint Martin of Antigny (Cher), nor the Gypsies of the Lower Rhine and the Pyrenees, nor the Lyselards and the Haut-ponnais in the Pas de Calais.

In following oral traditions in default of documents, we should discover in every French province "corners" distinguished by their dissimilar ethnical origins. The same phenomenon is found all over the earth.

In this way provincial psychology is also discovered to be

very complex and demands constant revision. The "ethnical fatality," false when applied to race and country and uncertain even in the case of provinces and districts, carries in itself the germs of death !

XI

As the peoples advance in history, a new factor comes in, viz. social and international imitation, the effect of which grows every day. G. Tarde has even tried to explain the age-long progress of humanity by its intervention.

Our life, in short, turns round imitation. This lies at the bottom of our social and individual activity. Man, from earliest infancy, spends his life in imitating. Animals merely follow this example. What is habit, which we call "second nature," if it is not the imitation of oneself?

The social man is a veritable somnambulist, hypnotised by all the surrounding atmosphere. Words, gestures, auditive and visual sensations, all kinds of sentiments, act on him and fashion his soul. Civilisation is only a great factory which pours forth into the world an incalculable quantity of facts and ideas to be imitated. Fashion, that is to say the imitation by some of the gestures and thoughts of others, is seen not only in the art of dressing, but also in art in general, in religion, in morals, in the way of thinking and in that of being. Our social organisation is subject to its ascendency in the same way as our morality. Place the descendants of any people whatsoever in the midst of another, and they will finally live and think like those who surround them. Lazarus tells us that the French Refugees in Prussia, although numerous, are no longer to be distinguished from the Germans either in character or intelligence. This vast "suggestion" encloses us as in a cage of brass. The dead themselves do not cease to hypnotise us. We imitate them without thinking, just as we submit to the action of past centuries. The older is our habit of imitation, the greater is its force; the more readily do we apply ourselves to it. We imitate more easily than our ancestors of a few centuries ago. Moreover, as civilisation grows, the horizon of imitation widens. We imitate, for example, many more countries, neighbours, brains and hearts.   Not only does our aptitude for imitation grow, but also our opportunities.   All our practical and moral progress tends towards the same end, viz. the *rapprochement* of peoples.

Now this causes in the first place a vast contagion.   Railroads as well as telephones and telegraphs ; science which is already international, and letters which tend to become so ; political and social institutions which unite nations across frontiers ; commerce and industry ; alliances between States and peoples ; peace and war ; the claims of social classes ; in one word, all the manifestations of our life have for final object the enlarging and facilitating of imitation.   National thought and customs which have taken the place of local thoughts and customs, evolve in their turn and become international !

Even modern criminality tends towards a sort of unity.   It grows in all civilised countries, for it develops under the influence of analogous economic and social conditions.   The black list of France becomes in this way a collective image of that of Holland, Germany, Italy or England.   We can remember with what astonishment the diminution of crime was received in this last named country.   But it was sufficient to confront the figures with the modifications of English penal law in order to perceive that this supposed amelioration was only due to a false interpretation of her penitentiary statistics.

The international register of crimes pleads thus by its uniformity for the supremacy of social conditions as compared with the voice of blood, otherwise unrecognisable and undecipherable !

Under the influence of the same "imitation," professional morality and mentality are born.   The commercial men of the civilised world, connected by analogous conceptions and laws, resemble one another more than merchants and artists living in the same country.   The unflattering picture which Spencer draws of the English merchant may be equally applied to those of Germany and France.   French, English, and German doctors and lawyers become strikingly like one another.   As the wave of the "intellectual proletariats" rises, the so-called liberal professions everywhere become debased as objects of aspiration and respectability.   There are now only semi-barbarous governments like the Russian and Turkish

Empires which would have us believe that the quality of the blood of certain peoples surpasses that of their social conditions in general and their professions in particular. The Athenian usurers of ancient Greece were equal to those of Rome, and these last were not inferior to those of modern France, Germany and Russia !

Schopenhauer has already made the remark that the superior classes have traits of resemblance all the world over, so true is it that our way of thinking and of living gives an uniform stamp to our being.

Max Nordau shows in his *Paradoxes*[1] how exceptional beings and geniuses succeed in modifying and in fashioning the state of soul of their peoples. They are for these last what superior cerebral centres are for individuals. The masses, he tells us, allow themselves to be impressed by their acts and their thoughts, and become under the influence of their suggestion either humane or bestial. How then can we speak of a national character which changes without ceasing ? The preceding generations of the German people were specially distinguished for their effeminate sentimentality and their dreamy souls ; that of to-day is remarkable for its practical aspirations and its thoughtful character. The English people were noted in the first third of the nineteenth century for their immorality ; to-day they are entirely devoted to moral improvement, temperance societies and piety. Exceptional beings thus act as hypnotisers with reference to the peoples, and direct them in the way of their own inspirations or suggestions. It is enough to recall the influence exercised by Bismarck on German mentality and morality or on the tendencies of modern Prussian politics and political parties. In another sphere poets and novelists impress vividly the soul of their readers and especially that of their fair readers. The same Nordau makes this piquant remark, that the modern Parisienne is the work of the journalists and novelists of Paris. They do exactly what they will with her both physically and

---

[1] *Paradoxes.* This work appeared in 1885 at Berlin, and consequently preceded all that has been written since on the psychology of peoples and of crowds. In a short chapter, entitled *Suggestion*, the philosopher of the *Conventional Lies of Civilisation* rails at the pretensions of the psychologists of ethnical collectivities which had already become very popular with the public and the powerful of the day. We have given above a succinct summary of it.

intellectually.   She speaks, she thinks, she feels, she acts, she even dresses herself and affects attitudes as suggested to her by her favourite writers.

Our religious ideas also leave their ineffaceable impress on our gestures, our looks and even our deportment.   An Englishman who has come into much contact with the adherents of different sects easily distinguishes them by their outward bearing.   The cult of a single idea and the infatuation for one single form of art often suffice to differentiate people.   The representatives of " Byronism," the " Parnassians " and the " Decadents," are easily recognisable.

European languages also, however divided they may be, exercise a levelling influence.   Between the tongues of Europe there is, owing to our civilisation, a continual exchanging even when it is not represented by visible loans, so that progress obtained in one particular becomes immediately the common property of all (Bréal).[1]

Congresses, which unconsciously emanate from our need of imitation and which swarm in every sphere of our scientific and social activity, in the same way as " Exhibitions" of the efforts and progress of peoples, accelerate the work of *rapproche-ment*, that is to say, the work of the " unification" of human beings.

What becomes of the psychological fatality of races under these conditions ?   Its foundations crumble, for everything seems to conspire against their solidity.   Problematic and unsubstantial as they are, the force of progress never ceases to inflict on them systematic and repeated blows.   The least scientific discovery often effects more changes than centuries of atavism.   The inventions of gun-powder, movable type and railways have destroyed more ethnical differences between races than common origins or centuries of cohabitation could or would have done.   This single consideration is enough to make barren all prophecies on the ethnical to-morrow of peoples.   Who could predict to-day the psychology of a people or peoples who had benefited by the discovery of a metal lighter than air ?

[1] *Essai de Sémantique.*

CONCLUSION

The character of a people is thus only an eternal becoming. The qualities of our soul and its aspirations are fleeting like clouds driven by the wind. They are born and are modified under the influence of innumerable causes. To speak of the stability or of the psychological fatality of peoples is like one who would make believe that circles caused on the surface of water by a falling stone retain their shape for ever. It is impossible for us to write anything durable on the ever changing page of races. Their real composition is beyond our knowledge, whilst their evolution in history, which is an incessant intermingling of eth- nical unities, laughs at all the formulas wherewith we pretend to arrange them.

Neither does geographical *milieu* alone suffice to explain the soul of a people, for man, according to Comte's happy expres- sion, socialises nature. The blood of our ancestors, becoming more and more complex with the march of generations, is neutralised by the manifold conditions of our existence. Social factors in addition contend with the influence of geographical and ethnical principles, and among their incalculable number imitation asserts itself with its immediate effect, viz. the levelling of international differences. All this revolutionises the moral and material life of peoples and races from top to bottom.

The recent progress of science actually hinders a racial psychology of the past. Everything which touches on the origins of races, and their formation or evolution, is a subject of controversy. How then can we create a true psychology of a race which should be a complete synthesis of its life and thought ? In the case of an existing ethnical group, the task is in itself paradoxical. The life of a people is attended with such a movement of phenomena that it becomes almost impossible to express them in a fixed formula. Suppose we admit that the number of data necessary to take into consideration, in order to formulate a judgment on a people or a race, does not go beyond 100, and let us then see how many chances of error we find on our path. We know from the example which has become classical that fifteen people round a table can be arranged in about

1,350,000,000,000 different ways! Now let us compare and conclude,—or rather let us abandon these disastrous experiments, which can only give chimerical results.

Racial and national unities do not lend themselves to this game of skill. What we can do at most is to confine ourselves to a " static " psychology, that is, to that of a given moment, which may be defended on the ground of curiosity, provided it be allowed that errors are inevitable.

Anthropo-psychology ought then to take leave of all dogmatism. It ought also to abstain from delivering its merciless decrees, and crushing us with its collective condemnations and apologies. What is more essential is that all its generalisations, whenever by chance they are at one with truth, can only have an ephemeral value in the case of living collectivities.

The nation of to-day is not that of yesterday or of to-morrow. In the eternal vortex of life everything evolves. The qualities of our soul are no exception. Our psychological " ego " is only a vast cemetery wherein are found buried all the metamorphosed consciences of our existence. The soul of a child is not like that of an adult, which in its turn is not like that of an old man. In the life of a people, these changes are still more accentuated and profound.

In the eternal flow of things and ideas, the souls of peoples change radically. A superior race or people becomes inferior, and *vice versâ*. A people praised for its morality becomes immoral; another deemed pacific becomes warlike; whilst a third, noble and generous, stumbles at its task and becomes barbarous and cruel. The psychological stability and fatality of peoples are not matters of this world.

All peoples evolve under the influence of external factors; consequently there are none predestined beforehand to be the masters or the slaves of others, as there are none who are predestined to an eternal immobility! Virtue and vice in peoples are only the products of circumstances. Civilisation, which tends to increase and equalise the number of those which act in a *uniform* way towards *all* peoples, produces as a direct result the increase of their similarities and the levelling of their differences.

PART IV

THE MYSTERIOUS OR UNCERTAIN ORIGINS
OF PEOPLES AND RACES

CHAPTER I

THE ARYANS, THE SUPPOSED ANCESTORS OF THE EUROPEAN
PEOPLES

WHEN we follow closely the errors committed by so many
eminent theorists with regard to prominent nations taken
individually, we can easily understand the entanglement in
which they find themselves on the matter of the racial origins
of humanity. For how can we solve the complex enigma of the
evolution of the whole human species if the scientific data which
we actually possess do not suffice to make us understand the
mystery of the ethnological formation of the most studied
groups? Our inability to explain a phenomenon is seen from the
moment when we have only a number of mutually exclusive
truths to make it clear. It is permitted us in this case not
only to arraign the premises of the judgment, but also the value
and method of the reasoning employed.

In judging the question according to the old juridical principle, viz. "Who can the most, can the least," anthropology finds
itself in a sorry plight, since, although aided by history, linguistics
geology, palethnology, ethnography, and so many other sciences,
it cannot succeed in explaining to us the origin and composition
of the leading nations! How then can it claim the right of imposing on us its solution with reference to all the subdivisions
of the human species?

We think it will be enough to examine the position of this
science towards a few leading problems touching the best known
peoples and races, in order to discredit its verdicts once and for
all on so many complex questions which it presumes to include
within its domain.

I

Whether it be Gobineau, Vacher de Lapouge, Tylor, Huxley or Pichat who are dealing with the French, English or Germans, they invariably deduce the origin of these nations directly from the Aryans. It has almost become an axiom. Following this doctrine, which is so deeply ingrained in the European mind, sociology, history, modern politics and literature never cease to oppose the Aryans to other peoples, such as the Semitic or Mongol. Our Aryan origin has become a sort of beneficial spring whence flow the high mentality of Europe and the virtues of its leading nations as opposed to other peoples, races and civilisations. When it is desired to compare in the usual sociological jargon two mentalities, or two sets of morals, the popular saying is "Aryan" and "non-Aryan." It is then supposed that all has been said. For the opposing of these two terms is held to imply a whole world of what is unexpressed. In the name of this belief the faggots have been lighted for thousands of the unfortunate who are guilty of having entered the world outside the Aryan fold and therefore against the Aryans. We see in the twentieth century the most civilised countries victims of the same superstition. The ravages which it makes in our thoughts can only be compared with a scourge which we have voluntarily summoned to afflict us. In order to maintain its vigour, new victims are daily immolated. In the theatre, in a book or a discourse, the reasoning or rather the lack of reasoning among people contaminated by the Aryan malady is always the same. They are perpetually babbling of the vices or virtues of a whole portion of humanity, though ignorant of the first foundations of its existence. The Aryan is imposed on their minds as a sort of invisible Being in whom one believes just as we do in the reality of spirits which no one has ever seen.

But when we come nearer to this dogma, the central position of which has been so long indisputable and undisputed, we perceive that we have only to do with a phantom. It disappears at the approach of impartial criticism. At the same time all the phraseology, the consequences of which are so disastrous to peace and the rational evolution of the human species, dissolves in ruins. It is only recently, however, that we have learnt that "these so-called Aryans never existed as a primitive people but only as an invention of armchair savants" (K. Hartmann), and that "the Aryan in a condition of local unity has never been discovered" (Virchow).

A century no doubt will pass away before the opinions engendered under the influence of unreflecting savants shall have disappeared in their turn. During this time abused humanity will not become weary of regarding this "discovery of the study" as an entity having a real existence.

Nevertheless, when we examine the contradictions of which the partisans of the Aryan doctrine are dupes, we are surprised at the ease with which writers who are generally very prudent have adopted an unjustifiable theory.

For no one has ever been able to show a single authentic Aryan. The descriptions of him, both moral and physical, his measurements, and also the description of his inner life, are all purely fantastical. Theories have succeeded one another according to the temperament of the writers and the fertility of their imagination. Journalists, politicians, literary men, artists, and in short the great public have with or without reason become enthusiastic about the inventions of some and against the discoveries of others. These products of a quasi-scientific imagination are received blindly without the least criticism and have moreover passed into manuals of history and instruction. To-day out of a thousand educated Europeans, 999 are persuaded of the authenticity of their Aryan origin. In the history of human errors this doctrine will some day without doubt assume a place of honour, and will serve as a decisive argument for the credulity with which both professional savants and the multitude allow themselves to be duped.

But the flagrant contradictions into which the representatives of the Aryan school have for a long time fallen should have aroused the attention of savants and men of letters. To give a simple idea of it, let us examine the most accredited principles of their doctrine.

II

We are first made to believe that a people of this name, viz. Aryan, came from Asia. They had been settled there from a remote period, especially in India and Persia. Afterwards they planted their stock in different parts of Europe. We know, according to the studies of very many distinguished palethnologists, that man appeared and evolved in ancient Gaul from the Quaternary epoch. Its first inhabitants could not have come from Asia into Europe, for the discoveries made in the caves of south-west France, as also on the banks of the Seine and Somme, prove that man lived there for numbers of centuries before the date assigned to the Asiatic immigration by the fervent believers in Aryan descent.

From this we gather that all the theories which would make of Europe a sort of colony founded by Asia considered as the real old world, appear to be ill founded. According to G. de Mortillet, man appeared in France more than 200,000 years ago. He lived there in company with two large elephants, the *Elephas antiquus* and the *Elephas meridionalis*. We only know that he possessed a single instrument, viz. a hard piece of stone roughly sharpened which now served as a weapon and now as a tool. This "punching" instrument was used directly with the hand, and man slowly and successively bettered it, cutting it with more care and with more art, and especially making it lighter. As the temperature diminished, man was driven to have recourse to clothing. A modification of the stone tool followed in consequence. Man begins to make clothes for himself out of skins. A long period of slow evolution, without intervention or foreign influences, characterises the palæolithic age, so the same author teaches us. De Mortillet even sees this persistence of local progress continuing without any intervention during the earlier and middle palæolithic epoch as well as during the Solutrian epoch. Without subscribing to all these details, which are given with so much assurance by this historian of the dark ages, let us state that he has for the reconstruction of the past as many decisive proofs as those who would show us ancient Europe as a desert peopled by Aryans. For everything is problematic and controversial in the case of these supposed ancestors of Europe. Thus, according to F. de Schlegel, they came from India to establish themselves in Europe. According to Link, they came from Asia and Georgia. According to Adolphe Pictet, the Aryans of Europe are from Bactria, and so on. But here we have a celebrated Belgian geologist, J. J. d'Omalius d'Halloy, giving the last stroke to this theory and demonstrating with the aid of ingenious arguments that the Asiatic Aryans were nothing more or less than simple Europeans. Europe, far from being conquered by the Aryans of Persia or India, sent there her fortunate conquerors. All durable conquests always proceed from West to East. Diving into the anthropological archives, d'Halloy brings another argument to bear on his theory, in demonstrating that the fair-haired as a rule prevailed in all times in Europe and only lived as exceptional types in Asia. From Europe, therefore, the fair-haired transplanted themselves into Asia! A number of savants, linguistic, geological, and anthropological, fought in favour of d'Halloy's opinion simultaneously with him and afterwards. Far from looking for the Aryan fatherland in Asia, they find it—and with what luxury of proofs!—in all parts of Europe.

Archæological discoveries which have been multiplied during fifty years have established the fact that Asiatic civilisation only influenced Europe from the thirteenth century before Christ. The finds, especially those made by Schliemann at Troy, and those of Mycenæ, Tiryns, Cyprus and Egypt, leave no doubt on this subject. At the time when the West came into contact with the East, its civilisation was already ancient by long centuries. It is thus that the dolmens of Northern Germany are of more ancient origin than those discovered in India. The bronze industry had prospered throughout the whole Mediterranean basin, and the swords exhumed in divers parts of France with handles of wood, gold and horn, are of the same type as those found at Mycenæ. Bronze, far from being invented in India, came only from Alexandria. The first cradle of civilisation, the knowledge of which we owe to the sciences of the past, appears everywhere as European, and it is only the second cradle which is of Oriental origin.

Clemence Royer tells us that the famous Aryan tongue was

originally formed and spoken in Europe, whence it penetrated into Persia and India through the Caucasus. This language was the special creation of the fair-haired peoples of Europe, and if the brown folk of Asia also spoke it, they must have learnt it from fair-haired European immigrants. Among celebrated linguists, Benfey declares in favour of the country situated between the mouth of the Danube and the Caspian Sea as the cradle of the Aryan language, civilisation and race. This savant tells us that since geology proves that Europe has been inhabited from time immemorial, all the explanations in favour of Asiatic immigration into Europe fall to the ground.

Moreover, recent researches give the last word to sceptics. Thus we perceive that Indian writing descends in direct line from the Greek and Aramaic alphabets, and that the Greek tongue is not the daughter of Sanskrit as it has been for a long time believed. The *Avesta*, which ought to constitute one of the most ancient literary monuments of the past, dates, according to James Darmesteter, only from the third century after Christ, whilst the famous *Vedas* are not primitive songs going back to the dawn of humanity, but learned works of a thousand years before Christ, redacted and versified twelve centuries later.[1]

Louis Geiger and Lœher even tried to prove that the Aryan fatherland was the centre and the west of Germany; according to Tomaschek, it was Eastern Europe; according to Th. Koeppen it was the west of Europe; and according to Penka the south of Sweden. Let us remark, however, that all Greek legends agree in making the Ionians, Achaians and Hellenes to have come from the north. As for the Thracians, who preceded them there, they likewise are said to have had a northern origin.

III

Among the anthropologists and naturalists we perceive the same dissensions. If Virchow holds for the East, Topinard declares in favour of Europe, and Huxley for the country between the

---

[1] Bergaigne, *La Religion védique.*

Ural and the North Sea. Pietrement, on the other hand, decides for the south-west of Siberia, Clemence Royer for Pelasgian Thrace on the borders of the Danube. V. Hehn defends the Asiatic theory entirely, and still another botanist and celebrated geographer, Jules de Klaproth, who wrote long before Hehn, concludes in favour of the North.

Some speak of Bactria, a legendary country of Paradise which has never existed, whilst others insist on the plateau of Pamir, a real country, as the land of the primitive dispersion of the Aryans.

But when we begin to study this fabulous country closer, we soon discover that it was scarcely habitable !

Among the philologists the contradictions are no less considerable. If according to Fr. Müller the south-west of Europe is the starting-point of many Aryan ramifications, according to Schlegel, Pott, Jacob Grimm, Lassen, Pictet, &c., it could only be Central Asia. Otto Schrader [1] declares in favour of the south-east of European Russia, near the middle course of the Volga. Taking his stand on a number of analogous words, he concludes that the cradle of the Aryans before their dispersion was a land of steppes. He notes among other peculiarities that the Aryans knew but few plants of the forest. It results from this that there could have been no forests where they lived. According to H. Hirt, their habitat could only have been near the Baltic. According to Cuno, the Aryan land extended from the Black Sea to the plains of Northern France, and from the Ural mountains to the Atlantic. M. Bréal,[2] on the contrary, says that the books of the Avesta, which have contributed so much to the formation of all sorts of theories, furnish us in reality with no serious basis either for the geography or the history of our Aryan ancestors. It is the first chapter (*fargard*) of the Vendidad (the first book of the Avesta) which has perhaps been the principal cause of the evil. In the enumeration of the countries which Ormuzd (addressing Zoroaster) pretends to have created, figures first the *Aryana-Vaeja* (*vaeja*, source, land of sources). As a result of the works of Rhode, Haug, Lassen, &c., one has wished to see in the *Aryana* the cradle of the Aryans.

[1] *Sprachvergleichung und Urgeschichte.*
[2] *Mélanges de linguistique et de Mythologie.*

Consequently we cannot affirm positively that the Aryans ever existed.

Even admitting that they did exist, did they really come into Europe ? Now, although lacking scientific proof as regards their real existence, savants have not hesitated to furnish us with pictures of their social organisation and their inner life. They have even been so kind as to provide us with all sorts of details concerning their physical appearance, favourite occupations and moral tendencies ! !

According to Huxley and Poesche they were big, fair and dolichocephalic. According to Isaac Taylor, the European Aryans, whom he identifies with the Celts, were big and short-headed. According to Pictet, the Aryans were a young and strong people devoted to agriculture and cattle-rearing. Their family life was very much developed and was distinguished by many Biblical virtues. According to Schrader, they were barbarous and ignorant and were acquainted only with copper among the metals. According to Quatrefages, the Aryans were of two types, viz. long and short heads. Whereas for some (Tylor, Taylor and Koeppen) they were of the same origin as the Finns, for others (Kremer, Hommel, &c.) they started from a point in Mesopotamia between the Oxus and the Jaxartes where they lived with the Semites.

They were big, dolichocephalic and fair, so preach Gobineau and his disciples. They were brown and small, so Sergi says. And when Ujfalvy went to see the celebrated Galtchas in the highland valley of Zerafchan (1876–1878), who are deemed the purest descendants of the genuine Aryans, he found among them fair, brown, brachycephalic, dolichocephalic, big and small ! ! Whom then can we trust ?

IV

According to certain savants, the Aryans rose on a Semitic basis, and according to others, like Tomaschek, their civilisation was borrowed from Finns and Tartars.

When it is a matter of recounting the details of their

migrations and the conditions in which they gave birth to the European nations, we fall again into a chaos of contradictory hypotheses. There were in Western Europe, Huxley tells us, in neolithic times four human types : the small with long heads (Iberians), the big with short heads (Celts), the big with long heads (Scandinavians), and the small with short heads (Ligurians). The Celts were pure Aryans and the other three were Aryanised.

According to Schleicher, a branch of the Asiatic Aryans entered Southern Europe and afterwards divided into three groups, the Greeks, Albanians and Italo-Celts. The Italians settled in Italy and the Celts in Gaul. We saw above that they are sometimes identified with the Semites and sometimes with the Finns, &c.

These strange contradictions resting on fantastical data, this general post of theories and hypotheses, which mutually annul one another, has little by little destroyed the belief in Aryans as the real ancestors of the Celts, and the many other branches of European peoples. We understand at last that the Aryan dogma was only based on a misunderstanding, viz. the existence of certain analogies between languages called Aryan and certain Asiatic and European languages.

We know that all languages may be summed up into these three groups, monosyllabic, agglutinative, and inflected idioms. Monosyllabism is without doubt the first evolutionary phase of every tongue, where we have independent and isolated roots, a certain number of which is required to form a phrase. At present it is represented by Chinese, Annamite, Siamese, Thibetan and Burmese.

In the agglutinative or agglomerate tongues, there are united to the principal root, which preserves its value, other syllables placed before (prefix), or after the said root (suffix), which thus modify its meaning. These composites thus created express all sorts of combinations of ideas and of relations. Among the agglutinative tongues we must count Finnish, Turkish, Basque, Japanese, Korean, and the Dravidian of India ; those spoken in the greater part of Africa from the Sahara to the Cape ; those of the various Oceanic islands ; and also those of the Negritos.

The third phase in the evolution of languages gives them the peculiarity of varying their roots. In languages with flexion the roots are no longer immobile and rigid, but "flexible," changing according to the circumstances. Three great families of languages enter into this group. First the Hamitic tongues, spoken in Northern Africa (Egyptian, Libyan and Ethiopian); then the Semitic languages (Arabic, Phœnician, Hebrew and Syriac); and lastly the branch of languages called Indo-European.

Now, after the science of philology had shown the striking analogy between the languages spoken in Europe and those of India, it was concluded that their origin was identical. According to A. Pictet,[1] who exercised a very lasting influence on the Aryan doctrine, the migration of peoples and also their descent are very simple matters. We must consider, as the starting-point, the place where the language from which the others are derived was spoken. This place was no other than Aryana, the vast plateau of Iran, the immense quadrilateral district which extends from the Indus to the Tigris and the Euphrates, and from the Oxus and the Jaxartes to the Persian Gulf. Here the initial language, Sanskrit, the mother tongue, was spoken. From this place the Aryans departed, and according to the purity of the language of each people, the date of its arrival was deduced. The vast Sanskrit or Indo-European family includes, according to Pictet, the Hindoo or Sanskrit, the Iranian, the Hellenic, the Italic, the Celtic, the Germanic, the Slavonic and the Lettic. Naturally behind these spoken languages, Pictet and his school did not forget those who spoke them. It is thus that, being in need of an hypothesis which would explain the relationship of a number of languages, they invented the romance of the migration of a mysterious people, namely, the Aryans, who carried their tongue all over the world, and who gave birth to different European peoples. But according to modern linguistics (see among others the works of Schrader) it is deemed necessary to repudiate this fantasy created and accepted with a light heart, and to condemn strongly the conception of the *Aryan race*. It is, in short, only a matter of *a family of Aryan tongues,* which does not suppose an Aryan

[1] *Les Origines indo-européennes ou les Aryens primitifs.*

people.   Has not the experience of modern and ancient peoples taught us that it is not permissible to identify races and languages?   The Latin tongue took possession of Gaul, but that does not say that the Gauls became Romans.   We see entire peoples adopting languages introduced or imposed from outside, without there being any manifest change in their ethnical origin.

We cannot even indicate exactly the filiation of **Aryan** tongues !

Here, for example, is the Etruscan language, which has played so important a part in the distant past.   Is it of Aryan origin ? According to Corssen, the Etruscan was only an Italic dialect, whereas according to Yanelli, Tarquini and Stickel, it belongs to the Semitic group.   According to S. Bugge, it shows a distinct relationship to Armenian, whilst for Sayce and Victor Henry the two are quite different.   Fligier tells us that, ethnically and philologically, the Etruscans have literally nothing in common with the Aryan peoples.   According to Tylor, the Etruscans are of Altaic origin; according to Brinton their tongue is only a Libyan idiom.

It would be fastidious to desire to remove the mountains of contradictions which divide the philologists in their explanations of the origins of other Aryan tongues.   Let us rather insist on this remark of Max Muller.   "The ethnologist who speaks of the Aryan race, the Aryan blood, the Aryan eyes or hair, is guilty of a heresy equal to that of which a linguist would be guilty if he spoke of a dolichocephalic dictionary or a brachycephalic grammar."

Aryan therefore only expresses a link of relationship between certain tongues.   When Fr. Schlegel for the first time (1808) recognised the numerous resemblances between the languages spoken between India and Germany, he proposed to call them *Indo-Germanic*, a name adopted by Pott, Benfey, &c.

Bopp thought it more practical to call them *Indo-European*. It was decided later to substitute the word *Aryan* as shorter and more expressive in order to designate this vast family of languages.

In lightly transporting this term into the domain of races,

we have been successively offered *Indo-Germanic, Indo-European,* and *Aryan,* expressions which are equal to one another, that is to say, which are equal to nothing.

V

It is, therefore, only a matter of a language and not of skulls, bones and hair.   But more!   For the cult of the Aryan tongue has undergone rude assaults.   To-day it is only for us an innate fetishism.   Easily disposed to believe in the supernatural, we readily adopted the miraculous origin of language.   According to many philologists, it could only have been an inspiration from on high.   This belief had numerous adepts, especially in Germany.   Some even supposed an unique tongue taught by divinity itself of which the modern idioms were degenerate descendants.   Others assured us that a special intuition was granted to certain privileged peoples like the Hebrews, Greeks and Hindoos.[1]   Perfection was universal at the beginning of things as the fruit of revelation, instinct or spontaneity.   As Grimm and Humboldt preached this doctrine with regard to the evolution of language, Creuzer applied it to the history of religions, Savigny to law in general, and Stahl more especially to political law.   The ideal Aryan tongue altogether benefited by this supreme disdain of reason, to the advantage of a mysticism which made ravages throughout all the sciences.

The languages, however, which the Europeans spoke who were settled in Gaul in the Quaternary epoch may have evolved under the influence of circumstances, and may have approached the Sanskrit.   Do we not see in the same way the Basque language, which is agglutinative, existing outside the whole influence of the other Indo-European tongues ?

The generic term " Aryan " seems all the more extravagant in that it is considered to include at least three clearly distinct types, viz. (1) the ancient Pelasgi and the ancient Iberi, who were small and brown with long heads ; (2) the big and fair with blue eyes, long skull, rosy complexion, viz. the Germani, Kymri

---

[1] M. Bréal.   *Essai de Sémantique.*

and Gauls ; (3) Celts and Slavs, with brown hair going from brown with light coloured eyes to fair with greyish complexion, long bust, and round head.

At the time of their appearance these three types are already very distinct from one another. How then could they have come from the same country and have the same ethnical origins ? If, moreover, we are obliged to admit that they had undergone such radical modifications in so short a time, is not that a condemnation of the most venerable principles of classical anthropology ?

In the face of all these irreconcilable contradictions, can we still decently speak of an " Aryan race " or of " Aryan descent," and oppose certain un-Aryan or non-Aryan elements which constitute a portion of the European population, to really " Aryan " elements which have never existed ?

This discovery, humiliating to the good sense both of those who propagate it and of those captivated by it, once buried out of sight, let us try to bury another misconception which has made nearly as many dupes as the Aryan myth.

CHAPTER II

THE GAULS AND THE GERMANIC PEOPLES

WE never cease to identify the two terms, French and Gaulish, German (*allemand*) and Germanic. Whereas the French are proud of thinking of the blood of Celtic Gauls which flows in their veins, the Germans on the other side of the Rhine think that they are obliged to hate in the French this very Celtic blood as being that of their age-long adversaries. Thus there is ingrained from time immemorial in the mind of the two peoples a conviction as to the difference in their origin, mentality and historic destiny. Do not ask from one or the other any justification for their animosity. One would think that they believed it to be almost instinctive quite apart from the misunderstandings and the quarrels of the moment. Have they not read in more or less serious books, and this for centuries, that from all time Gauls and Germans dwelt in separate camps and that each race had virtues and customs diametrically opposed to those of the other? They have ended in believing in facts, the genuineness of which has never to their knowledge been suspected. This belief going from father to son has become almost a legacy. All the incidents of life are commented on according to this precious dogma, and to-day it appears a sacrilege to express the least doubt that the French are the direct heirs of the Gauls or that the Germans are the descendants of the old Germanic folk. Now, in examining this theory in what concerns France and the French, we will demonstrate its inanity. Once we break up the Gaulish building, the Germanic structure will tumble down of its own accord.

I

In the present state of science there is no way of disputing the fact that France was inhabited in palæolithic and neolithic times. Man precedes the glacial period, the duration of which period alone extends approximately from 150,000 to 200,000 years. And we know that France has been the field of all sorts of discoveries of human bones dating from palæolithic times. Thus twelve years before the discovery of the cranial brain-pan of Néanderthal in 1841, there were discovered in the Haute-Loire (near Puy), in a bed of muddy lava of the ancient volcano of Denise, human fossils composed of many bones, teeth, cranial brain-pans, &c., all showing clearly defined Néanderthalian characteristics. The famous lower jawbone exhumed by Bourret and Régnault in 1889 in Ariège (near Montséron) has been attributed to the old palæolithic epoch. Many other discoveries in France, especially in the domain of palethnology, similar to those made in Belgium, confirm this opinion that France must have been inhabited from the most ancient times. Let us not, like certain palethnologists, try to find the anthropological qualities of these first inhabitants. Imagination, which never loses its rights in the science of the past, has made anthropological savants say, now that they were folk of the Néanderthal [1] race, now that they belonged only to the Laugerie race, who were settled in France much later, but in any case from the neolithic epoch.

The first were short, thick set, thick boned, and below the average height. Among those of the Laugerie race, the superciliary arches, so developed in the cranial brain-pan of Néanderthal, were much feebler. The high part of the skull forms a kind of vault, the chin is not so receding, and the thick and rounded shinbones of the men of Néanderthal are much flatter. Both according to this fine science are dolichocephalic. Were

---

[1] There was found, in 1856, in the Düssel valley between Düsseldorf and Elberfeld, near the ravine of Néanderthal, a human skeleton embedded in clay. A hundred feet from this place was found a grotto of the débris of rhinoceros, hyæna, and wolf. People have wished to see in this cranial brain-pan the remains of the first man living in this neighbourhood. The skull of Néanderthal had its superciliary arches very much developed, a low retreating forehead, the back part of the head very much widened, &c.

the Laugerie race the product of the simple evolution of that of Néanderthal, or were they invaders? Here is a mystery. Nothing can elucidate it unless it be the Supreme Force which has presided over all these evolutions! But as this Supreme Force thinks it wiser not to interfere with this kind of discussion, we find courageous savants stepping in. They proceed to discuss seriously concerning these facts of the past, guarding themselves the while against communicating to us the impenetrable reason for the formation of their convictions. Let us admit then, as our fancy bids us, all the phases of the evolution of the Néanderthalians and Laugerians, transformed in their turn into the people of Cro-Magnon,[1] popularised by Paul Broca, or the race of Baumes-Chaudes, favoured by Georges Hervé.

Whatever may be our conviction on this subject, it cannot hinder us from admitting that long before the appearance of Gauls on French soil there were other peoples and races who had been settled there for a long time. This is the essential point.

Prehistoric anthropology (otherwise called palethnology) even tells us that there was a period when all the population of France was exclusively dolichocephalic. Since we find in the neolithic epoch numerous brachycephalic folk, these could only have come from the outside. G. de Mortillet goes so far as to tell us with singular clairvoyance that " in prehistoric times, at the end of the palæolithic and at the beginning of the neolithic epochs, the greatest social revolution which ever happened, took place in France." Let us not sadden with our scepticism the believing souls of palethnologists. Let us wisely confine ourselves to saving out of all these complications of the past

---

[1] Paul Broca studied in 1868 in the shelters of Cro-Magnon in a little grotto in Dordogne, quite near the station of Eyzies (whence the name d'Eyziens), three human skeletons, one woman, one old man, and one adult. According to the description of Broca, these bones show dolichocephalic skulls and tall stature. The woman's thigh bone was very wide and of fabulous thickness, and both had wide and bulging foreheads. Thus Broca invented a special race of Cro-Magnon. A few years afterwards, in the sepulchral grottos of the Lozère, known as Baumes-Chaudes, the bones of about 300 dolichocephalic subjects were found, and near them several flint arrowheads and a few bronze objects. According to the anthropologists, the men of Baumes-Chaudes are very much like those of Cro-Magnon. Their height is 1 metre 61, their cephalic index varies between 64·3 and 75·1 ; the horizontal circumference of the skull, 543 and 533 millimetres for men and women respectively, the mean nasal index, 42·7, &c., &c.

the one certain fact that France was inhabited at the end of the
palæolithic epoch. We are even willing to shift this epoch for
people who are more incredulous, to the commencement of the
neolithic period.

II

The most serious historians who try to grasp the physiognomy
of France in the later periods represent it to us as originally
peopled with Ligurians. Who were these Ligurians ? Did they
come from the outside or were they but the descendants of the
primitive people who occupied the country in palæolithic and
neolithic times ? Opinions are very much divided, and it would
be more than risky to try to harmonise them. The poverty of
documents authorises all suppositions and does not suffer us to
adopt any one entirely ! For it must be acknowledged that the
data of French history before the eighth or ninth century B.C.
are as little precise as those of prehistoric times. We are told
of a certain movement of peoples which towards the tenth or
eleventh centuries B.C. entered the Mediterranean lands, but
opinions vary as to their origin, importance, route or ethnical
peculiarities. Everything is reduced to the fact that a displace-
ment took place.

When we examine more closely this Ligurian question, we
come to the conclusion that a people of that name must have
existed. In the time of Hesiod that name was given to the inhabitants of the countries situated towards the north-west of
Greece. They must also have been very numerous, for traces of
them are found not only in Gaul but also in Italy, Corsica, the
Netherlands and Spain. If the suppositions of the philologists
were well founded, we would have another element in favour
of the ethnical unity of the greater part of the European
peoples. What pleads for this doctrine is notably this theory so
ardently maintained by many authoritative philologists, viz.
that the language of the Ligurians had the peculiarity of
forming the names of mountains, rivers and inhabited places
in general by the use of the suffixes —*asco*, —*asca*, —*usko*,
—*uska*, —*osko*, —*oska*. In using this point, many of our savants,
after having found in France many places with names formed
in this way, conclude that the Ligurians made a prolonged

stay in these parts. But the presence of these same Ligurians in Italy has been proved, viz. on the shores of the Gulf of Genoa, where there still exists a mountain called *Pescasco* and rivers called *Carisasca*, *Sermichiasca*, &c. They also held Liguria, Piedmont, Emilia, Lombardy in the southern part of the Po basin, where are found about seventy names of places with the characteristic suffix of the Ligurians. They were also very numerous in Bavaria and in Portugal.

Without being able to solve the Ligurian mystery as we have been able to do in the case of so many other clouds which hang over the anthropological past of France, we must nevertheless admit the real existence of this people who entered Gaul long before the Celts, the Germanic peoples or the Normans. In our inability to provide an approximate number of these folk or their physiological description, let us confine ourselves to admitting the substantial portion of Ligurian blood in the composition of the French people.

The principal Ligurian tribes according to Polybius, Strabo, Pliny, Ptolemy, &c., were at first the Deciates (Antibes), the Ligaunes and the Olybes. Let us add the Sallyes (Salxuvii with their captial Aquæ Sextiæ, now Aix), the Vulgentes, Quariates, the Libiques, the Voconces, &c. West of the Rhone, the historians also show us many Ibero-Ligurian tribes and among others the Elezikes, occupying the Aude, the land where later rose the town of Narbonne ; in the eastern Pyrenees, the Sardones, whose chief town was Ruscino (Perpignan) and Illiberis (Elne). In the mountains dwelt the Consueranians, &c.

The time is doubtless far off when it will be possible to gauge the influence of this great Ligurian migration to which all the historians refer without being able to give precise details. It is in no way, however, detrimental to our theory, but quite on the contrary. For in adopting it, it must also be admitted that on the first ethnical stratum other strata superimposed themselves. When we come at last to the Gauls and to the more precise facts which accompany their appearance, we understand better that the latter could not have radically changed the composition of the ethnical elements of the country, considering their very limited number and their incessant peregrinations outside the frontiers of ancient Gaul.

III

What, in short, was this Gaul which La Tour d'Auvergne wished to consider as the cradle of humanity, and whose language as the mother language of all others?   According to this savant and his partisans, Gaul ought to claim all the rights which historians and linguists wrongly bestow on the mysterious Asiatic Aryana.   When it is a matter of defining the frontiers of Gaul, we are very much embarrassed.   Julius Cæsar [1] has included it within the Rhine and the Alps towards the east, the Atlantic towards the west, the Channel towards the north, and the Pyrenees and Mediterranean towards the south.   But the real Gaul extended far beyond these fictitious frontiers, and as D'Arbois de Jubainville explains with reason, one went to Rome for administrative purposes, for a precise geographical nomenclature and particularly for one which did not include too great an extension of territories.[2]   In reality the Gauls extended throughout the greater part of ancient Europe and even founded settlements in Asia Minor (Galatia).   At the time in which historians place the first conquest of the Gauls in ancient Gaul, about 600 B.C., another Celtic branch, the Goidels, had lived for over two centuries in the British Isles.   After having taken the south of the Netherlands and a great part of France and of Belgium, they invaded the Iberic peninsula and occupied it.

It is curious how history repeats itself!   Just as the English annexed the Transvaal for its rich mines of gold, the Goidels overcame Great Britain in times gone by because of its tin mines. Another Gaulish branch ventured into the Iberic peninsula for its mines of tin mixed with silver!

Towards the fourth century the Gauls established themselves successively in all the countries between the Danube and the Alps.   These vast territories constitute to-day the southern parts of Bavaria, Würtemburg and a great part of Austria (Styria,

[1] *De Bello Gallico.*
[2] See on the subject of Gauls and Celts the very remarkable works of the same author, viz., *les Premiers Habitants de l'Europe ; les Celtes ;* also those of Gaston Paris, viz. *Romania ; Cæsar, De Bello Gallico ; Tacitus, Germania ; Paul Broca, Mémoires de la Société d'Anthropologie* (Vol. I.) ; Am. Thierry, *Histoire des Gaulois,* &c., &c.

High and Low Austria, Salzburg, Carinthia, and lastly the south-west part of Hungary). They afterwards occupied a part of the Venetian territory, and invaded Italy. Pushed and worried by the Germanic peoples, they afterwards retreated towards the Balkan peninsula. The Tectosages, a Gaulish tribe, even succeeded in conquering, in Asia Minor, the little Gaul, viz. Galatia. In Italy their progress was more rapid. According to Livy, three Gaulish tribes settled towards the north of the Po, and three others to the south of this river.[1] When later (between 197 and 189) the Gauls were vanquished in their turn by the Romans, we find that they possessed towns like Bologne (Bononia), Parma and Modena (Mutina). Not satisfied with all these peregrinations, they pushed as far as Udine, where a Gaulish people settled under the name of *Carni*. Italy, Spain, the Balkans, anywhere satisfied them. In the epoch during which the Gaulish Empire flourished (figuratively speaking, of course, for there never was an Emperor or even any unity of as-pirations, or sentiments of relationship between the many Gaulish nations) Bohemia also became their prey, as also Servia, Bulgaria and Roumania. They are even met with in Russia on the banks of the Dniester, where they founded a town, *Carro-Dunum*, and on the Bug. A Gaulish people, *Scordisei*, settled before all others in the north of the Balkans; afterwards the Gauls conquered the numerous Illyrians and Thracians living in the territory held to-day by Bosnia and Herzegovina, and later they pushed as far as the Black Sea.

IV

The Gauls also settled in Germany. They planted their stock in the centre and the south. Those Gauls who invaded France in the third century arrived directly from the basin of the Neckar and the Main. Julius Cæsar even affirms in a formal way that the Gaulish tribe *Uolcæ Tectosages*, which lived near Toulouse, had numerous representatives in Germany in the neighbourhood of the Hyrcanian forest. The Gauls enjoyed there, so Cæsar adds, a great reputation owing to their justice

---

[1] The Cenomani, the Salluvii, and the Insubres in the north, and the Boii and the Lingones in the south.

and courage. Now this country mentioned in the *De Bello Gallico* comprises the territory between northern Bavaria, royal and ducal Saxony, and Silesia. It is in Upper Silesia that Tacitus finds a Gaulish people called Cotini.

If the name of the Germanic peoples was only known to the Greeks in the first century before Christ, if again, at the time of the invasion of the Cimbri and the Teutones, the Romans considered these two Germanic peoples as Gauls (even according to Cicero, *De oratore*, the Cimbri were a Gaulish people), it was because the Germanic folk had submitted to the Gauls for many centuries, and were politically confounded with them. The Gaulish invasion has left numerous traces in the life, language, and manners of Germania. Let us recall at this point that Tacitus speaks of the Helvetii as a Gaulish tribe living near the Rhine and the Main. In Germania there were also, according to the same author, Gothoni, speaking Gaulish, and Esthyeni, living on the southern coast of the Baltic, whose tongue was like that of the Celtic Breton.

When we reflect on these vast ramifications which the Gaulish tree pushed out into Europe in all directions, it is clear that unless one wishes to be "paradoxical," it becomes impossible to affirm that Gaul was France and that the Gauls were French. How many European countries are there, without speaking of an Asiatic land, which could not claim the benefit of the same favour or privilege—if it be a favour or privilege!

It is true that one could reply that all these peregrinations were for the purpose of conquest. But can we then forget that the Gauls were not the natives in France? If they came there, it was only for the same reason which drove other conquerors in all the directions of the world.

What is still more important is that at the time of Julius Cæsar's invasion, that is, in the midst of Gaulish prosperity, France counted among its inhabitants three peoples differing in manners, tongue and even in race.[1] The Aquitani lived between the Garonne, the Pyrenees and the Ocean; the Belgæ between the Seine and the Rhine; and the Gauls in the other provinces, from the Garonne to the Seine and from the Alps to the Atlantic. According to the anthropologists, the Aquitani belonged to a race with black hair whose type is now preserved among the modern Basques. The Gauls were divided into two distinct groups, the Galli and the Kymri.[1] The latter came from the Black Sea and constitute what we are agreed to call the Belgians. Whereas these last had light eyes and fair hair, so Thierry tells us, the Galli had brown or black hair and eyes. Following Thierry, the historians have recounted real romances on the respective life of the Aquitani, the Kymri and the Galli, and we are even told that *already* at that period they were mixed by way of marriage and were undergoing reciprocal influences.

We must not forget the existence of the autochthonous race, the Ligurians, of whom we have already found numerous and imperishable traces. All these ethnographical elements have to be combined, and even supposing that there were no other forgotten elements, they furnish us with a singular opinion of the "Gaulish" doctrine which reduces Gaul to France and identifies the French with the Gauls.

V

Something better follows. We know that in the third century B.C. the Gaulish power was the butt of attacks directed against it from every side. The Germanic peoples, Romans, Greeks and Carthaginians endeavoured by a number of invasions to crush the Gauls and to reduce them to slavery. Those of Italy had to fight against the Romans; those of the Balkans against the Greeks; those of the Iberian peninsula against the Carthaginians, and finally those of ancient France had to defend themselves at the same time against the Germanic peoples, the Romans, and afterwards the Normans. The Germanic and Norman tribes, profiting by the disunion of the Gaulish people, often joined themselves with certain Gaulish tribes in order to exterminate others. The Cimbri and the Teutones, Germanic peoples, allied themselves with two Gaulish peoples, viz. the Helvetii and the Tigutini, living in the modern lands of Baden, Würtemburg and Bavaria, and, strengthened in this way, they threw themselves on Gaul. After having inflicted many disasters on the Romans,

[1] Am. Thierry, *Histoire des Gaulois.*

they afterwards invaded Italy itself. If the Celtic period of Gaul gave way to that of the Roman conquest effected during the first centuries before and after Christ, this in its turn gave way to that of the Germanic invasion which was strengthened by the great migration of peoples (from the second to the sixth century A.D.).   Moreover, the following centuries did not bring the much desired peace to Europe, bleeding and torn in pieces.   But before examining the ethnical elements which all these turmoils brought into France, let us pause a moment before the Roman wars which devastated Gaul and had a decisive influence on its destinies.

We note in the first place that the Gauls, an added stratum like the Ligurians and the Aquitani, were for the most part destroyed during these deadly wars. " During eight years of war (Plutarch tells us) Cæsar had taken by storm more than 800 towns, subjugated 300 tribes and vanquished 3,000,000 fighters, of whom a million had perished in battle and a million had been reduced to slavery."

The silence of decay and death, H. Martin tells us, reigned then in Gaul.   The number of soldiers is no doubt exaggerated, but seeing that the condition of warriors was held in such high honour in Gaul, and that the circumstances were so critical, it may be admitted in principle that a third of the population able to carry arms disappeared, and that another third was taken away elsewhere.

The process of Gaulish extermination, begun under Cæsar, assumes frightful proportions during the first ten centuries after Christ.

During the interminable period in which the barbaric invasions succeeded each other with unparalleled ferocity, the soil of Gaul was strewn with numerous corpses of newcomers and also especially with those of the unfortunate inhabitants of the country. France became at that time a cemetery and a sort of funereal route, selected by all sorts of people who were thirsting for lands and riches.

We even find Mongolian Russians and Semitic Arabs coming in their turn in the same way as the Germanic and Norman invaders. The Wisigoths settled in Aquitaine, the Burgundians between the Rhone and the Loire; the Franks installed themselves everywhere, whilst the Normans took possession of the north of France.

Why speak to us any more of Gaulish blood dominating in France when we remember that towards the fifth century the Germanic invaders not only spoiled the land of its riches but transformed it into a desert, carrying into captivity all its able-bodied inhabitants ?

Henri Martin even tells us that in 406 they took away so many Gauls that the Belgian cities, according to the expression of a contemporary, *were transferred into Germania.* *There were no more seen in the country either flocks, trees or harvests.*

The first Germanic invasion took place about a century before Christ. This Cimbric inundation lasted fourteen years and cost the Romans the loss of five consular years. The immigrations succeed one another up to the time when Marius inflicted a great defeat on the Germanic barbarians near Aix in 102.

Besides the Cimbri and the Teutones, another Germanic people, the Suevi, also made an irruption into Gaul.

VI

We know almost nothing concerning the ethnical origin of the Germanic peoples. The whole of our knowledge is based on ancient authors who furnish us with nothing but contradictory information. For if according to Tacitus they were a separate people and very ancient, according to many other contemporary writers before and after Tacitus they were merely Celts.

When it is a question of indicating the ethnical character of the inhabitants on either side of the Rhine, we find historians contradicting one another in a singular way. Thus according to the four most trustworthy authors there were on the two sides of the Rhine :—

	Left Bank.		Right Bank.
Cæsar	Gauls.	Celts.	Germanic.
Dionysius of Halicarnassus	Galates		Germanic.
Diodorus of Sicily	Celts		Galates.
Dion Cassius	Galates		Celts.

Let us also remember that the arguments given by Tacitus in favour of a separate Germanic race, which arguments are drawn from their physiological appearance and also from their manners, apply equally to the Gauls. Thus the fair complexion, the fair hair, the striking courage and many other traits which Tacitus uses to construct a Germanic type, Livy and Polybius use to present us with a Gaulish type! Beginning with poets like Virgil and ending with Claudian, many were the writers who praised " the fair-haired Germania " and also the " fair and tall " Gauls, which proves how difficult it was even in Cæsar's time to find clearly distinct types and to make a collective psychology of peoples !

What is more certain is that the inhabitants of Germania invaded Gaul by land, rivers and even by sea. The most ardent and also those who left the most durable traces in Gaul were without doubt the Burgundians and the Franks. The first were part of the *Vindils* or *Vandals* who occupied the northeast of Germania. Driven back by Probus in the second half of the third century, they joined the Romans in 370 under Valentinian. The Romans succeeded in attracting them pacifically into Gaul in view of thus winning interested defenders against the barbarians. Lands were conceded to them and little by little their stock was established in the provinces between the Moselle, the Vosges mountains and the Rhine. Owing to the force of circumstances and as a result of unsuccessful battles against the Huns towards the middle of the fifth century, the Burgundians were obliged to retreat towards Ain and Savoy. In the sixth century they completely lost their independence and were incorporated into the Frankish kingdom.

As to the Franks, they only appear two centuries after the Burgundians. Of a much more mysterious origin than the other ·Germanic folk, we find the earliest traces of them only in 240 in the work of Flavius Vopiscus dedicated to the tribune Aurelian. Sometimes beaten and driven back by the Romans and sometimes victorious in their innumerable incursions, it may be said that the motto of the Franks was " Always to the front." They never ceased to place their landmarks in Gaul until the decisive moment when in 438, under their chief, Clodion, they succeeded in taking possession of a great part of the country. Clovis, who succeeded Clodion, beat back successively the Romans, the Alamanni, the Burgundians, and the Wisigoths. Under the rule of his successors they succeeded in transforming Gaul into a kingdom of Franks.

Besides these two peoples called Germanic, a dozen others invaded Gaul incessantly. Naturally their advent was followed by all the incidents which characterised the barbarous wars of other times, the violation and enslavement of women, the murder and sale of adults and children, &c. All this must have strongly modified the ethnical composition of the population By way of the Rhine came first the Alamanni, who settled on the left bank in Alsace and Lorraine. Piratical Saxons made incursions on the coasts of Gaul. The Vandals, a Germanic tribe according to some (Pliny and Tacitus), Sarmatian or Slav according to others (Lagneau, *Anthropologie de la France*), made several cruel invasions into Gaul during the first half of the sixth century. The Barbarians in retiring always left a part of their army in the land which they had invaded. Sometimes allured by the fertility of the soil and sometimes desirous of enjoying the fortunes they had acquired by pillaging, or simply weary of the hard work of soldiers, they settled in the new country and broke off every tie with their old life. There were thus in France towards the end of the fifth century numerous colonies founded by Alans, the allies of the Vandals, on either bank of the Loire and in a part of Armorica. These Alans were, according to Pliny, merely Scythians! During the fifth century Gaul was also the prey of the Huns and the Wisigoths. The first have no doubt left but few traces in the composition of the Gaulish blood, but it was otherwise with the Wisigoths, to whom Honorius ceded in 418 Aquitaine and Toulouse. In the place of the Gauls who perished in great numbers in battle or else were transplanted into Germany, numerous Germanic folk took possession. Nearly all these principal tribes planted their stock there. The country, however, was so devastated and the population was so thin that the blood of the Germanic people was bound to replace abundantly that of the Gauls.

VII

The Normans continued the work of destruction undertaken by so many predecessors.   It was all the easier in that they met with only few obstacles.   The north and south of France were equally devastated and equally defenceless.

" On one occasion two hundred Normans ventured as far as Paris, meeting with no obstacle.   No one arrived to bar their way " (Sismondi).

The author of the *Histoire générale du Languedoc* (Paris, 1730, Vol. I.) tells us again that the greatest desolation reigned in the south of France.   The inhabitants were scattered and the towns ruined.   The lands brought in nothing and the vineyards and orchards were abandoned.   Misery was so great according to Depping [1] that the people in the country "were reduced to eating dogs and even human flesh, whilst the mortality was simply fearful."

The Normans then came in their turn to take possession of the place which remained empty.   Here we have a new stratum of population superimposed on so many others arriving from all quarters and settling on French soil.   What was the origin of these newcomers ?   They have been regarded as Scythians, Vandals, Huns, Moors, Saracens, Germanic folk, and even Russians.   In the vast quantity of literature on this subject, all opinions find ardent and ingenious defenders.   The Normans have undergone the fate common to so many other peoples and races.   They burst through all narrow classifications and escape the limits within which it is desired to confine them.   Let us note, however, the opinion of Robert Wace (*Roman du Rou*), who sees in them men of different blood. To him the Normans were only an assemblage of pirates coming from the North. The position of the Norman was peculiar.   He was an adventurer and a plunderer by trade, and in order to belong to them there was no need to show any certificate of birth or of origin.

One must then be animated with a fine courage to presume

---

[1] *Histoire des Expéditions Maritimes des Normands.*

to state exactly the quality of blood which the Normans introduced among the inhabitants of Gaul.

Let us content ourselves with showing that its quantity is
not to be disregarded. For the Normans pushed far into the
interior of the country. Orleans, Auxerre, Burgundy, Nantes
and many other towns and districts retain numerous traces of
their invasion. In 854, after having taken possession of Bordeaux and after having burnt it, they reached Toulouse. Hasting
after his return from an expedition against Luna (on the Gulf
of Spezia, which the Norman hordes mistook for the city of
Rome), went up the Rhone and sojourned at Nîmes and at
Arles. Thus the Normans spread themselves over the whole
of France. Their expeditions succeed one another with prodigious rapidity, and without doubt they contributed largely, as
feared and respected conquerors, to the repopulation of Gaul.
It would be all the more unjust to disregard their merits in
this respect, inasmuch as the male population was more than
thinly sown, the inhabitants consisting mostly of women and
children.

The policy of Rollo, among other things, contributed much
to this result, for immediately after having obtained from
Charles the Simple a part of Neustria, which afterwards took
the name of Normandy, this chief of the pirates, afterwards
the first Duke of Normandy, undertook to repeople his country.
The task being too great for his army, he attracted with this
object numerous Germanic people into Normandy.

Let us add that already in the sixth century the country
of Bayeux (Depping) was peopled by a colony of Saxons from
Germania.

VIII

To give an account of the probable composition of the blood
of France, we must also consider many other races and peoples
who are generally forgotten when it is a matter of enumerating
its constituent elements.

Let us remember in the first place the Vascons and the
Basques. They held many spots in the south-west of France.[1]

---

[1] Fauriel, *Hist. de la Gaule méridionale*, &c.

In the reign of the Merovingians, Chilperic I. and Thierry II., *Vasconia* corresponded with the present departments of the Upper and Lower Pyrenees, Gers and Landes.

The Phœnicians founded numerous markets and colonies on the north-west coast of the Mediterranean, of which the town of Nîmes was one of the best known. The same applies to the Saracens (Moors) who invaded France in 721, and, after having taken possession of Narbonne and Carcassonne, went higher up towards the north. In spite of the defeats inflicted on them several years later, they settled in Septimania (a country bordering on the eastern Pyrenees near the Rhone). There joined this first stratum a supplementary immigration at the beginning of the seventeenth century, when numerous Moors, chased from Spain, sought refuge in France. Certain anthropologists believe that they can find traces of these Moors in France.[1]

What, again, shall we say of the Sarmatians and Slavs, whose descendants must be very numerous in France? In their number figured certain tribes already mentioned above, like the Vandals or Vindils and the Alans, to which there should be added the Taifali, the Agathyrsi, the Ruteni, and also the Burgundians, who, according to A. Gauguin, were simply Slavs.

The Alans, who are so frequently mentioned in the chronicles of the invasion, generally accompanied the Vandals, and were considered as of Slav origin. They have left numerous traces in France. Their descendants are found near Valence in the country of the Loire, &c. The Taifali, who also arrived with the Alans, settled in Poitou. They lived on the banks of the Sèvre (Nantaise), in the *Pagus Teofalgicus*, near the little town bearing the name of Tiffanges (Vendée). As for the Agathyrsi, called Hamatobes, of a Scythian stock, they also left descendants in Poitou, and, according to Le Play, certain customs of agricultural communities which are met with in Auvergne and Nivernais are of Slav origin.

Were the Sarmatians, Slavs and Scythians, whom the ancients

---

[1] M. Paul Guillemot sees them in Bugey; Elisée Reclus in Landes; between Chambéry and the lake of Annecy (Hudry-Menos, Cotte); near Plombières (Dr. Bens), &c., &c.

identified with such facility, really of common origin ?   This question appears all the more insoluble in that the chroniclers of the past apply these three names indiscriminately to the numerous peoples of whose origin they were ignorant.

Let us be content with adding that the Slavs in any case have descendants in France much more authentic than the Ruteni. Those who settled from the land of the Morini to the mouths of the Rhine came there from the north of England. But long before this immigration there were numerous Ruteni on the banks of the Aveyron.

The Greek and Roman races, viz. the Pelasgians, Sabines, Latins, Hellenes, Tyrrhenians and Etruscans who settled under the name of Protiades in the environs of Massilia (Marseilles), pretended to be the descendants of Protos, the son of Eutenius and Vesta.   Numerous Greek colonists, attracted by their prosperity, came to join them, and towns founded by them are there to bear witness to their presence and their ramifications into the neighbouring country.   Among these towns, let us note those which have survived the march of centuries like Αντιπολις (Antibes), *Portus Herculis Monoeci* (Monaco), *Arelatus* (Arles), Ἱερον (Hyères), &c., &c.   The Romans arrived later to continue the work of the Greeks.   Who will ever be able to define the quality of their blood ?   All sorts of tribes which, as conquerors or conquered, are associated with the history of Rome, contributed to its composition !

Without doubt we shall never know the exact truth on the subject of these many enigmas.   For each people introduces a dozen which are insoluble.   Thus with regard to the Pelasgians, we do not even know whether they were of white origin.   Did not Reinisch and Beeck maintain this revolutionary theory, that they were simply mulattoes, the result of a crossing between white and black folk ?   Who will ever say what the Sabines and Etruscans were ?

The Semitic race is represented in France not only through the Phœnicians and Moors, but also through the Jews, whose arrival at Diodorum (Metz) was noticed in the year 222.   Their number in Gaul must have been considerable, for the law of Gondebald in 500 contains many severities towards them. They were successively banished from France by Philip

Augustus, Philip the Fair, Charles VI., &c., and recalled by
Louis-le-Hutin and John II. the Good.   Nevertheless they have
been met with from all time in Provence, Lorraine and
Burgundy.   According to F. Michel, numerous and rich
Jewish families were found in the twelfth century at Béziers,
Montpellier, Narbonne, Marseilles, &c.   The persecutions in
Spain contributed to augment their number in France.   Chased
away by the Inquisition, they settled in the region between
Bayonne and Bordeaux.   According to the author of the *Races
maudites*, many Jewish colonies were collectively converted to
Christianity and lost in other peoples.   They were known by
the nickname of " Marrons " in Auvergne, "Polacres " in Lozère
and " Gets " in Faucigny.   Later, German, Russian and Polish
Jews came to augment the dose of Semitic blood which flows in
French veins.

The Uralo-Altaic races, that is, Mongol, Ugrian and Finnish,
have also numerous representatives in France.   The Huns, who
invaded Gaul, included in their train the most dissimilar tribes.
They themselves, composed of Tartars and Mongols (A. Thierry
and de Guignes), were in particular followed by Finnish
peoples.   L. Dussieux[1] mentions among the Huns, the Avars,
Uzes, Khasars, Cumans, the Finnish-Ostiac-Magyars, &c.

We are told, it is true (Fustel de Coulanges), that neither
the Huns nor the numerous Uralo-Altaic tribes who from 910
to 954 ravaged Alsace, Burgundy, Provence, &c., left children
behind them.   What does it matter ?   The anthropologists and
the historians who affirm it assure us at the same time of
the existence of numerous Mongoloid types among the French
of France.

Mahé de la Bourdonnais, Drs. Topinard, Beddoe, Guibert,
Collignon, &c., note numerous Mongoloids among the Bigoudens
in the south of Quimper in Brittany.   Dr. A. Roujon finds
this type in Picardy, Brittany, Auvergne, in Morvan, at Montpellier and even in the environs of Paris.   Professor Sabatier
says that he has even met them in the Cévennes, &c.

Our Mongoloids are distinguished, like their Asiatic brethren,
by a small flat nose, a flat and extremely large face, palpebral
eye-sockets, rather frequently oblique and only slightly opened,

[1] *Essai hist. sur les Invasions des Hongrois en Europe et spécialement en France.*

a chin somewhat effaced, a large skull (brachycephalic), a globular head, tanned skin, small stature, &c.

How can we explain the persistence of this type if the invasions which we have spoken of above had passed over France without leaving any traces like water off polished metal? Let us note on this subject the opinion maintained with so much authority by G. Hervé. According to him, the Celto-Ligurians themselves were simply far removed descendants of the Mongoloids!

Let us desist from any comments and bend to the fact of the influence of the Mongol element in the formation of the French people.

In more modern times, France, which is justly considered as the most favourable country in which to gain or spend money, continues to be the object of singular attraction to representatives of all the civilised peoples of the earth. Whereas in England the number of foreign residents is only 5 per 1,000, in Germany 8, in Austria 17, it attains to 40 per 1,000 in France ; and a circumstance which gives rise to meditation is that the foreign population grows thirteen times more quickly in France than the native element (see on this subject the studies of Turquan).

If we enlarge our limits and include the greater France with its numerous colonies, we shall obtain a veritable ethnical summary of all the peoples of the earth !

IX

But let us confine ourselves to Gaul, and endeavour to note as they come the names of tribes which have contributed to the formation of the French blood—Aquitani, Iberians, Vascones, Silures, Salians, Libui, Suevi, Vulgientes, Sardones, Conqueranians, Arverni, Bituriges, Santoni, Pictones, Cambolectri, Agesineses, Turones, Andegades, Carnutes, Veneti, Curiosolitæ, Redones, Osismi, Abricantuens, Lexovii, Aulerci, Vellocasses, Caletes, Parisii, Lingones, Helvetii, Ædui, Leuci, &c., &c.; Alans, Vandals, Teifales, Agathyrsi, Ruteni, Polonais, Venedes, &c., &c. ; Belgæ, Galates, Cimbri, Wisigoths, Burgun-

dians, Franks, Saxons, Germans, Suevi, &c., &c., with hundreds
of subdivisions ; Phœnicians, Saracens (Moors), Jews, Etruscans,
Pelasgians, Sabines, Tyrrhenians, Mongoloid peoples, &c., &c.,
without mentioning odd tribes like the Gypsies and many
other "accursed" races, the origin and ethnical links of which
are less known ; and also negroid peoples whose prior existence
in France appears to be proved by the discovery of the
Valaisan skulls dating from the thirteenth and fourteenth
centuries,[1] and neolithic skulls of Armorica of the same negroid
type !

When we reflect on the intermingling of so many disparate
elements, and when we also think that Germania for centuries
gave shelter to numerous Gaulish tribes, we are tempted to take
the side of M. d'Arbois de Jubainville, that " there is probably in
Germany more Gaulish blood than in France." [2]   The Burgun-
dian, Wisigothic, Frankish and Norman blood has perhaps in-
oculated France with more Germanic blood than there remains
in modern Germany.

Consequently two strange conclusions stand out from the
anthropological history of France and indirectly from that of
Germany.   On the one hand, France is the vastest and richest
reservoir of ethnical elements, and cannot claim the dominant
quality of the Gaulish people or country.   On the other hand
(a conclusion which is still more unexpected), if it were
absolutely necessary to attribute Gaulish descent to a European
people, it would be to that of Germany.

We thus arrive at a most unexpected imbroglio.   The
French have become a Germanic folk and the Germanic folk
have become Gaulish !

The truth no doubt is to be found elsewhere.   The two
countries, like so many other European States, have numerous
ancestors in common.   It is dangerous to wish to analyse their
blood and to disentangle its constituent elements.   For, when
the regular historical channel of facts is followed without

---

[1] This is the conclusion of a memoir read on this subject before the Academy
of Sciences (in April, 1904)—"By their general cranial form and cephalic
index, by their maxillary prognathism, the details of their dentition, by their
platyrhiny, all these Valaisan skulls of the Valley of the Rhone are negroid in
a very striking degree."

[2] Les Celtes (Preface, xi).

preconceived ideas, and when we have the courage to reject commonplaces which demand respect only on account of their age, we find ourselves face to face with truths which are in flagrant opposition to current phraseology. Our usual terminology thus loses all meaning, whilst our Aryan prejudices, Germanic or Gaulish, reduced to the questionable support of custom and tradition, are ripe, like all our prejudices, for rejection and ridicule.

CHAPTER III

I

THERE is reason to admire the persistence with which the French and the Italians never cease to proclaim themselves Latin peoples. At the moment when Spain, seriously attacked by a crisis of convalescence alarming for her future, draws on herself the witticisms of other lands; at the moment when so many little "Latin" republics still astonish the world with the incoherence of their social and political life; to wish in spite of all to belong to the family whose defects and failings never cease to be criticised, this surely borders on heroism. Nevertheless we find striking proofs of it in light and serious books, in the discourses of politicians and statesmen, and in the writings of journalists, thinkers and savants. For the power of error under the mask of truth is decidedly greater than that of truth itself!

Once the Latin doctrine is admitted, there is no hesitation in committing in its name all sorts of patriotic sacrileges. For is not accepting Latin descent the same as admitting the decadence of all its members, including of course the French nation? Starting from this point, the French-Latin people are contrasted with the insular Anglo-Saxons. The one have all the vices and all the failings, and the other all the merits and all the good qualities. Our would-be physicians, assembled round our bed, discuss gravely the state of our malady, nay rather, the date of our decease. Our irreparable ruin is certain to all. France is rebuked, among other things, for a lack of seriousness, for a lack of directing principles in life, for the corruption of her manners and that of her official life which must shortly consume her, and also for her diminished birth-rate, which presages her early exit. "For the last twenty-seven years there has been no pleasure in being a Frenchman," so cried Jules Lemaître one day, altogether abashed by the sad rumours which were current concerning his dear country. We recollect the stir which the works of M. Demolins made, who, like his numerous followers, did not believe in the possible salvation of the Latins except through a blind imitation of the Anglo-Saxons.

Quite a pessimistic and debilitating literature arose from these sentiments of disdain for France and discouragement for her future. We scrutinised the signs of malady among these Latin brethen like people condemned to a common torture, who look with anguish on the altered features of their fellows. Prophets of evil augury sprang up on every side. It became the fashion to bring into contempt French energy and the accursed propensities of its spirit. Nothing obtained grace in the eyes of these implacable Zoileans who, convinced of our inferiority, spent their lives in proclaiming it from the housetops. The "licensed" patriots distinguished themselves in particular in this concert of vociferations. The "nationalists," whose function is everywhere to claim a monopoly of patriotism for themselves while denying it to the other members of the community, never ceased praising the inhabitants of the two worlds at our expense. Did they not even prefer the Mongols of Europe and Asia to France and other "neo-Latin" countries!

In their strange love for their country, they never considered that this pessimism only weakened its living forces. For if confidence in ourselves and the exaltation of our powers augment their intensity, discouragement consigns peoples and individuals to impotence. Through hearing it repeated that they were irremediably condemned, the French ended in believing in the reality of their malady. The literature of "French depreciation" gathered strength with its growth. The foreigner, moreover, took us at our word. He accepted this suggestion coming from France, in order to hurl it back in the form of a most humiliating pity or hateful disdain.

Demoralised by all this diagnosis, France fell for a time into a veritable moral torpor. The enervated land seemed a prey to a kind of general weakening. The initiative and boldness of French ideas seemed to have disappeared, and pornography abandoned to its appetites of lucre invaded us on all sides. Saviours from every quarter threatened us incessantly with their "special cure," whilst the country, in order to justify its reputation of being "used up" and "decrepit," seemed to abandon itself to the enterprising energy of adventurers both from within and without.

Suddenly the abrupt awakening of Italy gave the lie to the neo-Latin decadence. Then the war in the Transvaal came to show up the grave and unsuspected weakness of Britain. Instances of corruption arising in Germany also opened our eyes with regard to that country. At the same time a troublesome affair happening in France moves her profoundly. Her sleeping energies awake under the impulse of the moment. The best of her citizens sound the tocsin of the revival of the national conscience, and France presents the unusual spectacle of a whole people impassioned and battling for years round an abstract idea. A little later the Russo-Japanese war causes her to see that the pretended youth of the Russian people does not spell moral and material health. France breathes more freely, and considers with justifiable satisfaction her *rôle* of a great nation, surrounded with universal respect, and guiding humanity towards nobler and better ends. She has at length understood that her past and present and the great moral future which is reserved for her, cannot be confined to the little ethnical tree to which her imprudent friends and envious enemies wish to bind her. In meditating on her destinies, France has certainly understood that her genealogical tree must be more widely human than narrowly Latin. Who knows even whether she remains Latin in any sense whatsoever !

II

Leaving on one side the great intellectual influence exercised by the Romans, let us for the moment confine ourselves to speaking of their ethnical force. Now in this respect it would be difficult to deny that it was almost nil. Let us not forget that Rome, including the adjacent districts, only contained an infinitesimal population as compared with that which lived in her vast provinces and dependencies. In taking possession of a new country, Rome could not think of sending there any part of her inhabitants. On the other hand, these were so content at home that they did not dream of expatriating themselves. The liberty which was so dear to them, the fruits of a civilisation which was advanced for the time, and which they enjoyed at home, what barbarous country was there which could provide them with the like ? In the conquered provinces we ought perhaps only to look for Roman officials and legionaries. But the officials sent out from Rome remind us of those appointed by France in her own colonies. All that attracted them was the desire to make or repair their fortunes, or to play a great part, with the hope of returning to the metropolis as soon as possible. Even these officials were not numerous. What constituted the strength of the Romans at all times was their grasp of the interests of the conquered country, and also the liberalism of the principles which they applied. In order to attach the new subjects to themselves, they respected their customs as far as they could, and their religion and their institutions. In their desire to forge links of sympathy between the capital and the conquered peoples, they chose the most distinguished among the compatriots of the latter in order to entrust them with lucrative posts and honourable places. Rome had in this way less need to remove her own citizens whilst at the same time creating a solid foundation for her territorial expansion. Let us remember also that, guided by their administrative genius, they had recourse to acts of astonishing liberality for that age. Did they not even go so far as to elevate certain inhabitants of the Gaulish capital to the rank of Roman senators! Moreover, the creation of local senates gave satisfaction to the ambitious spirits in the conquered lands. All these measures created an intense inner force, nourished as it was by elements drawn from the subjected provinces.

As for the Roman legions, let us not forget in the first place that, if the leaders were generally Romans, yet the soldiers were specially recruited from among the many peoples who comprised the Empire.   Urged on by the same administrative preoccupations, Rome, followed in this respect by modern England, always tried to form local armies.   Thus Cæsar, after the conquest of Gaul, at the moment when such an enterprise would have seemed most hazardous, did not hesitate to form the legion of the Lark, composed exclusively of Gauls.

The more we reflect on the distinctive characteristics of the Roman conquest, the more we perceive that it could bring no change into the composition of the blood of the so-called Latin nations.   The two principal roads which were bound to lead to an union of anthropological traits between the conquerors and the inhabitants of Gaul were, when all is told, only two little by-paths, along which only a few thousand Roman families passed at most.   Now when we consider that the Gaul of that time must have had many millions of inhabitants, we easily see that the interblending of Roman blood could not have changed the character of the whole.   Even admitting with Julian that there were about 30,000 Romans in Gaul, we can easily understand that these could not count for much in the anthropological formation of the modern French nation.

We shall see later on that the same remarks apply to the Italians, that pre-eminently Latin nation.   We have seen above that most of the peoples whom we have met with in Gaul, and whose origins were so diverse, also penetrated Italy, which country served for centuries as a meeting-place for all the human races.   According to M. Gebhart, we see there, simultaneously or successively, Gauls, Spaniards, Greeks, Asiatics, Egyptians, Jews, Germanic peoples, Bretons, Africans, Goths, Longobards, Byzantines (Ravenna), Slavs (Venice), Germans, Normans, Angevins, Saracens, &c.

According to M. Fouillée, what remains ethnically after this eternal procession of races is not the Latin element, but the Celto-Slav element with wide skulls in the North and numerous Mediterranean folk with long skulls in the South.

Nor can Spain prove her Latin origin.   She also for centuries sheltered numerous races and peoples.   We would have to pass a sponge over the momentous history of her past, blotting out a thousand years, in order to credit the Quirites with the blood which flows in Spanish veins. The anthropologists even tell us that what prevails in Spain is the brown and dolichocephalic Mediterranean type with a Celto-Germanic mixture. Most of the peoples who have traversed France and Italy have likewise contributed to transforming its blood, not to speak of Africans, who without doubt have contributed more to the present ethnical type of Spain than the Celts and the Latins put together.

What shall we say, lastly, of the South American republics? In the blood of their inhabitants flows that of all the races in the world. Noble blood, too, for it is essentially mixed; but have the Latins any part in it? These peoples, of whom it is the fashion to make fun as to their many origins and whimsical ancestry, ought rather to glory in it. For, and it can never be repeated too often, the nations who march at the head of humanity are above all things distinguished for their most extensive ethnical ramifications!

It might be said that a kind of irony presides over the baptism of all the Latin nations, so called because the blood of the Romans is conspicuous in them by its absence! When, moreover, we analyse the origins of other European peoples, we find likewise numerous common ancestors, so many indeed that the pure ethnological type remains accentuated only in the manuals of anthropology! It is enough to recall the ethnical history of France and to remember the names of all the peoples who have planted their stock there, in order to recognise that in the French blood the Latin addition must be treated as a negligible quantity.

III

But, unharmed anthropologically by Latin admixture, France and the other so-called Latin countries may perhaps be characterised as such intellectually. Therefore, not Latin races, but Latin mentality. The difference deserves to be noticed. For, whereas ethnical origin means fatal descent and connection, unavoidable if not eternal, Latin intellectuality is only a passing phase. However important may be the influence of the ideas which fashion our mentality, mentality itself is modified with the modification of the factors which create it. Germany by becoming Protestant changed the conditions of its soul. French Protestants themselves, having undergone an influence diverging from that which has contributed to the intellectual formation of the majority of French Catholics, are to be distinguished from them in many ways. The same applies to French rationalists, who in the second generation, after being brought up in a way contrary to that of believing Catholics, resemble these last mentally less than they do strangers nourished from the same source of independent thought.

Our soul evolves and is transformed under the influence of political and social institutions, for which cause the soul of modern France, like that of other Latin peoples, is assuredly not that of a few centuries ago. Let us take for example the intellectual evolution of France, and we shall see that even here Latin influence is far from being exclusive.

The language, administration, and also the civilisation of Gaul were developed under Roman influence. Yet can it be affirmed that French thought has followed from all time the unique direction given by Latin mentality ? Such was the case, no doubt, during the first centuries, just as English civilisation after the Norman Conquest was fashioned according to the French model. But just as England, becoming emancipated in time, pursued her own course while preserving at the same time as original bases the language and ideas from the other side of the Channel, so France, after having yielded to the Latin impulse and drunk sufficiently at its sources, proceeded later on towards an intellectuality more suitable to her situation in the world and the capacities of her people.

As a millionaire must not forget the debt of gratitude which he owes to the person who advanced his original capital, so France must remember what she owes to Roman civilisation. One would, however, fall into an unpardonable exaggeration in identifying the immense wealth subsequently acquired with the first Latin deposit. For what sources and tributaries have not contributed towards forming the French Sea !

The psychology of the French genius is most complex. It is the result of the widest comprehension and adaptation of the intellectual conquests of all other civilised countries, enriched and enhanced by the essential qualities of its own peculiar mentality. For as France ethnically is only the product of a mixture of divers races and peoples, the French mind and genius carry the impress of the intellectual travail of civilisations created elsewhere. The French language took much time to become an independent organism, but it succeeded nevertheless in becoming such. More time was necessary for her to emerge out of chaos than was necessary for the Greek and Latin languages put together. In Homer, that is, a few centuries after the formation of the Greek people, the language is already formed and crystallised. The same applies to the Latin tongue, which in the *Twelve Tables* (451 B.C. and 200 after the foundation of Rome) is seen in all its beauty and energetic vigour. The French language took eight centuries to get into shape. It took twice that time to conquer the world. For the *lingua romana rustica*, the language of the peasants, which in evolving became the French language, existed already in the seventh century. Under the Carlovingians it held its own before Teutonic and Latin. The priests were forced to preach in this vulgar tongue, like the Abbot of Corbie (in 750), in order to be understood of their parishioners. In 813 the Councils of Tours and Rheims ordered the priests to preach in the *vulgar* tongue and in *Roman*. The history of its diffusion is the history of the valiant struggles maintained with vigour against the Latin to begin with, and also against the Greek, Spanish, and Tuscan. Always fought against but never vanquished, the French tongue developed itself painfully but surely. It gained in richness and strength and commended itself more and more to the usage of the peoples. From the thirteenth century the Italians adopted it. From that date it " spread in the world ": so tells us the Italian savant, Hartino de Casare, who translated *into French* the Latin history of Venice " because the French tongue is more refined for reading and speaking than any other." As it developed it emancipated itself from the Latin tongue and became an independent language. When in the sixteenth century the respect due to a clearly defined idiom is paid to it, this has been gained by its wonderful virtues.[1]

[1] See Jean Finot, *La France devant la lutte des langues*. Paris, 1900.

Latin played the same part with regard to French as the latter exercised for many centuries with regard to English. The French language prevailed in that country till the reign of Henry VIII. The English writers themselves until the end of the fourteenth century tried to write in French (R. de Grosseteste, Pierre de Langtoft, &c.). Instruction and education were given in French, for even in the fourteenth century English students were more numerous than any other foreigners at the Paris University.

All the phenomena of English life are impregnated with French influence, its romance, philosophy, political constitution, poetry, science and arts. The Anglo-Saxon literature of the fourteenth century has scarcely anything but translations of French romances of chivalry. Again, in the fifteenth century many poets wrote the first part of their verse in English and the second in French. The number of French words in English is twice that of words of Germanic origin.[1] Hume tells us that the most beautiful parts of the English tongue, without considering the quantity of its borrowed elements, are drawn from the French and their language. Nevertheless English, born under the influence of the French language and nourished so abundantly by its roots, also became in emancipating itself an independent idiom, and holds a glorious position in the domain of languages.

IV

When we examine the many sides of the formation of the French genius, we perceive that the Latin impress has had with time to give way to other influences acting outside its sphere and often in a contrary direction. Thus the national consciousness in evolving has become finally altogether distinct from its primitive formulas. Note, for example, that French syntax has become radically different from Latin syntax. This is an important difference, for it influences the evolution of French thought in the way of research, individualism and criticism. Moreover, all those who exalt the influence of Latin according to their fancy, seem to forget that the same tongue under the influence of other factors has become Spanish, Italian,

[1] See Skeats's *Etymological Dictionary*.

and even Roumanian, and one may even add English on account
of its Franco-Latin formation.   They surely forget the effect produced by climate and so many other factors of the *milieu* on
language.   Yet this truth has already been formulated with
admirable precision by President des Brosses.   "Every people,"
he says, "has its own alphabet which is not that of another, and
in which there are several letters which it is impossible for
another to pronounce.   Climate, atmosphere, skies, waters, modes
of life and nourishment are the causes of this variation."

We are familiar with the violent discussions of these later
times on the subject of the prevailing tendencies and mission
of France.   To thinkers and writers like Paul Bourget,
F. Brunetière or M. Barrès, French is Latin and nothing but
Latin.   M. Brunetière even sums up all its history as "efforts
to maintain, vindicate and defend its Latinity against external
invaders and internal foes."   Pursuing to the end his Latin
paradox, the eminent critic tells us that the great preoccupation
of the Latin genius was the tendency to universality and
catholicity : "France is Catholicism and Catholicism is France."[1]
But Latin influence, which is nil ethnically, is far from being
exclusive in what concerns the formation of French thought.
Even in the religious world, where Latinity ought to be the
synonym of catholicity, history breaks irreverently the barriers
which "nationalists" assign to it.   It shows us that catholicity
as conceived by MM. Brunetière, Bourget, and their numerous
followers is in flat contradiction to French tradition and
genius.   Gallicanism is old in France by many centuries.   The
enemies of this "catholicity" are especially recruited from among
the old families, as the indignant cries of their mouthpiece,
Agrippa d'Aubigné, prove, who contrasts his French blood with
the "Spanish vermin" and the "Italian poisoners," introducers
of a "catholicity foreign" to the traditions of his beloved France.

> " L'air encore une fois, contre eux, se troublera,
> Justice au juge Saint, contre eux, demandera,
> Disant : Pourquoi, Tyrans et furieuses bestes,
> M'empoisonâtes-vous de charognes, de pestes ?
> .   .   .   .   Pourquoi
> Changeâtes-vous en sang l'argent de nos ruisseaux ? "
> —*Les Tragiques.*

---

[1] *Discours de combat.*

Architecture, painting, sculpture, and also philosophy and jurisprudence in France, all throw off the Latin influence with the march of centuries. The same liberating movement goes on in the other domains of literary, political and moral life. Mixed with so many other factors, the Latin element loses its preponderance and its decisive character.

It is enough to study French literature and to examine the origin of its principal tendencies in order to see how much it owes to foreign sources. We could fill several volumes, if we desired to discuss thoroughly the influences which foreign countries have exercised on all phases of our literary activity. French romance and philosophy, for example, in these last centuries have grown and developed under English influence. Voltaire, Diderot and Rousseau were permeated by English ideas and submitted to their force willingly or inevitably. The *Lettres Anglaises* of Voltaire, one of the most sensational works in literary history, were written as a direct consequence of travels in England. "Diderot is quite English" (F. Brunetière). As for Rousseau, with "his bourgeois romance, and eloquence of heart, the tone of his sentiment is absolutely Richardsonian" (Fréron).

The case of Richardson and the English is all the more significant in that Rousseau and the other romanticists owe to them not only the plot of the bourgeois romance but also their way of treating human feeling. It is to them we owe the 1789 of letters which permitted the introduction of the poor and downtrodden, and the description of their sufferings and miseries, illuminated with rays of poetry and softened with tears of compassion and human fraternity.

What is more original and more essentially French than the genius of Voltaire, Diderot and Rousseau, in spite of the influence which moulded it? The whole skeleton of the *Divine Comedy* is found in the rhymed visions of the Friar Alberic of Mount Cassin, just as *The Menœchmi* of Plautus contains the subject of Shakespeare's *Comedy of Errors*! And yet who would presume to doubt the originality of these two geniuses!

And Goethe? Do we not find his influence in Taine, Renan and Paul Bourget? The *Capitaine Fracasse* of Th. Gautier, essentially French as it is, owes more for all that to *Wilhelm Meister* than to Scarron!

These characteristic examples explain how France has always been able to draw from foreign sources without losing anything of her own national genius. The more she is given to this exchange of ideas, the more she prospers intellectually. A kind of ideal comprehension always accompanies her methods of borrowing. In bringing in richness from abroad, she transforms and revalues it and then places it at the disposal of humanity.

Thus all peoples are amalgamated in her, not only ethnically, but also and especially in an intellectual sense.

CHAPTER IV

THE FRENCH CONSIDERED AS AN EXAMPLE OF A SUPERIOR PEOPLE BEING AT THE SAME TIME THE PRODUCT OF AN EXCESSIVE MIXTURE OF RACES

FRANCE presents an invincible front against all the exaggerations of the anthropo-sociologists or anthropo-psychologists. Peoples, we are told, perish owing to mixture of races. But here is France, which has the honour of being, if not the first, yet at least one of the first peoples in the world, and which includes in its blood that of all other peoples and races. It is sufficient to trace the story of its historical evolution and to compare this with its present condition in order to perceive the incalculable benefits which ethnical and intellectual crossings procure for humanity Let us try as briefly as possible to make this clear in a few pages of historical synthesis.

What in the first place is French mentality? It is the quintessence of civilisation and of universal progress enriched by the fruits of French genius, which is at the same time both comprehensive and creative.

In the course of centuries France has become a kind of gigantic factory of ideas at the disposal of other countries and peoples. The original material comes sometimes from herself and sometimes from all other quarters. But what does it matter where it comes from? Polished up " à la française " it goes round the world and feeds the civilised nations. Romanticism, which has revolutionised modern literature, forestalled by forty years the works of Chateaubriand through the pen of Young and his school. Nevertheless, romanticism only dates from France. The same applies to the conquests of the Revolution. England furnished us with a model, but that was only for her own personal advantage. France was able to make it a work for humanity!

The same remarks apply to the influence exercised on France by German, Italian and Spanish thought, and by that more recent thought of the Scandinavians and Russians.

A national mentality, like that of individuals, is all the more perfect when the elements which contribute to its perfection are numerous.

The crossing of thought produces a still more beneficial effect than that of blood, in which respect France is also highly favoured. For, being the result of so many ethnical types, she has always had the germ of an innate sympathy for other peoples and races. The English love to speak of the Americans of the United States as their cousins. With how much more reason can France claim ties of blood and relationship of thought with the peoples of the two worlds! They are all chained to her destinies not only biologically but also in the formation of their souls and mentalities.

Wherefore instead of a communion on the grounds of similar cephalic index, or of Aryan, Gaulish and Latin origins, which are extravagant and doubtful principles, it is more worthy to lay claim to the great heritage of the French genius and of French thought.

Moreover, what would be the advantage of a narrow nationalism founded on certain external bodily marks? "Let everyone look about him," says Paul Broca, "or merely within his own family, and he will nearly always see eyes of different colours, white skins and brown skins, high, medium or low statures. The features of the face and the forms of the head also show but slight stability. This one has the features of the Celts, but not the colour. That one has the head of the Cimbri, but not the stature."

The fact that so ardent an expert in the doctrine of races should make an avowal which destroys the reality of his theory even within the frontiers of his native land, shows that doubt is no longer permissible on this subject. The existence also of various types and the commingling of characteristic traits of races are met with in all our provinces, a fact which constitutes a permanent challenge thrown down by every Frenchman against the most sacred principles of the anthropological science and which gives him the value of a symbol.

What is perceived to-day with regard to the French is also noticeable in all other Latin peoples. It is sufficient to study the formation of Italian, Spanish or Argentine mentality, in order to see that these also are connected with the progress of humanity in general and not exclusively with that of one of its branches. Moreover, such also will be the destiny of the civilised races of to-morrow, so much does the mixture of races tend to destroy their salient and distinctive traits.

If only by its geographical situation, France seems to have been called to symbolise the civilised world. As the French people belong to all ethnical types, the soil of France presents a kind of synthesis of all climatic, agricultural and geological properties. And yet these diverse qualities are invariably resolved into a complete harmony. It has been observed more than once that even the richness of its geological strata corresponds with that of its surface. A manufacturing country, France is also agricultural. A mining country, it is also commercial. The harmonious rhythm of its configuration has at all times stirred the admiration of travellers and thinkers.

Strabo about twenty centuries ago, with that enthusiasm which marked the Hellenic genius, wrote naïvely : "Such a happy disposition of places, arranged so as to resemble the work of an intelligent being rather than the effect of chance, is enough to prove the existence of Providence." It might be said that it was purposely chosen to be a vast anthropological laboratory. In this ideal crucible there have been blended the numerous physiological and psychological qualities of peoples. Its geographical unity has, on the other hand, contributed much to this work of internal pacification.

The soil of France, so profoundly humanised according to the happy expression of one of her demographs, has from all time beneficially controlled the oscillations of her history. When a slow and cruel retrospect is made of the innumerable disorders which she has suffered in the past, and when these are contrasted with her present condition in the world, we cannot help thinking of these lines of André Chénier—

> "O France, beautiful country, generous land
> Which the kindly gods destined to be happy!"

The numerous elements which enter into the composition of the French people have also contributed to the triumph of the humane principle, making it victorious over racial restrictions and physiological divisions. On the ruins of these levelled "differentiations" has been erected a "French type" admirable both morally and physically. It unites in itself numerous moral and intellectual gradations. It is not Aryan, nor Gaulish, nor Latin, but what is more than these. It is human.

Throughout her long historic existence, France has been able to assimilate everything which came into her and also everything which was directed against her. Her constant and continued progress may be compared with those rivers which suddenly disappear and remain invisible under the ground, to reappear later on enriched by the hidden elements which they have gathered up in their invisible course.

As we observe it to-day, the French nation is a living proof of the benefits of the interpenetration of peoples and of the unlimited commingling of their blood, intelligence, vices and virtues. In this beautiful union of human beings the horizon of French thought was fashioned and enlarged.

We are not in any way the victims of an unblushing optimism. We acknowledge that France often seems to deviate from the broad way which has marked her ethnical past and the formation of her intellectuality. From time to time specious saviours have arisen and have preached her their puny gospel of hatred at home and enmity abroad,—sentiments, both of them, cruelly at variance with her proper destiny. Some there are, no doubt, not insignificant numerically, who have allowed themselves to be overpowered by the pestilent odours of the gutter. What matters it? The civilisation of Hermopolis has never ceased to be admired because many of its inhabitants gave divine honours to greyhounds. We still continue to be enthusiastic over that of Lycopolis or Sais, although we know that the citizens of the former prostrated themselves before wolves and those of the latter before sheep.

After all, in spite of her momentary weaknesses, France always goes forward. Often, like an army exhausted by fatigue, she advances through dark nights in an almost lethargic condition. But the dawn always finds her fresh and valiant at the van of other peoples in their progressive work.

Who would dare to deny that the qualities of goodness and justice and the level of the general conscience of modern France are not above those of fifty or a hundred years ago ? Her humanitarian ideals are in any case superior to those of neighbouring lands. The sympathy between social classes, which is an essential standard of progress, has become stronger and intenser. Add also the fact that the sentiment of solidarity between the French and the outer world has increased by several degrees !

To confine her origins of blood and thought to a single ethnical and intellectual element is to misunderstand, together with the significance of past centuries, the true greatness of France. It is also perhaps committing a sin against the dominant virtue of the formation of her people and of her genius. For the multiplicity of her ethnical and mental origins, which involves as logical sequence her understanding of the soul of the world and her faculty of directing it, is precisely the cause of her brilliant and exceptional position.

Although weakened by the war of 1870, France has been able after thirty years to regain her place as the directing force of the world.

Owing to her social genius she has succeeded in unifying the many diverse elements gathered together on her soil. The same genius which has made her beloved by other peoples, allows her in addition to accomplish her civilising mission of creating the great Human Family as she has already created the great French Family. Never let us forget that among all nations it is still France which has the least ethnical prejudice and the most innate sentiment as to the equality of individuals notwithstanding the colour of their skin or their craniological differences.

While "Yellow" writers are already proclaiming this French

virtue, those of the " Black " peoples bless her and look to her for assistance in their social emancipation.

Let us hope that she may realise this supreme desire, voiced by one of her most glorious poets and the one who best expresses her historic genius. " She will be " (he loved to say) " the heart and the brain of other peoples ! "

CHAPTER V

A FEW OTHER EXAMPLES OF THE IMPOSSIBILITY OF
ANALYSING THE ETHNICAL COMPOSITION OF PEOPLES
AND RACES

I

ALL that we have said in the preceding chapter about France
can be also applied to Germany. We have seen above that
Germany is the more Gaulish in origin, whilst France, to say
nothing of the many other ethnical elements which have contributed to her formation, deserves rather the name of a Germanic
country. From the moment when we proceed to a concrete
analysis of the different German States, we see in addition what
an imposing part the Slav element has always played there.
The Slavs and the Teutons, who appear to be so profoundly
disunited and who never cease to fill the world with the noise
of their quarrels and implacable hatred, are nevertheless very
closely related. Nearly all the branches of the Slavs, like the
Oborites, the Poles, the Servians, the Wends, &c., have settled
in Germany, whilst numerous Germans have contributed in
their turn to the formation of Slav peoples. Here also a continual coming and going of peoples is noticeable from the most
far-off times. Germany is so much more in the wrong to claim
purity of blood, in that to her happiness and honour she has
from all time benefited from foreign deposits, as considerable
biologically as intellectually. "The German race," Waitz [1] tells
us, "could not by its own forces arrive at a superior development,
without impulse from outside and a cleavage with its own
peculiar traditions." "All true Teutons," Nietzsche tells us,
"went abroad. Modern Germany is an advanced station of

[1] *Deutsche Verfassungsgeschichte*, III.

the Slav world and prepares the way for a Panslavic
Europe." [1]

II

We generally imagine that we have better knowledge of the
origins of modern Italy. Consult its historians, and especially
the glorious representatives of its letters, and they reply with
serenity that they are descended in a direct line from great and
illustrious Romans. Have we not seen an imperialist or rather
a nationalist school founded quite recently in Florence, finding
the ethnical origins of modern Italy in the patrician Quirites ?
And yet the Longobards, Byzantines, Egyptians, Gauls, Greeks,
Spaniards, Slavs, Normans, Angevins, Jews, Bretons, Saracens,
Teutons, &c., have also mingled their blood with that of the
other inhabitants of the peninsula.

But were these last Romans, in the sense which we give to the
word ? Not in any way. The few rays of light which anthropo-
historical science has thrown on the darkness of the past have
only destroyed all the accredited legends on this subject.

Not to speak of the prehistoric, and therefore doubtful
peoples, we see in Italy, at the dawn of the period accessible
to science, two great branches of African peoples, viz., the
Liburni and the Sicani. They were checked in their continual
invasions of Mediterranean lands by the Pelasgi and the
Liguro-Siculi.

Among the Pelasgi figure, among others, the Apulians,
Japyges, Messapians, Peucetians, Opici, Oenotri and Argivi
(who, according to Virgil, occupied the Palatine, one of the
seven hills). What were all these tribes ?

It would be very presumptuous to wish to solve the innumerable mysteries which surround them. Let us be content
merely with saying that these yield in nothing to the thick clouds
which envelop the origin of the Liguro-Siculi. We note among
their tribes the Taurini, the Siculi, the Itali, &c.

Elsewhere, near the Adriatic, we see the Venetians, an equally
mysterious tribe, and also the Umbrians, who during several
centuries ruled in central Italy.

---

[1] *The Germans and Civilisation.* Fragments of a posthumous volume.

According to some, these Umbrians were Celts; according to others, they belonged to the Ausonian branch. These Umbrians were in any case not Latins, for, according to the data of comparative grammar, their language is distinguished from the Latin by the formation of its words, by its construction and syntax, by its sound, and also by its flexion and termination.

With the arrival of the Etruscans, the composition of the Italian blood becomes singularly still more complicated. They were called Rasena in Italy, and Livy tells us that they settled in Rhaetia at the time of the Gaulish invasion. In truth they finally spread themselves all over the peninsula. We see them at Ravenna, Modena, Bologna, on the coast of ancient Umbria, in the valleys of the Arno, and also in the environs of the Tiber.

What were these Etruscans who were also called Etrusci or Tyrrheni, or just simply Tusci? All sorts of origins are ascribed to them. Sometimes Slavs, Libyans, Celts or Lydians, they are also regarded as Hittites and Semites. D. Brinton brings many proofs to bear on the theory that the Etruscans were Africans, whereas d'Arbois de Jubainville speaks eloquently in favour of their Asiatic origin. According to many anthropologists (an opinion maintained by A. Lefèvre among others) they had negroid features. In any case it was (already!) a race dreadfully mixed with nearly all the races on the earth.

Philologists (M. Bréal), on the grounds of their language, deny that the Etruscans had any affinity with the Indo-European peoples. It is true that it borrowed certain forms from Umbrian, Oscan and Latin, but in its endings one finds no trace of declension or conjugation, or anything which one might regard as belonging to a system of flexions.

In the matter of their cephalic index, we meet with the most opposed statements. They were dolichocephalic (63 per cent.) and brachycephalic (37 per cent.), so Nicolucci affirms with assurance; no, says Carl Vogt, they were simply sub-brachycephalic. Baer tells us, on the other hand, that they were pure dolichocephalic; whilst Retzius says they were quite the contrary, being vulgar brachycephals.

To this insoluble problem many others are joined. Scarcely had the Etruscans taken possession of Italy, when all sorts of so-called Gaulish peoples, including the Boii, the Senones, the Langres and many others, made a number of irruptions into it. They bring in their train a multitude of other nations, whom we have seen throwing themselves in like manner into France and Germany. Although we can affirm nothing positive in what concerns the dark origins of so many peoples and races, who contributed to the formation of the modern Italians, still we can draw a negative conclusion, namely that, strictly speaking, the Latins only played a quite inferior part in it. Let us remember on this subject that even the famous seven hills, whose territorial dimensions, as also their population, were insignificant when compared with the terribly mixed population of the whole of Italy at that period, were not in any way exclusively Latin. By the side of Pelasgic Argives, there were Etruscan Luceri, Sabini, &c. What remains, then, for the Latins ?

Those Italians who are somewhat chagrined on this subject have only to contemplate the lot reserved for so many other races ! For all those who have in any way participated in the progress of civilisation, and who on that account have deserved the attention of historians, find themselves in the same situation. As soon as we discover their past, we are impressed by the imposing spectacle of the ethnical mixtures of all sorts which have contributed to their formation as a race or people, and which have never ceased co-operating to that end.

The universal commingling, the mixture of all with all, seems to be the dominant law of their historical evolution. The first and the last in the scale of civilisation, nations great and small, enter, in this respect, within the limits of this essentially human law. Just as progress consists in the passing from the simple to the complex (from the homogeneity to the heterogeneity of Herbert Spencer), so the development of a people outside the incessant mixtures of its ethnical elements is not to be thought of.

III

Let us turn to the prehistoric and historic ethnology of the peoples of Great Britain. Its isolated situation ought theoretically to have preserved it from many and repeated invasions of foreign elements! But its past also furnishes matter for doubts which are not to be solved. It is sufficient to listen to the reasoning of the most authoritative ethnographers on the native peoples who were settled there before the Celts in order to understand the impossibility of arriving at a clear and decided conclusion. The race which Daniel Wilson christened *Kymbekephalic* and which Beddoe identifies with that of *the Dead Man* has left but few traces. We are told that it was distinguished by a long skull with an index of about 71 in width. It preceded the race of bronze or that of round barrows, who resemble the men of Borreby in Denmark.[1] What are all these peoples whose remains, found in dolmens, do not allow us to divine their origins or state of culture ? We know, on the other hand, that the blood of the inhabitants of Great Britain since the historic period presents as rich a mixture of divers elements as that of Germania and of Gaul. It would be necessary to repeat the diversified history of the first centuries after Christ, in order to show the variety of ethnical elements which have taken root there. It is enough to state with Beddoe that Mongoloid and African types appear, and with von Holder that we come across numerous Iberian and Sarmato-Germanic types. Let us take another no less significant example.

What can be more radically opposed in appearance than the Poles and Lithuanians. Yet it was enough for proximity and historic evolution to intervene in order to amalgamate these most divergent ethnical elements. According to Sigismond Gloger,[2] the ancient tribes of Poland, viz. Poles, Mazovsians, Lechites, Zmoudzines, Dregovisians, Krivisians, Drevlanes, &c., once so dissimilar, present to-day anthropologically, as the result of their incessant crossings, a unique Polish-Lithuanian type ! " How can you find a pure type (asks the celebrated Polish ethnologist) when to-day there is not a single man in Poland in whose veins does not flow the composite blood of so many divergent tribes who dwelt there ? "

The ethnical composition of the Russian people has for

---

[1] Beddoe, *Sur l'histoire de l'indice cephalique en Angleterre.* See also his *Races of Great Britain.*
[2] *Album etnografiezne Glogera.* See also his *Encyklopedya Staropolska.*

centuries exercised the fancy and learning of demographists and anthropologists. Are the Russians Mongols, Slavs, Aryans, Sarmatians, Teutons, Tartars, or a disparate mixture of peoples? All these doctrines have had authoritative representatives who, with an unheard-of wealth of arguments, plead in favour of their respective theories. Whereas Duchinski only sees Mongols in the Russians, and Sickerski the purest of Aryans, Fouillée mentions forty-six non-Aryan peoples who have entered into the ethnical composition of the Russians. Even among the partisans of the mixed blood of Russians some speak of their Finno-Mongol composition, whilst others bring out in succession the honour, or the dishonour, for the Russian blood of being merely a Slavo-Finno-Tartar mixture (A. Leroy-Beaulieu); Ugro-Finnish, as much as Slav (Penka); Celto-Slav, Slav-Norman (Léger), &c., &c.

The same cacophony breaks out in characterising the Russian skull. Sometimes it is presented to us as brachycephalic with a mixture of dolichocephalic and mesocephalic, or pure brachycephalic.

Nevertheless, when, delivered from all preconceived doctrines, we survey the history of the formation of the Russian people in its true aspect, we also perceive here the triumph of universal commingling.

In the first place we must note that the ancient Normans, who contributed to the formation of other great European peoples, likewise aided in the creation of the Russian State. Its name, moreover, only comes from a Norman tribe, the *Rous,* who arrived at Novgorod with their chief Rurik (862), just as that of France is derived from another Norman tribe, the Franks, and that of Allemagne (Germany) from the Allemans, and that of England from the Angles. But Russia long before the arrival of the Normans shows, like other countries, a mixture of peoples and races who met there and intermingled as everywhere else. When archæology brings us the fruit of its arduous studies in the Kourganes (funeral monuments which are found in the form of artificial hills in the south and centre of Russia), we notice there, above everything else, an extraordinary mixture of cranial types. The anthropologists, condemned to see here characteristic signs of races, must in this way bend before the fact of racial diversity on Russian ground. R. Weinberg,[1] in taking his stand on the study of about 7,000 measurements made in different parts of Russia, proves the extreme variety of types. The crushing majority, however, of the population in Russia is brachycephalic as in the other parts of Europe. M. Weinberg, moreover, makes singular avowals. He states, for example, that in the governments of the south of Russia, where the distribution of cranial types ought to be fairly uniform, one meets with the most considerable digressions. It is thus that in the governments of Kief, Kharkoff, and that of Poltava the percentage of dolichocephals was from $1\frac{1}{2}$ to 20 per cent.

Another Russian anthropologist, A. A. Ivanovsky, in his " Anthropological Examination of the Russian Population," tells us in his turn that the brachycephalic number 64 per cent. among the white Russians, and 72 per cent. among the Great and the Little Russians. In other words, the ethnical agglomerations considered in Russia to represent racial unities are reduced to a sort of craniological uniformity. In Russia, therefore, as everywhere else the different parts of the population are not to be distinguished by their physiological composition, but by the aspirations of their souls and the diversity of intellectual, moral, social and political interests. Between Russian officials of St. Petersburg, Moscow or Warsaw, connected with the form of autocratic government, there is no doubt more resemblance, in spite of their Polish, Finnish, Tartar or Slav origins, than between two Great Russians who have received an opposite education and show totally different mentalities.

Between the appearance of a free man and that of a slave the difference is, in short, much more striking and more essential than between all the craniological variations which anthropology could establish from their comparison.

---

[1] *Rassen und Herkunft des Russischen Volkes* (Pol. Anthrop. Revue, Nov. 1904). Let our readers remember the reserve with which anthropological measurements must be accepted.

IV

We are apparently more agreed on the history of Jewish anthropology, and yet the conquests of Hebraists have proved that even in this domain our science is only supreme ignorance!

What is this Jewish race whose name has been heard for so many centuries and which, from time immemorial, has exercised the curiosity of politicians, philosophers and historians? What we know of it to-day is limited to the almost certain fact that it is not a matter of race, but of religion. The Jews, who are far from constituting a race in our day, are not even justified in claiming that privilege in the past. When they arrived, few in number, in Palestine a dozen centuries before Christ, they found there all sorts of peoples and races, viz., Hittites, Arabs, Philistines, &c., with whom they finally blended. Dispersed after the time of Alexander, they never ceased making proselytes. On this subject let us recall the conversion "en bloc" of a whole Turkish tribe (the Chazars). Scattered throughout the whole world, they mingled in the life of other nations and underwent, not only the influence of *milieux*, but also those of crossings. They finally gave their blood to all peoples and received theirs in exchange.

To-day the most rigorous anthropologists acknowledge that there is no Jewish type, but rather Jewish types proper to Germany, Poland, Russia, Spain, France, &c. In all countries, we are told, the marked characteristics which distinguish them from their environment are reduced to their political and social position. When the barriers which separate them from other co-inhabitants disappear, the Jews come at last to resemble more and more both intellectually and biologically their immediate surroundings.

Let us take another example as it comes. The Japanese have been considered as the brothers of the Chinese. In this quality they have even furnished Europe with a bogey as to her immediate future, under the form of the "Yellow Peril." Their origin has never been a subject of doubt in the past. But now, having entered within the pale of white civilisation, they excite greater curiosity on the part of savants, who try to lift some of

the clouds which hide their impenetrable past. Suddenly
their yellow origin has become a disputed matter. Certain
distinguished ethnologists even connect them with the Turko-
Tartar families.[1]

But, really, we know nothing of it, just as we know nothing
of the Chinese race itself.

V

The more we study the beginnings of races on the earth, the
more we perceive the absolute impossibility of obtaining light
on their origins. According to Renan's justifiable complaint, we
are in the wrong to apply our habitual methods to periods
" wherein rivers have sons and mountains give birth."

The truth is that we know nothing of their prehistoric phases
and very little of that which preceded the fusion of peoples
and of races. What we know, on the other hand, after a more or
less certain fashion, is that the primitive Aryan, the primitive
Turanian, and the primitive Semitic groups had no physiological
unity.

At the time when we perceive the formation of modern
peoples, it is still more noticeable that ethnographical and
anthropological considerations had no place in it. States, as
they exist in our days, were formed in spite of the ethnical
origins of their inhabitants and even in opposition to them.

Historical anthropology having already furnished us with
negative lights, we remain stupefied before the amount of child-
ishness and ignorance necessary for pretended savants in order
to preach hatred between races amalgamated for centuries.

We do not intend to show the mistakes made with regard to
all these peoples and races. It is enough for us to note certain
obvious errors, with the object of demonstrating the lack of
prudence which characterises the generalisations habitual to
the sociologists and psychologists of ethnical collectivities.

A singular coincidence is that the more a people or a race
appears to be known, the less exact are our ideas on its ethnical

---

[1] See on this subject the curious work of Dr. E. Neumann, *Vom goldenen
Horn zum Euphrat*. The author, a Munich professor, was for a long time a
director of the Geological Institute of Japan. He notes numerous links of
relationship between the tongues and mentalities of the two peoples.

past. Our ignorance grows as the direct consequence of the
efforts made to elucidate the past. This means to say that true
science touches on total ignorance. Let us console ourselves,
however, with the thought of this maxim of Pascal : " It is true
that it is miserable to know that we are miserable, but it is also
great to know our misery. This makes us great lords ! "

Science can proclaim with pride her reasoned ignorance of the
composition of peoples and races, just as she can the absolute
impossibility of grouping them in irreducible partitions. Her
laborious efforts, however, have not been in vain. Having
established the mixture of races as a law, and their age-long
and continued interfusion as a general rule, she can easily
remain content with her inability to gauge their consecutive
elements. She has done something more in rendering impossible
and laughable, anthropologically, the notion of pure races, as
also that of inferior and superior blood.

But has this classification of human beings, which is
biologically and physiologically ephemeral, any chance of
success, intellectually and psychologically ?

PART V

ARE THERE PEOPLES CONDEMNED TO
REMAIN ETERNALLY INFERIOR TO
OTHERS?

CHAPTER I

THE NEGROES

AMONG the most decisive arguments which the partisans of human inequality oppose to their adversaries, the place of honour belongs to those drawn from the life and the evolution of Negroes. One might say that Nature only created them to serve as a dolorous proof of the impassable gulfs which separate the different members of our species. With the ineffaceable impress of colour and many other physiological stains, they are predestined, especially by their moral and intellectual faults, to remain in the bottom ranks of humanity. "A race which holds the middle place between man and monkey," according to some. According to others, it is even declared to be "below animals," for these at least do not desire to rob the White man of his privileged place under the sun! Savage in Africa, they remain savage, we are told, even in the United States, where they show the propensities of gorillas towards white women, or the unconscious instincts of thieving rooks. The repugnance with which they inspire the Whites is greater than that which most animals provoke. They are approached with disgust. In railway compartments and in hotels reserved for the Whites, dogs and parrots are admitted, but men of colour are unmercifully driven away. Everything seems to separate them from their White surroundings—their physiological characteristics, declared fixed and immutable throughout all time; their mentality, considered inferior; their morals, which we are told are deplorable; and, lastly, their animal propensities, which, always alive, wake at the first call of their sub-human instincts. Like the Gibeonites of the Scriptures, American writers tell us.

they were created to hew wood and draw water for white men. To wish to prove their equality with other mortals is a defiance of the Supreme will, so say the white bishops of the South. Mr. Charles Carroll, the author of the work, *The Negro is a Beast*, or *In the Image of God*, points out by texts drawn from the Bible that the Negro is a beast, created with an articulate tongue and hands, in order that he may serve his white master.[1] To bear out his theory, the author quotes among other things this proof, viz., that man has been created in the image of God, but God not being a Negro, as everyone knows, it follows that the Negro is not in the image of God, and therefore he is not a man. Teachers of the greatest repute, even those who are called to form and direct the American soul, try to inculcate this thought, that no instruction or education can take away from the Negro conscience its ineffaceable mark of inferiority. Judge Tilman, again, in his little work on the *Plant System*, brings forward, in favour of the general prejudice, this pious argument, that "He who at the dawn of creation placed moving sands as barriers to the impetuous waves, saying, 'Here is your limit!' placed also and forever his seal on the Negro in his black skin, woolly hair, thick lips, snub nose, and anatomy differing from that of a white man. His limited intelligence is announced in this prophecy made thousands of years ago, no less true to-day than then—*Thou shalt be the Slave of Slaves!*"

Thus in the Negroes we have the true type of human inferiority! Let us study it closer, to see what truth there may be in this conception of the most degraded race.

I. *Physiological Characteristics*

In examining the question of long and narrow skulls, hair, colour of skin, Negro odour, &c., we have discussed the different traits which rouse objections against the Blacks. In the light of impartial observation, the fundamental and immutable qualities of Negro physiology undergo perceptible modifications.

---

[1] Quotation borrowed from the remarkable work of M. Urbain Gohier on the *Peuple du XXe. siècle* (*i.e.*, the American people, whom the author deals with socially, politically, educationally, &c.

The Negroes only confirm this general rule, that everything which divides humanity is not immutable.

This incessant transition of different characteristics prevents the human species from degenerating into a number of fixed types. Negroes, whom it is desired to regard as forming a separate human species, tend, like other human beings, to become similar to other human races when they are subjected to similar conditions of physical and mental *milieu*.

Their resemblance to the Whites in the United States baffles every artifice resorted to in order to recognise them. We even have at the present time numerous American novels, the tragic plot of which is based on the *entrée* of "perfected" negroes into the life of the Whites.[1] But in truth can one regard these brilliant specimens of the evolution of races as true negroes? This identification of Whites and Negroes goes very far, as is proved by the curious example quoted by John S. Durham (*Atlantic Monthly*, vol. 81). Two brothers (coloured), printers by trade, came to Philadelphia a few years ago to look for work. The one entered a printing-house where none but white men worked, and became foreman. At the end of two years, a workman became acquainted with the fact of his colour and denounced him. The Whites immediately sent a delegation to the proprietor demanding that the coloured man should be immediately dismissed. The proprietor, although appreciating the merit of his foreman, informed him of the cruel necessity which compelled him to give way to the remonstrances of his subordinates.

The unhappy "Negro" asked him as a favour to accept his brother in his place. "In that way," said he, "I shall be able to live on his wages as he has lived on mine." It was done. The workmen, ignorant of the origin of their new foreman, worked under him for a long time, until the fact was discovered.

---

[1] Among others we note the novel of Mrs. Gertrude Atherton, *Senator North*. A rich Southern heiress, Miss Madison, receives under her roof her young sister, the offspring of a *liaison* of her father with a coloured woman. Nothing in the newcomer betrays her origin, so that Harriet Walker easily passes for a white woman. Astonished at her beauty, Miss Madison exclaims, "You will be happy. I will make you forget *everything!*" But Harriet answers, with a despairing glance, "Not *everything*, for somewhere in me, hidden but present, is a black vein swollen with the blood of slaves." This is an allusion to her finger nails. A white man, however, falls in love with her, and as no one in her circle of acquaintances has recognised her degraded origin, she marries him. The tragedy only breaks out when Harriet herself undertakes to inform her husband of "her hereditary stain."

This is how Mr. Durham concludes:—"The first of the two brothers gave up the struggle in despair. He fled into a vaster world, viz., that of the Whites, who, ignorant of his origin, allowed him to live their life and to enjoy all the privileges which in the United States are reserved for Whites alone."

Booker Washington dwells pleasantly on the embarrassments of railway guards in the United States. "Is such a traveller a Negro or is he not?" so the perplexed employees often ask themselves. If he is, he must be made to enter the compartment reserved for people of colour. But *if he is not*, and if one undertakes to assign him a place which is considered humiliating for the Whites, what a responsibility!

The American tribunals have had to judge cases in which Southern European women, who had been taken for coloured women and compelled to enter the special Negro carriages, have demanded and obtained heavy indemnities.

M. Jules Huret, in the interesting souvenirs of his travels, *En Amérique*, tells us the same thing with regard to the transformation of the Negro type. After a close observation of the pupils of the Tuskegee Institute, he states that not one of the 1,400 young people who receive their education under Booker Washington carries any longer the stigma of slavery. Besides the quite pure offspring of Soudanese Negroes we have the most finished types of the human race, figures of "amber tinted women with delicate and almost haughty profile, eyes ardent, melancholy, and as though bathed in liquid mother-of-pearl, lips just full enough to denote sensitiveness, chin raised with a gracious curve, noble oval face, figure delicate and supple, hand small and distinguished." Now, all these women are merely quadroon and octoroon negresses of Jamaica, Porto Rico, and other parts of the globe. This Parisian, free from all prejudice of race, concludes with justice that in France and in Europe all these women would be surrounded with the praises of men, whereas in the Southern States they are penned up like lepers in special schools, special railway carriages, and special hotels.

Mrs. Mary Church Terrell, the honorary President of the large "Association of Coloured Women," confirmed in my hearing this frequent impossibility of distinguishing Whites from Negroes.

She herself, belonging to the most beautiful Southern type, can both travel as she likes in railway carriages reserved for Whites, and also enter their hotels. And yet, as she told me with her pleasant smile, " My parents were slaves, and, like so many others of my brothers and sisters, I only owe my liberty to the War of Secession." She personally could have lived among the Whites, if she had not preferred to fulfil her duty towards her unhappy and humiliated ' sisters. The number of coloured men and women mixed with the Whites and participating without hindrance in their ordinary life is incalculable. If ever the white portion could fall from the face of those who have no right to it in the Southern States, their social life would be singularly revolutionised. And not without cause. The influence of the *milieu*, including cross-breeding with the Whites, has effected radical modifications.

At the present time it is a vain task to seek distinctive characteristics among certain products of Negroes crossed with Whites. Dr. Pearce Kintzing, who has devoted several years of his life to the study of this question, mentions the same fact in *American Medicine* (July 1904).

He tells us we can no longer find means of distinguishing mixed blood from white blood, except in American novels. In real life everything deceives us, including the colour of the nails, which, according to certain lady novelists of the South, is so infallible. In order to dissipate all illusions, Dr. Kintzing for three years submitted to close examination 500 · patients from among the Whites and the Blacks. The students were called to decide as to the origin of the subject, who was completely covered excepting the nails. But the errors were so obvious and so frequent that Dr. Kintzing finally rejected the nails as a characteristic sign. Other significant traits deceive us in a like manner. The same author quotes cases of coloured children in the hospital who were entered as Whites.

The persecution and injustice of the Whites, however, continue their work. Worried and despised, the " Blacks," including even those who have ceased to be such, become more and more united, and constitute a kind of State within a State. The humiliations suffered by them all in common hasten this unifying process. It may be said that the Negroes are being driven back upon themselves, whilst the present miseries of their existence are impeding the process of their moral and intellectual liberation.

Everything in the meantime permits us to believe that this is an arrest of a somewhat sentimental nature. The Negroes, far from being discouraged, resume their efforts, and are working valiantly for the emancipation of their thought and their persons. The school of sorrow is the best of schools. It has been proved by nearly all people (and one observes the same phenomenon among individuals regarded singly) that adversity and privation only quicken and develop the intellectual faculties and ameliorate the moral life. The Negroes, always in the school of misfortune, become more moral and more enlightened, more rich and more independent. Their physiological progress (!), to use anthropological language, being aided by their intellectual progress, an impartial observer can already foresee the time, not too far distant, when the two hostile races shall arrive at understanding and unity.

The psychology of primitive peoples, and especially of Negroes, strangely resembles that of the uncultured classes of Europe. The inhabitants of a Negro village in Central Africa are like peasants living far from railways in the extreme north of Russia or the extreme south of Italy. Travellers who go among the Negroes without preconceived ideas notice the narrowness of their minds, their strongly accentuated *misoneisme*, the littleness of their daily preoccupations, and their love of noisy knick-knacks. The women gossip, get jealous, and quarrel. The men fight and envy each other, whilst the children grow up anyhow under the tender eyes of their mothers and the indifference of their fathers. A similar state of things is also met with among trading Negroes. The Negro palavers themselves are in certain respects strikingly like the communal assemblies of villages in outlying parts of the Old World.

Whilst showing virtues and vices common to other men, the Negro, living closer to nature, has certain sides of his character more accentuated and certain others less so than those which characterise White populations. African Negroes resemble one another much more than the White population of Europe. The process of the differentiation of individuals, which is effected

under the influence of the innumerable factors of culture, has
scarcely as yet touched the Negro soul, which from this cause has
remained more whole, more one. But in following their
evolution in the United States, we see how that, when exposed
to the action of the factors which have fashioned the soul of the
Whites, the same stupid Negro, careless and often even cannibal,
assimilates the mentality and the intellectual conceptions of
the latter.

Cannibalism is often but the result of the cult of ancestors
wrongly understood. They are killed and eaten in order that
their family virtues may be preserved. All explorers are at one
in marking the disappearance of this custom through the
influence of more civilised tribes. The contempt with which
these last regard cannibals causes their number to diminish
rapidly. The moment is close at hand when cannibalism
shall have completely vanished from the earth.

CHAPTER II

NEGRO MENTALITY

IT is fruitless to maintain the theory of the mental inferiority of Negroes, and the consequent impossibility of civilising them.

Everything which explorers tell us of their life in general, even of that of the primitive Negroes of Central Africa, furnishes us with proofs to the contrary. Let us not forget that it would be thoroughly unjust to measure their psychological life and moral aspirations by the standard of peoples who have behind them centuries of civilisation and intellectual progress. Those who undertake to compare the mentality of European peasants with that of the White *élite* would no doubt find between them a much greater gulf than between these same peasants and the Blacks of Central Africa. Their prepossessions, ideas, and superstitions betray a similarity which draws them singularly together. This resemblance becomes still more striking when we compare Negroes and peasants living in an analogous *milieu*. The men of the forest (the Pahouin) are radically distinct from the Negroes of the valley. The numerous works of M. Cureau, who, as chief administrator of the French Colonies, had the opportunity of studying the Negro soul during many years, teach us how the *milieu* and occupation succeed in fashioning primitive mentality and mode of life. Whereas the Pahouin coming out of his gloomy coppice and mixing with other men resembles the bat blinded by light, the man of the plains and of the great rivers is frank, gay, and exuberant.

The first is anxious and suspicious; he dreams only of returning beneath his sombre covert in the sad and melancholy woods. The second, ready to mix with new-comers, receives them with open arms as long as such new-comers do not abuse his confidence. Nay, his gentleness and hospitality surpass those of the popular classes in Europe. It is enough to examine his intimate life more closely to see how many common traits connect it with that of the Whites. The women love their little ones with the same tenderness and the same abnegation as those of Europe, whilst the fathers are similarly less tender. " If a mother passes through a village with her little one, a traveller tells us, all the others will come and take the child, hold it in their arms, lift it up, and make it jump! A cannibal who has just been enjoying a piece of human flesh is quite as capable of doing this as the most sensitive of our civilised folk."

Cannibalism itself does not there present such repulsive sides as are generally represented to us. It nowhere constitutes an instinct or an innate desire, but a simple custom. Those who practise it on a large scale are not on that account less sympathetic even with Europeans. "They are gentle, light-hearted, and have agreeable relations with their friends. To eat the bodies of their enemies seems to them as natural as an *auto-da-fé* of heretics would have seemed to a peaceful citizen of the sixteenth century." [1]

Cannibalism considered from this point of view is only a peculiar kind of warfare or the extension of the hunt for human prey. Let us acknowledge, however, that the civilised eat their neighbour in a much more cruel way, though no doubt with greater formality. An exploiting patron of the poor classes, or a financier who owing to his dishonest operations ruins thousands of families and is often the cause of numerous suicides, has on his conscience more victims than a whole tribe of cannibals.

We remember this sally of John C. Calhoun: " If I could find a Negro who knew Greek syntax, I would believe that the Negro was a human being and ought to be treated as a man." This happened in 1834, when the Senator of South Carolina was able with impunity to promise the Negroes his special consideration on impossible conditions. As the most severe punishments were meted out to any person who undertook to

[1] Dr. Cureau, *Psychologie des races nègres de l'Afrique tropicale. Revue Générale des Sciences*, 1904, Nos. 14 and 15.

teach the alphabet to a coloured child, it was improbable that any Negro would comprehend the tongue of Homer and Plato.

Negro education is of quite recent date. Before the War of Secession the instruction of the Blacks was formally interdicted in the Slave States.[1]

Persons accused of having violated this law were liable to be imprisoned or whipped. The first school for Negroes was founded at New York in 1704 by a Frenchman, Elias Neau. He brought together, with the permission of slave masters and at the cost of great personal efforts, about 200 children. Neau taught for nothing, regarding duty done to these unfortunate children as its own reward. The example given by this noble Frenchman was afterwards followed in the Northern States by many beneficent societies. In the South the hostile feelings directed against the education of the Negroes persisted up to the time of the War of Secession.

It is thus that in Carolina alone there were, in 1874, 200 Negro judges who did not know how to read or write. The same fact applies to the members of the School Commission, who, illiterate as they were, presided over the destinies of the schools. The majority of the Negro senators, Andrews tells us, during the eight years' reconstruction of the Southern States which immediately followed the war, were unable to write three lines. Some did not even know how to read, and yet these were recruited from among the Negro *élite*.

The instruction of the Blacks only began with the war of liberation. Under the supervision of Northern officials, schools were founded where Negroes might receive primary instruction. They were military schools of a special kind, giving lessons in citizenship instead of superior instruction in the art of killing one's neighbours. In the space of a year (1863–1864) General Banks succeeded in establishing in Louisiana ninety-five schools, with 162 masters and 9571 pupils. General Howard states in his report of January 1st, 1866, that there were already in the South 740 schools, with more than 1300 masters and 90,500

---

[1] See on this subject : *L'Education des Nègres aux Etats-Unis*, by Kate Brousseau ; G. W. Williams, *History of the Negro Race in America ;* E. B. Andrews, *Last Quarter of Century in the United States ;* Meriwether, *History of Higher Education in South Carolina ;* Booker T. Washington, *The Future of the American Negro ; Up from Slavery*, &c., &c.

pupils. This is the real beginning of Negro civilisation! It only happened forty years ago, from which about ten years should be subtracted, inasmuch as Negro instruction, far from meeting with ardent sympathy, was for a long time subjected to all sorts of persecutions. The impediments placed before the work of education by the fanatics of the South and by want of judgment on the part of the legislators of the North, caused irreparable harm. On the other hand, Negroes, deceived by their illusions on the subject of a liberal education, came to regard instruction with aversion. The Negro masses could only have a great contempt for an education which only served to make them more despicable and wretched. The unbridled ambition of these children of nature suffered cruelly in their contact with life and its mortifications. Their pride was wounded by the jests of the Whites and by their own unsatiated hunger. As all doors were closed to them they became subject to criminal temptations. In pointing to the results without seeking the causes, the best-intentioned Whites began to doubt the morality and intellectual capacity of coloured folks. It became the fashion to speak of their innate evil instincts, and of their inability to assimilate real White civilisation. The hatred of their enemies and the impatience of their friends had mournful consequences. Both the one and the other forgot this elementary truth, that the delay of a moral reaction is at least proportional to the duration of the original evil. The ill-omened work of centuries cannot be wiped out by the influence of a few years of justice.

Let us remember, therefore, in the first place, that during a very long period the schools in the South lacked masters. Professors refused to teach there, for fear of being despised and hated by their fellow citizens. It became necessary to approach the people of the North. These replied to the appeal with the ardour and faith of true missionaries. People went to instruct in the South as they went to convert savages in Central Africa.

Contact with the prejudices of the Whites, however, was exceedingly dangerous, for their reception was more hostile and their hatred more implacable than that of savages. The White professors of both sexes who came from the North were banned by society. They were regarded with disgust and shunned like people infected with the plague. A pastor of Georgia declared, in a reply to a commission of inquiry, " I know nothing of those females from the North who have come to teach in our coloured schools. I have never spoken to one of them. They are rigorously excluded from society " (K. Brousseau). The professors, discouraged, took refuge in the North, abandoning their schools. Teaching was thus often interrupted. If scorn and innumerable petty artifices did not suffice to deter masters from their duty, violence was resorted to. Schools were burnt, at the risk of destroying both the accursed buildings and their evil genii, the teachers. If these attempts failed, they did not hesitate at nocturnal attacks. White teachers, male and female, were often beaten and whipped.

In these resorts to intimidation or violence, numerous secret societies were particularly prominent, of which the Ku Klux Klan was the most formidable. It was founded in 1866 in the State of Tennessee, in order to hinder negro electors at the ballot-box and to forbid coloured people from attending elective functions. In burlesque disguises the members of the Klan entered the huts of Negroes, and tried to terrify their imagination by means of divers extravagant ceremonies. Sometimes, with a bag on the arm in the shape of a heart, they proclaimed in a loud voice that they were carrying the flesh of a fried nigger. At other times, wearing india-rubber stomachs, they astonished Negroes by drinking bucketfuls of water. But in addition to these puerilities they were also given to downright murders. They paraded about in bands, wearing horrible masks and white robes, and throwing themselves on the Negroes, whom they crippled or beat for the least fault. The Whites who were accused of conniving with the Negroes, and especially the teachers, both male and female, suffered the same fate. In this way the members of the Ku Klux Klan succeeded in closing the numerous schools in the State of Mississippi. The Governor, R. C. Powers, even announced this monstrous fact at the Congress, that for eight months no Negro school had been tolerated in the county of Winston, and that all the houses which had served as schools save one had been burnt down (Andrews). The other Slave States were in the same predicament. In Georgia, for example, there was in 1871 a great number of localities where no school for people of colour was tolerated. The burning of schools and churches was very frequent.

The persecution of schools was prolonged for a number of years. The Whites ostensibly showed greater sympathy towards illiterate Negroes than to those who had had the misfortune to pass through the schools. Nevertheless, in spite of all these obstacles, Negroes have succeeded in realising a progress which is altogether astounding.

Towards 1899 the position of people of colour in the United States, according to the 11th census and other administrative documents, was as follows:—There were only 8 per 1,000 destitutes among the Negroes. The Whites show as many, but these last had 64 rich for 1 rich Negro. Of 100 proprietors there were 75 Whites for 25 Blacks, but *proportionately* the latter should not have exceeded 12 or 13. Of 100 Negro houses, 87 were free from all mortgage, whilst of 100 houses belonging to Whites there were only 71 such.

The value of 130,000 Negro farms represented in round numbers 2,000 million francs (£80,000,000), that of their churches about 1,190 millions (£47,000,000), that of 150,000 landed estates, excluding farms, about £70,000,000, whilst their movable property amounted to about £32,000,000. What is more significant is that four-fifths of the work done in the South was done by Negro labour.

In his inaugural address in April, 1904, Mr. John Gordon, President of the Howard University, stated that this university "of colour" had in the thirty-seven years of its existence conferred university degrees on more than 2,000 students, of whom 200 were pastors, 700 doctors, 200 solicitors, &c.

The Fisk University in 1900 could account for 400 diplomas of colour, of which 17 were doctors, 9 lawyers, 46 headmasters of schools, 165 teachers, and 19 ministers of religion. The same applies to the thirty-six other universities, which all do their utmost to elevate the Negroes. It must be stated, however, that the general level, with the exception of Howard, is much inferior to that of White universities. Owing to lack of resources, they were obliged to be satisfied with less capable masters, poor laboratories, and a rudimentary organisation. But

owing to the enthusiasm and zeal of professors, their instruction gives very satisfactory results. Coloured women, unwilling
to be behind their brothers and husbands, contend advan-
tageously with them in the sphere of higher education. Nearly
all the Negro universities open their doors to women, and
accord to them equal treatment in what concerns studies
and official diplomas. We lack data for the period which
follows the year 1898, in which the feminist movement made
the most considerable progress, but it is sufficient to note that
up to that time the United States already counted 82 women
of colour who had obtained university degrees in the North
and 170 in the universities of the South.

These brilliant results have been acquired in a short time.
Certain writers of the North have raised objections against the
Southern Negroes for having spent 250 million francs, since the
time of their emancipation, for purposes of education. This
sum is astonishing for its very moderation. According to
Kelly Miller, the city of New York spends as much every two
years. The Negroes, however, number 10,000,000, cover an
immense territory, while the statement applies to a period of
forty years. With reason does Booker Washington insist on the
poverty of schools of colour. We are told that about 100 francs
is spent on each child in the States of New York and Massa-
chussetts, and only 2 francs 50 in the South. He mentions
certain schools in the South where neither the State nor the
public authorities possess a pennyworth of scholastic materials,
school, black board, or pencil. In the State of Georgia 200,000
Negro children have not been able to enter any school !

The disillusions which came to poor coloured graduates
through their unfruitful diplomas created among the Negroes
an admirable movement in favour of industrial schools. Those of
Hampton and that more recent one of Tuskegee are real models
of the kind, worthy of imitation by the Whites. This last contains to-day about 50 buildings, of which 47 have been built
by the hands of the scholars, and also 2,500 acres of ground
tilled by the same hands. The teaching body is composed
of 112 professors, teachers, &c. During the year 1901, 1,324
were taught 28 different industries. For the immense building
raised in 1901, 800,000 bricks were necessary, which were all

manufactured by the students of Tuskegee. The plaster, masonry, wood-work, painting, lead-roofing—in a word, all the supplies, including electricity—were done by the pupils on the premises. The machines, of which one was of 125 horse-power, were also installed by students. When the latter have not sufficient to pay for their schooling (about 400 francs per year), they work in the day, and the money they earn is devoted to the free schools in the evening. Owing to the Slater foundation, a number of other professional schools have been established, where, besides special instruction, the attempt is made to give pupils a general instruction.

Great activity has also been shown in the world of women. Together with agriculture, they are taught the best way of pro-fitably managing dairies and farmyards. Coloured women in this way work for the regeneration of their sisters. Their work and spirit of initiative is enormous. They have formed a nucleus of "farming societies," societies for village improvements, &c., which exercise a great educating influence.

If we would talk of the creative faculty of the Negro it would be necessary to mention their numerous poets, novelists, *savants*, engineers, and inventors, like Paul Lawrence Dunbar (the Negro Victor Hugo); Kelly Miller, the mathematician; Dr. Blyden, lin-guist; Booker Washington, the genial schoolmaster and a public man of the first order; du Bois, political writer and historian, &c. To see with what difficulties the Negro *litterateurs* have had to struggle, let us remember that Dunbar, who died quite recently at the age of thirty-two, was the son of a simple slave who had found refuge in Canada. His youth, full of miseries and of pri-vations, and his most simple education had ill prepared him for the trade of writer. After having started as a lift boy, he began to educate himself and to write poetry, which he took to like measles, as he loved to say. Everything was against him, even the language, that detestable jargon of American Negroes, in which he wrote touching poems of humble life and the fireside.

W. E. Burghardt du Bois tells[1] us with reason that the Ne-groes perhaps best incarnate the fundamental spirit of indepen-

---

[1] See his curious work, *The Souls of Black Folk*, recently published by A. Constable, a mixture of the dreams of a poet and the meditations of a philosopher on the miseries and hopes of his black brethren.

dence of the United States ; that America has no more national
music than that of the gentle and at the same time wild
melodies of black souls, just as American folk-lore would be non-
existent were it not for that of Redskins and Negroes. The
Negroes form in America, the land of dollars, the only oasis where
the Ideal and where Faith may find refuge, so says somewhere
the same du Bois. Elsewhere he goes on to tell us that the
United States would not be the imposing United States of our
day without the help of the Negro race. There is no doubt a
partial truth behind this exaggeration. The Negroes have
become flesh of the American flesh and blood of her blood in
having suffered and toiled with the great founders of the United
States as also in the love which they bear to their common
country.

In spite of the lateness and insufficiency of the technical
instruction which American Negroes have received, they have
found the means of distinguishing themselves in this sphere.
The Patent Office of New York, for instance, proves that up
to 1900, 357 patents were taken out by coloured people.
In the United States, where aptitude for industrial and commercial affairs is considered as a proof of intellectual superiority,
it is interesting to note that coloured commercial men are
already so numerous that they have been able to establish a
special association, viz., the *National Negro Business League,*
whose members are counted by the thousand.

CHAPTER III

NEGRO MORALITY

BUT when the slaves of the prejudice of races see themselves forced to render justice to the Negro intelligence which is equal in every way to that of the Whites, they console themselves, at the risk of being taxed with partiality, with the thought of the "innate" immorality of the blacks.

Herein we find a regrettable inferiority, so say the detractors of Negroes, and with them all the anthropologists who believe in the "fatality" of blood and of colour. This accusation must fall before facts. In vain do the enemies of the Negro race endeavour to convince us that their bad qualities increase with education. Statistics, to which belongs the decisive voice, are a standing refutation of their assertion. Moreover, where Negro criminality is very great, it deserves a special absolution.

The coloured population is still going through one of its most critical periods. In one day it found itself thrown from slavery into freedom, without any moral or material resources. It was necessary to cut a path through life at the cost of superhuman efforts. Far from being encouraged by its old masters in the way of moral perfection, it has never ceased to be the butt of their railleries and persecutions. The North, in its desire to humiliate the South, did the greatest harm to these children of nature in according to them there and then the fullest political rights. Called to vote, the Negroes, with all their limitations and illiteracy, did their best to envenom still further their relations with the Whites. Vain like children and intoxicated with the power which came so suddenly into their hands, they lost all sense of reality. Work being to them synonymous with slavery, they considered all occupation to be incompatible with liberty. Idle and vain, they played with life like dogs do with objects which fall between their paws. In their heedlessness and want of comprehension of the world which they entered without the least preparation, they very soon lost all balance, together with that little Christian morality which had been taught them in servitude. Those who had had the benefit of a liberal education were soon discouraged by the disdain of the Whites and the difficulty of earning their bread.

The number of coloured *declassés* was growing, as all could see, and with it the number of criminals. Little by little their eyes were opened. Men of goodwill and initiative from among the Whites of the North, like General Armstrong, and from among Negroes, like Booker Washington, saw that in the present state of things the future belonged to professional teaching, and they directed their efforts on this side. Thus a second revolution took place in the inner life of Negroes which made them better men and more dignified. Even apart from these extenuating circumstances, the Negroes need not lower their heads before the Whites. It would be fastidious to compare in detail the number of white criminals with that of coloured people. Let us note, however, that the increase of coloured inhabitants in a locality does not increase the rate of criminality. The proportion remains the same. The Negroes are especially accused of being at variance with the Code in the North. In this, Negro writers like Booker Washington and Professor du Bois, &c., tell us there is nothing astonishing. The Negroes come there especially from the South, living on the outskirts of society sometimes for reasons known to the police of the localities from which they come, and sometimes as immigrants looking for work.

But when they have reached the North, they find themselves subject to the persecutions of the syndicates of work. Discouraged and famished, they often succumb to the temptations of despair and misery.

But in the North as well as in the South the number of convictions in no way corresponds with the criminality of Negroes. The jury composed of Whites is frankly hostile to them. Not only do the police harass them and bring them before tribunals for the least thing, but these tribunals also condemn them for the smallest offences. In certain Southern States there is even a kind of special premium which gives an impetus to the conviction of Negroes. For their keep in the prisons brings in considerable profits to the States, to say nothing of the middleman. A Negro prisoner as such is obliged to work on farms and in mines and industries. It is calculated that a prisoner generally brings in about 750 francs to the State (J. A. Hobson). In most cases White contractors, worse than the old planters, harshly exploit their work and enrich themselves at their expense. Everyone, from the State to the contractor, is thus interested in heavy penalties. For the longer the imprisonment, the more the revenues of the State and of the exploiter of Negro labour increase.

Owing to the prejudices and the hatred of the judges, the Negroes have to put up with convictions which are often unjust, and which are nearly always more severe than those meted out to Whites. Frequently, when a disorder breaks out in a Negro centre, a disorder the causes of which are often mysterious, a kind of raffle takes place among them. Arrested, accused, and condemned to pay large fines, the poor Blacks find it impossible to pay. A White benefactor then appears, and, after having reimbursed the sums fixed by the tribunal, takes the Negroes into his service in virtue of a public contract.

These shocking abuses of judicial power ought rather to increase the sum of White criminality, which is thus weighted with the charge of partiality and injustice! They are made, however, to increase that of the Blacks.

After all, can one decently ask from a race exasperated by all kinds of barbarous and unjust treatment, that self-respect and moral dignity which constitute the best barriers against criminal leanings?

Let us add that certain of their crimes are only of a transitory character. Such are the small thefts which are so objected to in Negroes. During the period of slavery the Blacks were deprived of all property. Everything which they succeeded in acquiring belonged by right to their masters. The Negro, not being able to take possession of the property of another, did not really steal. He displaced but in no way diminished his master's wealth. The latter in any case remained the proprietor of everything which belonged to his slaves. Booker Washington tells the funny story of a slave who after stealing his master's chickens justified himself in this way: "Now, Massa, it is true you have a little less chicken; but, Massa, you have a little more Negro." Conceptions rooted in the Negro conscience for centuries cannot disappear in a summer's night. Let us content ourselves with saying that really educated Negroes are unharmed by them. This is an evident proof that theft is not in the Negro blood. It is only the temporary result of a special mentality, of a particular state of soul, of which the Whites are in the first place the most guilty.

The same applies to their family life. One reproaches them with immorality, forgetting that marriage and the family only date among coloured folk from the emancipation. In the time of slavery there were neither husbands, wives, parents, nor children. The master disposed of the life and well-being of his slaves as of his other chattels. Mulattoes, who number more than two millions, are there to bear testimony to the respect of the planters for the chastity of negro women in general and for their own conjugal life in particular! The women were separated from their husbands as it pleased their masters, the children were transported if necessary far from their parents, the young girls were delivered to the caprice of the planters and their employees, and all this with the aid of the law, which admitted no resistance on the part of those interested; such is the account of family life in the old days. How could it flourish in a *milieu* from which one never ceased to banish it ?

The liberty accorded to men of colour was powerless to revive in a day virtues which perhaps never existed. One must allow time to work. Seconded by the moral and intellectual culture which Negroes of to-day enjoy, they will be allowed to rise to the level of the Whites. Already a perfect morality is established among Negro women who have passed through the school. The inquiry made by Mrs. E. C. Hobson and Mrs. E. C. Hopkins, at the request of the administrators of the John Slater Foundation,[1] furnishes us with proofs of it.

[1] *The Trustees of the John Slater Fund Occasional Papers*, No. IX. 1896.

Whenever the vitality and the future of the White races are dealt with, there is much concern as to the birth-rate amongst them. With reason or without, there is seen in the numerical increase of the population a symptom of health and a criterion as to the part which history has in store for it. From this point of view, the coloured folk of the States are far ahead of the Russians and the Italians, who are regarded as the most prolific of peoples. Whereas other Americans, by themselves and not including immigrants, are diminishing in number, the coloured population never ceases to grow.

Since 1860 (we must leave out the period before the liberation of the Negroes, which was marked by an incessant arrival of slaves from Africa) the Negro population has more than doubled. From about five millions in 1870 it became six millions and a half in 1880, seven millions and a half in 1890, and about nine millions in 1900.

At the present time about 280 American counties, with an extent of about 150,000 square miles, contain a Negro population numbering far more than that of the Whites, there being about 130 Blacks to every 100 Whites.

A serious crime against chastity weighs heavily on the Negro conscience, viz., the rape of White women. This fact saddens profoundly the best among the Negroes, as also those Whites who really sympathise with them. Without wishing to find excuses for Negro criminality on this matter, we must observe that its gravity is apt to be measured by the indignation of the Whites rather than by the true number of crimes committed. Lynching singularly changes the nature of justice in very often making people suspected of a crime first the accused and then the victims. The Negroes reply, however, with reason that the crime of rape is not unknown among the Whites, who indeed practise it on a large scale.

Immoral men are equally to be despised, whatever may be the colour of their skin. White men who commit this crime against Negro women are equal to the Negroes who are guilty of it against White women. Let us not forget, however, that all the cases of lynching are not solely due to outrages against White women. According to certain American statistics, there were lynched in the Southern States, from 1891 to 1902, 1,862 persons, of whom only 1,448 were for attacks against women, 770 for murders, &c.

This kind of justice, however, or rather injustice, has the effect of giving rise to the very crimes which it is intended to stifle.   Exasperated by the stupid ferocity of crowds, Negroes avenge themselves in multiplying the crimes which seem to touch their persecutors the most.   American legislators understand this so well that they are now waging a war to the death against lynching in general, and against that caused by the rape of white women in particular.

The profound transformations which are being effected in the lives of the Blacks will alone cause this crime to cease.   Both coloured agriculturists and educated Negroes are exempt from it.   Its complete disappearance only depends on the Whites themselves.   Let them try to be more just towards the Negroes, let them strive to make amends towards them for the crimes of the past, let them be penetrated with the idea that the virtue of a coloured woman is equal to that of a white, let them beware of lynching in particular (that incomparable breeding ground for the multiplication of evil instincts), and this crime which desolates the Whites of the South will gradually die away.   It will entirely disappear when the two races shall have understood that they only form two arms of the same body, and that on their friendship and fraternal work depends the happiness of the Southern States.

CHAPTER IV

THE NEGRO FUTURE AND THE TRIUMPH OF THE MILIEU

To understand the extent of the progress effected by the coloured people, one ought to compare the point they have reached with that from which they started. Negroes have only been on the territory of the United States two hundred and fifty years.[1]

The historians, it is true, mention certain transportations of slaves brought there before 1650, but the number of these "immigrants" was very small, and never exceeded from two to three hundred.

The period of the forced immigration of the Blacks into North America begins in 1672 with the activity of the *African Royal Company*. According to Bancroft, the number of slaves rose in 1754 to 293,000. Forty years later it exceeded 700,000. At the time of the enfranchisement of the negroes in 1863, it was already four and a half millions.

It is important to notice that the importation of Negroes continued incessantly during all this time. If it is impossible to state precisely the annual arrivals, we can nevertheless conclude that they were very considerable. Here is an indirect proof of it.

Between 1790 and 1860 the Negro population had mounted up from 757,000 to 4,450,000—that is to say, it became six times greater in seventy years. Between 1860 and 1900 the Negroes increased from four millions and a half to nine millions (in round numbers)—in other words, they doubled in forty years. It is also generally supposed that their birth-rate even

---

[1] Bancroft, *History of the United States*, vol. I. ; G. W. Williams, *History of the Negro Race in America*, vol. I., etc.

increased during the first years after the emancipation ! Now this fact shows that the extraordinary increase of Negroes, in the period between 1790 and 1860, ought to be attributed to the fresh slaves who never ceased pouring in from Africa. In reality the slave trade continued to prosper in the United States up to 1860.[1]

Several authors mention scandalous captures by English cruisers about this time of slave-ships belonging to American citizens. " In the space of a year and a half, 1859–1860, eighty-five slave-ships were armed at New York, and these ships alone transported in a year from 30,000 to 60,000 slaves " (du Bois).

In 1858 twenty-one Negro slave-ships were seized by English cruisers. Although the Puritans of the North condemned slavery among themselves, perhaps because the climatic and industrial conditions made it profitless, they did not, therefore, despise the very lucrative commerce in human flesh. They armed slave-ships, transported slaves into South Carolina, and brought back materials for the construction of ships.

The city of New York was the chief port in the world for this infamous trade. It shared this sad celebrity with Portland and Boston. From these three places there sailed frequent cargoes for the Southern States.

It follows from all these data that the length of time the full Black population has lived in the United States, can only be fixed on an average at about one hundred and twenty-five years, because for the small number which came in the seventeenth century we have an immense number only dating from the eighteenth century, and a still greater mass which only arrived in the nineteenth century. Moreover, the geographical origins of the American Negroes are very varied. Slaves were obtained from the Congo, the Gambia, the Niger, Zanzibar, Central Africa, as well as from Guinea and the Gold Coast.

They arrived from everywhere. Among them were the Nigritians of Soudan, the Bantus from southern equatorial Africa, and the Guineans, with their subdivisions including the Kroo, Grebo and Bassa, etc. When they embarked they were real savages, and were long kept in the same condition by the planters. They laboured like domestic animals and were

[1] Prof. du Bois, *Suppression of the Slave Trade.* See also *The American Slave Trade*, by Spears.

regarded as such by their masters. "The slave constituted a piece of personal movable property, and could be sold or mortgaged, or given in bail as his master wished" (G. M. Stroud). "I tried on the 22nd of June to prevent the Indians and Negroes from being placed on the same footing as horses and pigs, but I did not succeed." [1] And still, in spite of these persecutions, in spite of the relatively recent date of their arrival in the United States, we have seen the manifest progress which the Negroes have realised.

Already very distinct biologically from their African brothers, they serve as a living proof of what the influence of the *milieu* can accomplish in the case of very distinct races. In addition, their intellectual and moral progress, achieved in so short a lapse of time, demonstrates that all human races are capable of rising to the level of the Whites.

When we examine the position of Negroes in the other countries of the world, we arrive at the same conclusion. With the change of *milieu*, understood in its widest sense, their physical and moral type changes.

Let us take, for example, the island of Jamaica, in which the Negroes were enfranchised in 1838. The beginning of their liberty was not of the happiest. Aroused from their age-long torpor and given the dignity of free men, whilst having at the same time the mentality of beasts of burden, the poor Blacks made themselves conspicuous by their extravagance of unbridled savagery and the heedlessness which characterises schoolboys freed from their master's control. But twenty years were enough to recall them to reality. To-day Mr. W. P. Livingston, the conscientious historian of the Negroes of Jamaica, states that the 610,000 Negroes of that island form an honest and hard-working population. We can only marvel at their progress. This incessant forward march authorises us to entertain the best hopes for the future. Far from being the victims of civilisation, the Blacks grow and develop under its influence.

It thus becomes hazardous to doubt their possible amelioration and their capacity for drawing near the Whites morally, intellectually, and physically. It is useless to try to have us believe in the persistence of the Negro type throughout the

[1] *Slavery in Massachusetts*, extracted from the *Journal du Juge Sewall*, 1716, quoted by Kate Brousseau.

course of centuries. This affirmation altogether lacks logic from an evolutionary point of view. Since it is the *milieu* which has fashioned the Negro, it is impossible to question its transforming influence. The fact that Negroes residing in certain places and exposed for centuries to the same influences of climate and culture succeed in retaining their type intact, forces on us a conclusion in favour of the action of the *milieu*. The adversaries of its decisive action in the formation of races love to quote the population of the valley of the Nile. That of to-day resembles in a striking way that of some thousands of years ago, as represented in the images and sculptures of that time. But, in truth, a change in these conditions would have been rather surprising. In this classic land of immobility nothing has changed. Why then should its population be an exception to the rule?

The *milieu* being identical, including the way of working (even the tools have scarcely varied), mode of nourishment also and climate having always remained the same, the type ought to be more stable, more crystallised, and more difficult to modify. But let us be patient. Let but civilisation begin to operate there for one or more centuries, let the inhabitants undergo the equalising influence of its conditions of living and thinking, and it will follow that traits considered immutable will melt like wax under the influence of heat.

The conclusion therefore forces itself on us that there are no inferior and superior races, but only races and peoples living outside or within the influence of culture. The appearance of civilisation and its evolution among certain White peoples and within a certain geographical latitude is only the effect of circumstances. The Negroes, wrongly considered as occupying for ever one of the lowest rungs on the ladder of humanity, bring, by the fact of their raising themselves to the level of the most civilised Whites, a powerful argument in favour of the equality of human capabilities. When, in addition, we consider the progress accomplished by Black Americans in a century and a quarter, in the midst of almost insurmountable difficulties, it is not an exaggeration to affirm that under the influence of the same causes the Negroes in the space of one or two centuries will have acquired physiologically and intellectually the type which prevails in the American *milieu*.

CONCLUSION

I

WHEN the thermometer is powerless to indicate imperceptible modifications of heat, our physicists use a much simpler method ; they transform this heat, by means of the thermo-electric battery and the thermo-multiplicator, into electricity, whose slightest gradations can be easily seized and controlled. Our method has not even had to have recourse to transformation of facts. It has been enough to examine them in their simplest expression. Instead of losing ourselves in clouds of thought and in vague formulas, repeated without discernment for centuries, we have thought it possible and useful to look more closely at their contents. Sweeping away articles of faith which have become obsolete, we have simply recalled the logical processes which occasioned their genesis. Instead of studying races according to the divergences of their cephalic index, their colour, their height, their facial angles, or their collective psychology, we have commenced by redoing the work already done, and submitting the accepted ideas to a preliminary verification of their constituent elements. And just as a light in a dark field illumines the dark parts and gives them an unsuspected appearance, so everything has been changed in the domain of races. From the moment when, renouncing acquired ideas, we only wished to admit those based on observation and controlled by the recent conquests of science, the facts have assumed a new significance.

The analysis of all the successive theories on inequality created in us before everything else a profound astonishment at the credulity and the inertness of our thought. Successive generations only added faith to the same error, and this faith which always favoured its growth also favoured its persistence. As all the appearances seemed to support the dogma of inequality, it was adopted with the first superficial sensations which affected us from without. This belief was thus as deeply rooted as was long ago the faith in the movement of the sun round the earth.

Some time will no doubt elapse before science, emancipated from the prejudices which have prevailed and multiplied for centuries, will succeed in making the truth triumph. All these measurements, with their imposing numbers and scientific pretensions, as also the theoretic observations and deductions, resolve themselves, as we have seen, into a nebulous doctrine which affirms many things and explains nothing.

The exact instruments which anthropologists and especially "craniometrists" use, offer us fantastical data. The results of their operations are deposited in thousands of volumes; and yet what is their real bearing? In examining them closely one can hardly attribute to them even a descriptive value, so much do they contradict and destroy each other.

We have seen, for example, how precarious are the affirmations of craniometry, which constitutes, however, the most developed section of anthropometry. Although the instruments which it places at the disposal of *savants* are very numerous, yet the ways of using them are still more varied. The lack of unity in the observations and the contradictory ends which those who use them seem to pursue, cause numerous misunderstandings, which end in chaotic affirmations. In bringing forward the most indisputable data and in proceeding to a kind of cross-examination, we arrive at a conclusion quite different from that which the adherents of the dogmas of races are anxious to impose on us, and which so many learned demographs, politicians, novelists, and statesmen blindly accept.

When we go through the list of external differences which appear to divide men, we find literally nothing which can authorise their division into superior and inferior beings, into masters and pariahs. If this division exists in our thought, it only came there as the result of inexact observations and false opinions drawn from them.

The science of inequality is emphatically a science of White people. It is they who have invented it and set it going, who have maintained, cherished, and propagated it, thanks to *their* observations and *their* deductions. Deeming themselves greater than men of other colours, they have elevated into superior qualities all the traits which are peculiar to themselves, commencing with the whiteness of the skin and the pliancy of the hair. But nothing proves that these vaunted traits are traits of real superiority.

"If the Chinese and the Egyptians had judged our ancestors as we too often judge foreign races," says Quatrefages, "they would have found in them many traits of inferiority such as this white skin in which we take so much pride, and which they might have regarded as showing an irremediable etiolation." This is what dogmatic anthropologists seem at all times to have forgotten. Human varieties have not been studied like those of animals and plants, that is to say, without conventional prejudices as to their respective values and as to those which are superior and inferior. Facts have often yielded to sentiments. We have been persuaded, with the help of our feelings, to accept our own preferences rather than impartial observations, and our own prejudices rather than scientific laws.

In pursuing this course the elementary commandments of experimental science are transgressed. The majority of the anthropologists, faithful in this respect to the scholastic teachings, have begun by assuming the inequality of human beings as an axiom. On this preliminary basis they have built an imposing edifice, but really one of fictitious solidity.

A radical condemnation of principle weighs on anthropology each time that it exceeds its descriptive limits in order to affect the attitude of a dogmatic science. It becomes teleological, and in that way is deprived of all value. If "*anthropo-sociology*," this too much vaunted branch of anthropology, had adopted this indispensable maxim of the experimental method, that every theory is only true till facts are discovered which are opposed to it, or which coming within its limits burst its barriers, this quasi-science would have had a short career ! With what justice could not one apply to dogmatic anthropology and to the phalanx of its disciples what Claude Bernard says of the "scholastic" method, so severely judged by positive science ? "Scholasticism never doubts its starting-point, to which it wishes to attribute everything. It has a proud and intolerant mind, and never accepts contradiction, since it does not admit that its starting-point can change." It is thus that all the main data which hurl themselves against the theory of races are empty in its sight. Deaf to the appeal of hostile facts, its adepts are specially distinguished for their intrepidity in maintaining their theory against evidence itself.

Commenting out of sight on the doubtful facts, and rejecting with scorn as worthless the observations of its adversaries, anthropo-sociology continues to live in its romantic hiding-place. It builds there, it is true, impassable walls between men with wide and narrow skulls, yellows and whites, tall and short men, those with thick and thin joints, those with small and large nostrils, those with straight and curved foreheads. But life passes above all these artificial partitions, and marches on their ruins towards unity.

Hypnotised by their primordial idea, they thus bring together without examination everything which seems propitious to their theory, a theory by the way which is political rather than scientific. In their comparisons of the cerebral index, what does it matter to them to know the age or the sex of the subject, his occupations, his intellectuality, or the state of his health? Naturally, if they wish to take all these points into consideration, they must reject nine-tenths of the constituent elements of their pretended truth.

We know, for example, that the weight of the brain varies in man, increasing up to the age of forty-five, and diminishing after that period; that the brain grows under the influence of occupation; that sex also plays a considerable part in it; that the subject's state of health reacts on his cerebral structure; that the form of the human head is often influenced by the pelvis of the mother; and still with what lightness do they not lay hold of their rough measures, leaving on one side the causes of the effects observed? They proceed with no less unconcern in distributing certificates of superiority among the ranks of human beings. After having stated that superior races are furthest removed from the anthropoid apes, whilst the inferior ones are nearer to them, they bring together all the facts which in this respect favour the Whites, and entirely forget those in which Negroes are shown to be more favoured. For example, we are told of the angle of the condyles that the Whites are in this respect nearer the monkeys than the Negroes. When dolichocephaly is regarded as a trait of incontestable superiority, they seem to forget that the majority of Europeans are to be classed in the miserable category of brachycephals, whereas the Negroes belong to the dolichocephalic aristocracy !

If you wish to take as element of comparison the facial angle of Jacquart, you will be forced to arrive at the conclusion that the French and Spanish Basques, a nobly pure race, approach the Esquimaux and the Chinese.

If we keep to the length of the forearm, or to that of the tibia, we fall into a number of eccentricities, where Oceanians accompany Europeans and Bushmen cut no sorry figure. The more we study the many variations which distinguish human beings, the more we perceive that these are in no way intended. They are due to accidents of climate, occupations—in one word, of the surrounding *milieu*, the almost exclusive creator of the phenomena which vex certain obstinate anthropologists, who deny its incessant activity.

It must not be forgotten that the different parts of the body among races called inferior do not vary simultaneously and in every respect from the ideal type which is adopted as basis for comparison. Whereas certain limbs in a Negro or an Australian seem to approach the simian type, other traits preserve their nobility (?) of form, and all this according to no preconceived plan, and especially with no respect for the colour of the skin or the relative beauty of civilisation. Thus are explained the supposed anomalies of races called inferior which are superior to us in many respects, and also those of superior races which so often deserve to be styled inferior. The beast and the angel are mixed in all human beings. All peoples seem equally good and bad, perfectible or susceptible to moral and physical degradation. A kind of enchanted dome covers humanity. It is in vain that it exerts itself, for it never succeeds in surpassing certain limits. Humanity has its boundaries, like the earth which holds it.

II

We have made good progress in the sciences and in the increase of discoveries, but we have not succeeded in altering the planet. Man has grown morally and intellectually, but he is only, after all, a great *man*. He surpasses his fellows by a few inches morally and physically, but he never succeeds in differentiating himself from them so far as to overstep his species. In vain are irreducible physiological qualities sought for among human varieties, and when we examine the facts impartially we come finally to see their inanity. The greater our field of observation becomes, the more we perceive that organic demarcations and differences are only passing traits, born with time and susceptible of disappearing under its influence.

The work of centuries caused humanity to advance considerably, but all the same it has not permitted it to go beyond certain limits. Biology teaches us that there is a limit outside of which modifications are produced with more and more difficulty. A moment comes at length in which they no longer take place. It is within this imaginary enclosure that humanity has evolved for thousands of centuries.

An athlete might exercise his muscles for ever, but he cannot get more strength in them after certain efforts. A porter would vainly try to accustom himself to increase the weight of his burdens; he would never succeed in raising 1000 kilos. A singer breaks his voice if he attempts too high notes, just as beyond a certain amount of intellectual overwork our nervous system breaks down.

We are without doubt free to progress, but only like a goat tied to a post browsing within the range of the circumference. The space reserved to us is great, but it does not fail to be restricted. Change of conditions and hereditary improvement can do much, but their action does not overstep the real though invisible barriers.

Thus it is dangerous to nourish oneself beyond certain limits fixed by nature. Each excess compromises our organism. As our nourishment is subordinated to our faculty of assimilation, so do all our intellectual and physical efforts depend on the circumscribed capacities of our organism. Giants constitute pathological cases, as certain geniuses border on neurosis and insanity.

This is why human beings imprisoned within these inexorable limits have had to move or die.

To this teaching of the past prudent minds have even added a curious indication for the future. Thus many biologists regard the White race as having arrived at the limit of its evolution. It cannot go higher without exposing itself to a great danger which "will come" to it from its own over-developed brain.[1] (On this subject see, among others, the studies of Professor Le Damany.) But what is more important is that all peoples and races may attain this distant frontier which the brain of the Whites has reached.

We bow before the efforts and the perseverance of the dogmatic side of anthropology. For if the results are almost nil, it is not for lack of ingenuity, tenacity, and ardour that it fails to erect a solid structure on moving sands.

In addition to these numerous obstacles which bar the way of the experts of inequality, there is another kind of insurmountable obstacle which makes all their efforts sterile. This is man's peculiar nature, which, owing to the impressionability of his being and the influence both of the levelling milieu and of that psychical life which is common fundamentally to all human beings, tends towards the realisation of the solidarity of races or (to use a more correct expression) to that of human varieties.

III

In examining the world of our psychical and intellectual life, we have been struck with analogous phenomena. From all sides voices are raised in favour of our mental unity. Savage peoples enter triumphantly into our civilisation just as

[1] The hip of the new-born amongst white people, which is the pivot of flexion before birth and of deflexion after birth, is always at present at the limit of the normal and pathological conditions. The enlargening of the brain—so says Le Damany—causes this defect to grow, the consequence of which is a frequent or constant pathological condition—that is, a physical degeneracy contrary to the actual laws of the preservation of species.

civilised peoples fall back into barbarism. The Negroes, regarded as occupying the last rung on the human ladder, have furnished us with proofs of an unexpected evolution. Within the space of fifty years they have realised as much progress as many white peoples have done in five or six centuries. From the time of Julius Cæsar and Tacitus until Charlemagne—that is, eight centuries—Germany realised less progress than the American Negroes have done since the War of Secession. After all, we have seen the impossibility of attributing immutable psychological qualities to certain peoples or races. Their virtues and their vices are only the effects of historic circumstances or of the influence of the *milieu*.

The psychology of peoples has shown us the unity of their mind. The three principal faculties which assure us of man's exceptional position in the scale of living beings—the faculty of abstraction, that of mastering his impulses, and the power of choosing among his perceptions and his actions—are to be met with among all human races. What varies is the degree of mental exercise on which the application of these faculties depends, and also the sum of accumulated tradition, to use the expression of certain psychologists. Herein lies all the difference which separates the savage from the civilised man! Change his environment, and at the end of a certain number of generations, often even in the space of one, he will regain lost time.

In vain is the attempt made to endow certain privileged nations with every virtue by overwhelming their adversaries with condemnation to eternal inferiority! Reality irreverently destroys our puerile classifications, and, according to the words of the Gospel, makes the last to be first.

The history of civilisation is only a continual come and go of peoples and races! All, without distinction of their biological characteristics, are summoned to this great struggle for life wherein we fight for human progress and happiness. All the ethnical elements can take part in it, all can contend for places of honour in it. Such is the general import of our biological and psychological equality, which remains intact underneath all our superficial divisions.

In the present state of science it has become impossible for us to distinguish the ethnical origins of peoples. The constituent

elements are so much intermingled that the most ardent partisans of inequality must admit the relationship of all the races.
The "purity of blood" which we create at will, and which we
find in the animal world, becomes impossible in the human
milieu. The Negroes are related to the Whites, who are linked
to the Yellows, as these last have common links both with
Negroes and Whites. On the road which separates them we
only meet with links which unite them.

Nevertheless, we foresee an objection which certain minds
who are satisfied with simple arguments are sure to make.
"Does the Negro ever cease in spite of everything to be a
black, or the Chinese a yellow? Would the author have us
understand that between a Redskin, a Papuan, or a White there
are no differences?" Far from wishing to hide them, we have
done nothing but look for them. They exist, and we have laid
stress on a considerable number of them, but they are only the
passing products of the *milieu.* Having come about as the
result of external circumstances, they disappear in the same
way. As it is impossible to shut up human souls in dogmatic
and eternal formulas, it is equally impossible to enclose human
beings in immutable racial moulds. But more. As we have
had the opportunity of proving, the word race cannot be used
to determine the specific character of the floating distinctions
between members of the human unity.

In one word, the term race is only a product of our
mental activities, the work of our intellect, and outside all
reality. Science had need of races as hypothetical limits, and
these "products of art," to use Lamarck's expression, have
become concrete realities for the vulgar. Races as irreducible
categories only exist as fictions in our brains. They exist in us
but not outside us. We can never sufficiently insist on this fact,
which is elementary and undeniable to all truly scientific minds
and to those desirous above all of ascertaining the truth.

There are thus human varieties based on the differences
caused by the changing influences of the *milieu.* Owing to the
increase in the number of the factors which will be common in
the evolution of future humanity, these varieties will gradually
lose their over-marked differences. But humanity, whilst
advancing towards unity, will hardly attain it in the absolute

meaning of the word. Its fragments, dispersed all over the
globe, will naturally retain under the influence of different
milieux certain distinctive traits. The duration and intensity
of these, however, will be all the more transient in that the
relations and intercourse between human beings will become
easier and more active. Let this reassure all those who tremble
in anticipation of a sort of uniformity in the humanity of the
future. For human unity does not signify human uniformity
and monotony.

IV

The truths concerning man are confirmed when they find
their application and their confirmation in his everyday life.
The conception of human races in a "conventional" or
"conditional" sense prevents us before everything else from
regarding them as fatally divergent. On the ruins, therefore, of
the belief in superior and inferior races, the possible development and amelioration of all human beings arise. Their
evolution, having become of universal application, makes their
extermination criminal.

The principle of human equality takes away the right of
killing so-called inferior people, just as it destroys the right
claimed by some of dominating others. If all peoples are equal,
if their different appearances are only the result of changing
circumstances, in virtue of what principle is it allowable
to destroy their happiness and to compromise their right to
independence?

Humanity, looked at from this point of view, becomes a
concrete conception. Its solidarity is seen to be its real good.
Regarded apart from the equality of races, or rather varieties,
integral humanity becomes an expression devoid of meaning.

Once the "prejudice of races" has disappeared, we must
acknowledge the beneficial reaction of this belief on the
"inner" life of peoples. As we have shown, modern nations
have been formed outside and very often in spite of the conceptions of races. When once amalgamated, ethnical principles
regarded as most hostile have contributed towards creating
the national principle. There are no longer "pure" peoples,
if ever there were any.

The more advanced a people and the greater its vitality, so much the more intermixed with others is it found to be. Those which march at the van of civilisation, like the French, English, German, Italian, or those of the United States, all possess blood which is richest in heterogeneous elements. What Paul Broca said of the inhabitants of France—namely, that they exhibit every known type of cephalic index—is applicable to all civilised peoples. All those whose origins have been studied show the same richness of ethnical elements, which, intercrossed, have contributed towards forming their national unities.

Purity of blood is thus only a myth, and its talismanic virtue is found to be irremediably compromised. Unity of blood retreats to the background. What constitutes modern peoples is the solidarity of their moral and material interests. Switzerland, officially known as the union of four different races (really we find some dozens here as elsewhere), constitutes, for all that, a people united in an ideal way, owing to the moral cohesion of all its inhabitants. The same applies to other peoples. Between a Frenchman of the Pas-de-Calais and a Frenchman of the Alpes-Maritimes there is without doubt more divergence than between a Dane and a Norwegian. Yet the two former have one common country and the latter two diverse countries.

Once the nightmare of races is dissipated, we easily understand what Fatherland in the *human sense* of the word means.

How miserable seem to us to-day all the political and sociological doctrines founded on the principle of blood!

Of all the vulgar methods of sparing oneself the trouble of studying profoundly the moral and social factors which influence the human mind, the grossest, according to John Stuart Mill, is that which consists in attributing diversities of conduct and of character to those *natural differences* which are as proper to peoples as to individuals.

In the light of the facts brought together in this volume, we see the immense amount of nonsense connected with the racial theories of peoples. If patriotism was bound to our conceptions of races, what incessant metamorphoses would it not have to undergo? France, believed for centuries to be Gallic, is suddenly revealed to be Germanic! Must we under these

circumstances embrace our German brothers, and at the same
time espouse German hatreds and sympathies ?   Through such
historic discoveries as to races, we should logically have to
modify our loves, hopes, ideals, and sentiments !

The true conception of humanity, far from destroying the
sentiment of patriotism, only fortifies and enhances it.   It is
no longer a brutal instinct of blood, but a high expression of
community of ideals and of moral and material interests.   With
the erroneous principles of pure and irreducible races, and with
the false theory of organic inequalities, we arrive, fatally and
inevitably, at internal strifes and inextricable misunderstandings.   Once, however, these principles are abolished, we understand the obvious and absolute fraternity of the inhabitants of
the same country, together with the possibility and the necessity
of advancing towards its political and social realisation.

As the differences among men are thus only individual, there
will theoretically be no more room for internal and external
hatreds, as there will be no more for the social and political
inferiorities of classes.

On the ruins, therefore, of the falsehood of races, solidarity
and true equality arise, both founded on a rational sentiment
of respect for human dignity.